HOW TO BE AN EFFECTIVE TEACHER

THE FIRST DAYS OF SCHOOL

by Harry K. Wong & Rosemary T. Wong

*Some people go into teaching
because it is a job.
Some people go into teaching
to make a difference.*

*We are pleased to share with
the teaching profession
our contribution to making
a difference.*

Harry K. Wong Publications, Inc.
www.effectiveteaching.com

In a Nutshell, What Is *The First Days of School* About?

How to Be an Effective Teacher

For Whom Is This Book Written?

- ✔ EXPERIENCED TEACHERS
- ✔ PRESERVICE TEACHERS
- ✔ NEOPHYTE TEACHERS
- ✔ NEW TEACHERS
- ✔ MENTOR TEACHERS
- ✔ ADMINISTRATORS
- ✔ STAFF DEVELOPERS
- ✔ COLLEGE PROFESSORS

Why Was This Book Written?

The First Days of School **is written to help all teachers "jumpstart" by beginning school successfully.** This book is the result of the myriad ideas and techniques that have been shared by the legions of educators who have interacted with us. We thank these people for their contributions, and now we share them in return.

We thank the more than 500,000 people who purchased the first edition of *The First Days of School*, and we are proud to present the second edition.

COVERS: A tribute to REAL educators in working classrooms in actual schools. You are making a difference in the lives of students and in the world.

Dee Blassie, Debby Branscum, Betsy Brooks, Richard O. Butt, Jeane A. Cagle, Beth Ann Dixon, Richelle Dodoo, Sue Flynn, Gililland Elementary School (Fort Worth, Texas), Rita Gorang, Jim Heintz, Edward Hockenberry, Stephanie Hosack, Hilton Jay, Laurie Jay, Catherine M. Joefreda, Kenya N. Kilpatrick, Kenyette Kilpatrick, William R. Machay II, Kim Migliore, Joann Moreland, Holland Myers, Wendy S. Ong, Alicia Osland, Magda Porras, Anita Richardson, Roosevelt Elementary School (Port Huron, Michigan), Lois Rowe, St. Mary's Central School (St. Clairesville, Ohio), Carolyn Schramka, Barbara D. Stark, Art Vlahon, Kathy Weston, Katrina Wong, and Equilla G. Wright

Executive Producer: Rosemary T. Wong
Original illustrations: Heidi Heath
Additional illustrations: Jin Hei Kang
Editors: Bruce Emmer, Mary Carman Barbosa

Harry K. Wong Publications, Inc.
943 North Shoreline Boulevard
Mountain View, CA 94043
TEL (650) 965-7896   FAX (650) 965-7890
www.effectiveteaching.com

ISBN: 0-9629360-2-2
Library of Congress Catalog Card Number: 97-91202
25 24 23 22 21 20
Printed in Singapore

Dedicated to my father and mother,

who wanted me to be a brain surgeon.

I exceeded their expectations.

I became a scholar and a teacher.

—Harry K. Wong

Dedicated to Mr. Frederick McKee,

my first principal, whose
evaluation of me said I needed
better "classroom management"
skills. Thank you for telling me
I needed to improve my skills.
I did. It worked!

—Rosemary Tripi Wong

A Magnificent Future Awaits You

Before you start planning the first days of school, take a quick look at what's ahead during the next decade.

- ✔ Approximately 200,000 new teachers will enter the profession each year.
- ✔ The corps of 2.8 million teachers who teach presently, will increase to 3.3 million by 2003.
- ✔ Fifty percent of the teachers teaching in 2000 will have been in the classroom seven years or less.
- ✔ Of the teachers teaching in the year 2000, 75 percent will have been trained after 1990.
- ✔ Up to 50 percent of new teachers will leave teaching within their first seven years.[1]

The message is clear. The entire teaching profession will all but turn over during the turn of the century.

If you are a new teacher: You have a magnificent future awaiting you, with teaching positions and educational opportunities galore. Prepare yourself for these opportunities.

If you are an administrator or a staff developer: This is the chance of your educational lifetime to affect reform within 10 years. The vast majority of the teachers will change in the next decade. Education can be reformed if we change the culture of the new generation of teachers. Use a new teacher induction program to establish a culture of effective teachers. They are the future of education and humanity.

If you are a veteran teacher: This is your chance to leave a legacy to education. This book explains how you can be a masterful and effective teacher. Use this knowledge to help the new teachers entering the profession. Be a mentor and a positive role model.

This Is a Critical Time

Given the fact that fully half of the teachers who will be teaching in the year 2005 will be hired over the next decade (and large-scale hiring will continue into the decade thereafter), this is a critical time to transform the quality of teacher preparation.

— Linda Darling-Hammond
  "The Quiet Revolution: Rethinking Teacher Development."
  (March 1996).
  Educational Leadership, p. 6.

---

[1]Wilkinson, Gayle A. (Summer 1994). "Support for Individualizing Teacher Induction." *Action in Teacher Education*, p. 52.

Do not become one of the 50 percent who will leave the teaching profession discouraged, overwhelmed, and abandoned. Use *The First Days of School* to help you become a supersuccessful teacher.

How to Change the Culture of Education

Educational reform can be accomplished in the next 10 years by changing the culture of the new teachers coming into the profession.

> *A major attribute of a profession is that there is a systematic enculturation of its new members.*[2]
> —Jon Saphier

"I had the key to this room in June. I cleaned the room inside and out. I knew every corner. But I was overwhelmed; I didn't know where to start."

—Alicia Escobar
Santa Cruz, California

The enculturation of new teachers begins with an induction program. Without help and enculturation, beginning teachers perpetuate the status quo by teaching as they remember being taught. And if we do not reach these teachers, they will in turn listen to the same people with the same message and have things validated in the same way, and we will repeat the same cycle generation after generation in education, going nowhere.

What Is Induction?

Induction is a structured program that takes place before the first day of school for all newly hired teachers. During the induction process, effective schools and districts teach their teachers how to become effective teachers.

> ✔ Fully 95 percent of beginning teachers who experienced support during their initial years remain in teaching after three years, and 80 percent of the supported teachers remain after five years.[3]

Training is one of the best ways to send a message to your teachers that you value them and want them to succeed and stay. Much worse than training people and losing them is not training them and keeping them!

---

[2]Saphier, Jon. (1994). *On Becoming a Professional.* Carlisle, Mass.: Research for Better Teaching.

[3]Wilkinson, Gayle A. (Summer 1994). "Support for Individualizing Teacher Induction." *Action in Teacher Education,* p. 52.

That Noble Title
Teacher

As we begin each new school year, let us remember the fine nuances and the distinguishing essence of that proud word Teacher.

Let us be reminded of the tools you have at your command, because of your talents, your traits, and your training . . . and because you chose to become a Teacher.

Teacher — you are a poet, as you weave with your colorful magic language a passion for your subject. You create a vast and grand mosaic of curiosities to imagine, secrets to unfold, connections only to begin the cycle of learning.

Teacher — you are a physicist, as you bring magic, logic, reason, and wonder to the properties, changes, and interactions of our universe.

Teacher — you are a maestro, a master of composing, as you conduct and orchestrate individuals' thoughts and actions from discordant cacophony into harmonic resonance.

Teacher — you are an architect, as you provide each student a solid foundation, but always with a vision of the magnificent structure that is about to emerge.

Teacher — you are a gymnast, as you encourage the contortions and gyrations of thoughts and the flexing and strengthening of ideas.

Teacher — you are a diplomat and the ambassador of tact and sensitivity, as you facilitate productive, positive interactions among the multiplicity of personalities and cultures, beliefs, and ideals.

Teacher — you are a philosopher, as your actions and ethics convey meaning and hope to young people who look to you for guidance and example.

As you prepare for your first day and each day, when your students enter and you encounter their attitudes, ranging from eager, enthusiastic anticipation to uncomfortable, uncertain apathy, recall the powers you have within . . . from poet to philosopher . . . and present yourself to those students as a person worthy of the noble title . . . Teacher.

— *Trish Marcuzzo*
Omaha Public Schools

Five Units at a Glance

Basic Understandings — The Teacher

The successful teacher must know and practice the three characteristics of an effective teacher.

First Characteristic — Positive Expectations

The effective teacher has positive expectations for student success.

Second Characteristic — Classroom Management

The effective teacher is an extremely good classroom manager.

Third Characteristic — Lesson Mastery

The effective teacher knows how to design lessons to help students reach mastery.

Future Understandings — The Professional

The teacher who constantly learns and grows becomes a professional educator.

Contents

A   *Basic Understandings — The Teacher*

The successful teacher must know and practice the three characteristics of an effective teacher.

B   *First Characteristic — Positive Expectations*

The effective teacher has positive expectations for student success.

C   *Second Characteristic — Classroom Management*

The effective teacher is an extremely good classroom manager.

D Third Characteristic — Lesson Mastery

The effective teacher knows how to design lessons to help students reach mastery.

E Future Understandings — The Professional

The teacher who constantly learns and grows becomes a professional educator.

How to Use This Book

> *The First Days of School* **is not a novel,**
> **so it is not necessary to read it in sequence**
> **from beginning to end.**

The First Days of School **is more like an automobile owner's manual. You will be able to turn to the right section to solve a problem if something doesn't work right.**

Every effort has been made to make this book user-friendly. All the techniques suggested are nonthreatening. Use them as a springboard to your success. Please familiarize yourself with the parts of this book.

Step 1. Look at "Five Units at a Glance" on page vii and note the framework of this book. For general understanding, read Units A and E. If you want specific techniques, read units B, C, and D.

Step 2. Read the table of contents. This will give you a quick overview of the organization and chapters of the book.

Step 3. Thumb through the book and note that each chapter has a "Key Idea" that states the purpose of the chapter. If this is where you want further information, read the chapter for the accompanying text and techniques.

Step 4. Each chapter ends with a summary list of concepts. Use these for implementation and success.

How to Get Quickly to the Meat of This Book

If You Want to Know	Read the Key Idea for Each Chapter	
How to understand why you are teaching in the first place	Unit A	(page 2)
How to motivate and inspire your students	Unit B	(page 34)
How to manage a classroom that is uncontrollable	Unit C	(page 80)
How to have your students do their assignments and pass their tests	Unit D	(page 196)
How to cope with the years still ahead of you and retire with dignity	Unit E	(page 270)

Have You Ever Watched a Slow Reader Read?

Slow readers start at the beginning and read every word, one by one, in the order in which they occur, at the same slow rate of speed. They are slow not necessarily because they cannot read but because they do not know how to read effectively—that is, with speed and efficiency.

Intelligent, effective readers—like you—scan, browse, overview, organize, survey, . . .

This process is called SQ3R:
Survey
Question
Read
Recite
Review

That is how *The First Days of School* should be read. It's not necessary to read it from cover to cover. Browse through this book to familiarize yourself with its structure so that you can refer to the right parts when you need help.

Now please go back and follow **Steps 1 to 4** in "How to Use This Book" on the preceding page.

Why You Need This Book

> **If you are going to be a teacher,
> you've got to know how to teach.**

Experienced teachers know that what you do and what you say in the first few seconds of the first day of school can make or break you. That is why you need this book, because you've got to know what you are doing. **The First Days of School will bring positive results to your teaching and from your students.**

Do not call this the Wong model.

Since there are no foolproof plans or models for successful teaching, you need this book all the more. This book does not contain a PLAN. Nor is this a MODEL.

The First Days of School will help you start the school year properly so that the remainder of the school year can run smoothly. This book has been written to **HELP** you formulate your own plan, your own model.

Innumerable ideas, techniques, and skills can help you improve your performance as a teacher. Here are some ways that *The First Days of School* will help you:

- ✔ You will have FEWER PROBLEMS in the classroom.
- ✔ You will PRESENT YOURSELF POSITIVELY to your students.
- ✔ You will feel LESS STRESS.
- ✔ You will feel BETTER about your CAPABILITIES in the classroom.
- ✔ You will be much SOUGHT AFTER and ADMIRED.
- ✔ You will be RESPECTED as a professional.
- ✔ You will have greater STUDENT SUCCESS.
- ✔ You will be a SUPERSUCCESSFUL TEACHER.

Best wishes as you master the first days of school!

The Key Word Is *Help*

This book will only help you become the teacher you were meant to be.

There is no teacherproof method of education.

There is no one way to teach.

There are no pat answers, quick fixes, or foolproof plans for teaching.

There is no way to reduce teaching to a simple and predictable formula.

To do so would "de-skill" and deprofessionalize education.

What you need to do is continually try and learn.

What This Book Will Teach You

> **If you dare to teach,
> then you must dare to learn.**

The Key Word Is *Free*

This book is long on practical techniques.

It has just the right amount of research and common sense.

Implementation of the techniques suggested costs no extra money.

Learning the techniques suggested requires no extra in-service training.

You can do everything on your own time and at your own pace.

Money and materials cannot buy an ideal learning environment. Only **YOU** can provide that environment.

You want results? You've got them! This book is teacher-specific and excellent for getting results.

This book has nothing to do with educational reform. No controversial, cutting-edge, sacrilegious, or outrageous ideas are proposed. All the ideas and techniques explained in this book are used by hundreds of thousands of teachers. They are tried and true, fundamental, basic things that good teachers know and practice to get results in the classroom.

We haven't invented any of the ideas and techniques featured here. They have simply been gathered over years of watching good teachers and reading about effective teaching and then adapted to our particular classroom setting.

Certain basic classroom techniques can help you manage a classroom for high-level student success. Here are some techniques you will learn from *The First Days of School*:

- ✔ How to have your CLASSROOM PREPARED for instruction
- ✔ How to establish CREDIBILITY with your students
- ✔ How to have a DISCIPLINE PLAN that works
- ✔ How to have PROCEDURES and ROUTINES that cause a classroom to run smoothly
- ✔ How to have students who will work together in COOPERATIVE LEARNING
- ✔ How to maximize ACADEMIC LEARNING TIME
- ✔ How to give ASSIGNMENTS that are clear and concise
- ✔ How to write a CRITERION-REFERENCED TEST

Welcome to the world of lifelong learning!

For Those Helping Teachers Become Effective Teachers

✔ **Administrators**

✔ **Staff Developers**

✔ **Mentor Teachers**

✔ **College Instructors**

To enhance the understanding and implementation of *The First Days of School*, an eight-part video series, *The Effective Teacher*, is available. Each segment of the video correlates to a portion of this book, as indicated in the box that follows:

The Effective Teacher Video Parts	Corresponding Unit in *The First Days of School*
1 — The Effective Teacher	A — The Teacher
2 — The First Days of School	B — Positive Expectations
3 — Discipline and Procedures	C — Classroom Management
4 — Procedures and Routines	C — Classroom Management
5 — Cooperative Learning and Culture	D — Lesson Mastery
6 — Lesson Mastery	D — Lesson Mastery
7 — The Professional Educator	E — The Professional
8 — Positive Expectations	B — Positive Expectations

The Henry County school system receives the Georgia Staff Development Council's award for its new teacher induction program. The program successfully incorporates the book and video series.

UNIT A

Basic Understandings — The Teacher

The successful teacher must know and practice the three characteristics of an effective teacher.

Basic Understandings — The Teacher

The successful teacher must know and practice the three characteristics of an effective teacher.

Unit A is correlated with **Part 1: The Effective Teacher**
in the video series *The Effective Teacher*.

KEY IDEA

Your success during the school year will be determined by what you do on the first days of school.

The First Days Are Critical

> **What you do on the first days of school will determine your success or failure for the rest of the school year. You will either win or lose your class on the first days of school.**

The first days of school can make or break you. Based on what a teacher does or does not do, a teacher will either have or not have an effective classroom for the rest of the year. What happens on the first days of school will be an accurate indicator of your success for the rest of the school year.

The Purpose of School Is Learning

Douglas Brooks observed a group of teachers in his research. The ineffective teachers were those who began the first day of school with a fun activity and then spent the rest of the school year chasing after the students. The effective teachers spent time organizing and structuring the classroom for student success. Fun is fine in the classroom, but the purpose of school is learning.

Effective teachers have classrooms that are caring, thought-provoking, challenging, and exciting. They have this because they begin with classroom management procedures.

Students like well-managed classes because no one yells at them and learning takes place. Effective teachers spend the first two weeks teaching students to be in control of their own learning. **Unit C in this book may be the most important for you to read and implement as you start the first days of school.**

School is a serious place. You go to school to study, work, and produce —just like in an adult workplace. School is where you go to learn skills that help make you a productive citizen and grow to your fullest potential as a human being.

Douglas Brooks, in his article "The First Day of School,"[1] discovered two things:

1. Very few teachers receive any instruction on what to do on the first day of school.

2. Very few teachers get any experience or training during student teaching on what to do on the first day of school.

[1]Brooks, Douglas M. (May 1985). "The First Day of School." *Educational Leadership*, pp. 76–78.

3

Nearly every teacher goes out to teach with no instruction or knowledge and no experience on what to do on the first day of school. **Yet there is overwhelming evidence that the first two to three weeks of school are critical in determining how well students will achieve for the remainder of the year.**

The first two or three weeks? How about the first two or three days? The first two or three minutes! The first two or three seconds!

> **Student achievement at the end of the year is directly related to the degree to which the teacher establishes good control of the classroom procedures in the very first week of the school year.**

The effective teacher establishes good control of the class in the very first week of school. Control does not involve threats or intimidation. Control means that you know (1) what you are doing, (2) your classroom procedures, and (3) your professional responsibilities. It is urgent also that your students know that you know what you are doing.

You must have everything ready and under control when school begins. **Your success during the school year will be determined by what you do on the first days of school.**

This teacher is ready on the first day of school.

Effective People Know What They Are Doing

People who do things right are **EFFICIENT**. And people who do things right over and over again, consistently, are **EFFECTIVE**.

"My, he's efficient!" This is what you say about someone who does things right. "She is very effective" is what you say about someone who does the right things or makes the right decisions so that the office is effectively run.

> **Efficient:** Doing Things Right
> **Effective:** Doing the Right Thing
>
> The **Effective** teacher
> **Affects** lives.

Effectiveness has to do with **DOING**. To be effective, you must be doing something, constantly working toward improved performance.

The Four Stages of Teaching

1. Fantasy
2. Survival
3. Mastery
4. Impact

There are four stages to teaching,[2] yet many teachers never progress beyond the second one, survival. Which stage are you presently in? The purpose of *The First Days of School* is to get you to the third stage, mastery, so that you can make a difference in the lives of your students.

---

[2]Ryan, Kevin. (1986). *The Induction of New Teachers*. Bloomington, Ind.: Phi Delta Kappa.

Stage 1—FANTASY. A naive belief of neophyte teachers is that they are infallible. They believe that to be a successful teacher, all they need to do is relate and be a friend to their students. They also believe that teaching means doing activities, especially fun activities.

Stage 2—SURVIVAL. Teachers are in survival when they rely on ineffective practices just to make it through the day. To them, teaching is a job, and they do it for the paycheck and vacation benefits. Teachers in survival spend much time whining about work conditions and making excuses. They find busywork for the students to do, copy notes from a chalk board or transparency, show videos. They exhibit no accountability: "I teach the stuff; if they don't want to learn it, it's not my fault." So they come each day to put in time and baby-sit.

Stage 3—MASTERY. Teachers who know how to achieve student success employ effective practices. These teachers know how to manage their classroom, teach for mastery, and have high expectations for their students. Effective teachers strive for mastery by reading professionally and going to professional meetings. They teach to make a difference and exhibit accountability: "If the students are not learning, I need to find another way or discuss the problem with my peers to see if they have answers. I am an adult; I am responsible; I am a problem solver."

Stage 4—IMPACT. Effective teachers are able to affect or make an impact on their students. A teacher's role is to open the door to learning. Effective master teachers know how to get their students to enter for learning. To make an impact on your students, you need to use effective teaching practices. Students learn only when the teacher has an appreciable effect on a student's life. You have arrived as a teacher when you reach this stage. You have gone beyond mastery.

Don't Be a Pal

Our heart goes out to all the neophyte teachers who want to be their students' friend. Be friendly, caring, loving, and sensitive, but do not be their friend. They have enough on their hands with their own friends.

The students of today need you to be an adult role model that they can look to with admiration and pride. If you become a student's friend, the student will start asking for favors, as people do of friends. And if a favor is not granted, the student becomes incensed, — "I thought you were my friend. I hate you!"

It is better to be a paragon than a pal.

Effective Teachers Affect Lives

Teachers who are efficient and effective are more capable of affecting the lives of students than teachers who are not efficient and effective. Perhaps you have heard the definition of education, as shown on the graphic to the left.

For instance, what is the difference between a student who is tardy and a student who is not tardy? Between one who turns in the homework and one who does not? Between one who studies for the test and one who does not?

It is not height, age, sex, race, religious affiliation, or socioeconomic background.

It is behavior or attitude. You change or affect the attitude of a student, and you suddenly have a student who is not tardy, participates in class, does the homework, and studies for the test.

You were hired to affect lives. You were hired not so much to teach third grade, history, or physical education as to influence lives. Touch the life of a student, and you will have a student who will learn history, physical education, even science and math, clean the erasers, staple all the papers, and turn cartwheels to please you.

EDUCATION
IS NOT
teaching people
what they do
not know.

EDUCATION IS
teaching people
to behave as
they are not
already behaving.

The effective teacher affects lives.

The beginning of school is the most critical time of the school year. **What you do in the first days of school to affect the lives of your students will determine your success during the rest of the year.**

7

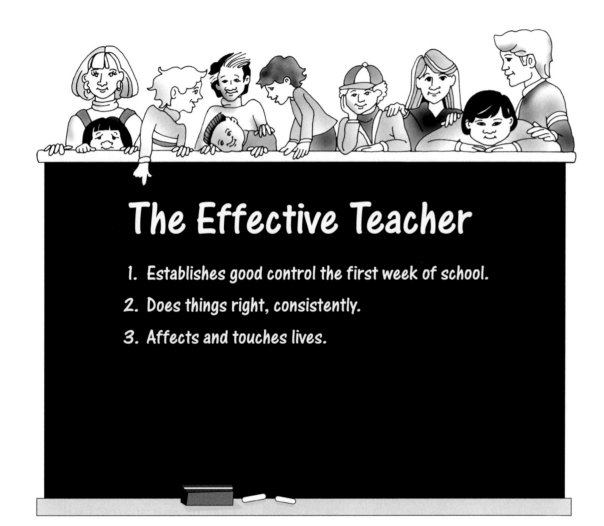

The Effective Teacher

1. Establishes good control the first week of school.

2. Does things right, consistently.

3. Affects and touches lives.

The effective teacher must be proficient in the three characteristics of an effective teacher.

The Effective Teacher

The Three Characteristics of an Effective Teacher

An effective teacher . . .

1. has positive expectations for student success.

2. is an extremely good classroom manager.

3. knows how to design lessons for student mastery.

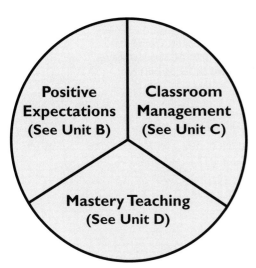

The three characteristics of an effective teacher and where to find them.

There are three characteristics of an effective teacher, and they apply to all teachers.[1] Note that none of the characteristics have anything to do with grade level or subject taught. These characteristics are known, and you can easily learn how to be a very effective teacher.

You are probably eager to present your lessons, do your exciting activities, and share your wonderful knowledge. None of these will be successful until you become skilled in the characteristics of an effective teacher. Teaching is not covering chapters or doing activities. **Teaching is a craft, a highly skilled craft that can be learned!**

Every one of us is both a student and a teacher.

We are at our best when we each teach ourselves what we need to learn.

[1]Good, Thomas L., and Jere Brophy. (1994). *Looking in Classrooms.* New York: Harper/Collins, pp. 376–377.

Positive Expectations

Ways to convey positive expectations are discussed in detail in Unit B.

Positive expectations, sometimes called high expectations, should not be confused with high standards. Having positive expectations simply means that the teacher believes in the learner and that the learner can learn.

The belief in positive expectations is based on the research that whatever the teacher expects from the learner is what the learner will produce. If you believe that a student is a low-level, below-average, slow learner, the student will perform as such because these are the beliefs you transmit to the student. If you believe that a student is a high-ability, above-average, capable learner, the student will perform as such because these are the expectations you transmit to the student.

It is essential that the teacher exhibit positive expectations toward all students. It can only benefit both the teacher and the student, as well as the total classroom environment.

Jane H. Smith
Principal, Haughton High School

High Academic Standards In A Controlled Environment

210 E. McKinley Dr.
Haughton, LA 71037   (318) 949-2429

Jane Smith is now superintendent of the Bossier Parish schools. But when she was principal, the standard she set for her school was reflected on her business card.

Classroom Management

The management techniques that a teacher must use in the first days of school to get the students to develop good classroom habits are discussed in detail in Unit C.

Classroom management consists of practices and procedures that a teacher uses to maintain an environment in which instruction and learning can occur. For this to happen, the teacher must have a well-ordered environment.

> **Well-Ordered Environment + Positive Academic Expectations = Effective Classroom**

Discipline has very little to do with classroom management. You don't discipline a store; you manage it. The same is true of a classroom. Unit C explains how to manage a classroom, applying the principle that a well-ordered environment leads to an effective classroom. The teacher must establish a productive and cooperative working environment. **The effectiveness of such an environment is the result of how well a teacher manages a classroom.**

How to design lessons to reach mastery is discussed in detail in Unit D.

Lesson Mastery

Mastery is the student's demonstration that a concept has been comprehended or a skill can be performed at a level of proficiency determined by the teacher.

When a home is built, the contractor receives a set of blueprints from the architect. The blueprints specify the degree of competence that will be acceptable. The inspector who periodically checks on the construction always looks at the blueprint first and then checks the workmanship to see if the work has been performed to the degree of competence specified.

Teaching is no different. To teach for mastery, an effective teacher must do two things:

1. Know how to design lessons in which a student will learn a concept or a skill.

2. Know how to evaluate the learning to determine if the student has mastered the concept or the skill.

Student success in the subject matter of the class will be the result of how well the teacher designs lessons and checks for mastery.

Students Work Without the Teacher Present

Dear Dr. Wong,

In my 23 years in the classroom, I have always felt that one of my greatest strengths is in the area of classroom management.

To illustrate, I called the administration one evening to inform them that I was ill and would not be present the next day. The following morning my students were standing in the hall outside my room when the first bell rang. The other teacher in the department opened my door to let the students in. As the day progressed, the classes came and went. In the afternoon a counselor came looking for me. My students said that they had not seen me all day, turned the radio up again and went back to business as usual.

My standing joke with the administration is that if I could get my students to keep quiet about my absence, I could stay home all week or maybe even take a trip to some South Seas island!

In closing, I have not had a serious discipline problem in over 15 years and my day is free to spend however I wish at 3:15 p.m. Thanks for pointing out to me that I am doing something right.

Richard L. Crewse
Concord High School
Elkhart, Indiana

The classroom of Roberta Ford, middle school English teacher and Colorado's Teacher of the Year, is structured for success.

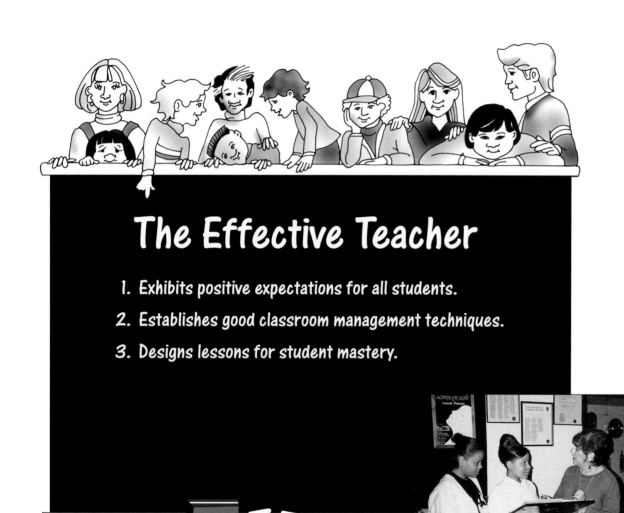

The Effective Teacher

1. Exhibits positive expectations for all students.

2. Establishes good classroom management techniques.

3. Designs lessons for student mastery.

Pam Ware of Gainesville, Georgia, is a national Milken award-winning drama teacher. She produces and directs 13 shows each year—with ease. Pam says, "I am a planner of the first order. I pride myself in management skills, selling the theater program and its value, explaining procedures, and presenting a calendar of time expectations and commitments from my students. I have very high expectations. Then I light a spark that will flame toward brilliant success."

KEY IDEA

The beginning teacher must perform the full complement of duties while learning those duties.

Yes, the Hardship Will End

> **The first day of school or a class—even the first few minutes—will make or break a teacher.**
>
> **It is those first few minutes and first few days of school that are the subject of this book.**

The First Year of Teaching Is the Most Critical in a Teacher's Career

Richelle Dodoo, first-year teacher.

New teachers feel
    Isolated,
    Vulnerable, and
    Deeply concerned with how
       they will be perceived, yet
    Afraid to ask for help.

They are hired,
    Given a key,
    Told which is their room, and
    Given no support.

They are given the worst assignments.
    They feel frightened.
    They feel humiliated.
    They are given no help.
    They want someone to
      give them hope,
      to tell them when their
      hardship will end.

Clueless may be the best way to explain the plight of neophyte teachers. Their bag is brimming with a five- or six- or seven-step lesson plan, boxes of activities, the state performance appraisal instrument, five interpretations of educational foundations, nine theories of child development, and a collection of buzzwords. But they have no clue as to what to do in the first days and weeks of school.

Your first day of teaching will be an exciting anticipated event but very frightening at the same time. **Yet you can succeed if you learn how to be effective on the first days of school.**

> **The First Year of Teaching Can Be Frightening**
>
> 1. Teacher education will not have prepared you.
> 2. Student teaching will not have prepared you.
> 3. The district may not have prepared you.
> 4. Yet you will be expected to perform immediately.

Teacher Education Will Not Have Prepared You

Teacher education rarely prepares the student teacher for noninstructional tasks. You will have lots of ideas for instructional tasks: bulletin boards, activities, projects, books, and media.

But you probably will have received no training in such noninstructional activities as how to maintain discipline, conduct a parent conference, keep a grade book, act and dress for success, teach procedures and routines, or deal with negative, nonsupportive, and energy-draining students and colleagues.

The schools of education are not to be blamed. No one ever said that education ends with a college degree. The best teachers are also the best students. Good teachers are continually improving themselves by going back to college; joining professional organizations; attending conventions, conferences, and workshops; paying attention at in-service meetings; and working cooperatively with others on the staff to improve student achievement.

Selected Professional Educational Organizations

American Alliance for Health, Physical Education, Recreation, and Dance
American Association of Physics Teachers
American Council of the Teaching of Foreign Languages
American Library Association
American School Counselor Association
American Speech-Language-Hearing Association
American Vocational Association
Association for Childhood Education International
Association for Children and Adults with Learning Disabilities
Association for Educational Communications and Technology
Association for Gifted and Talented Students
Association for Supervision and Curriculum Development
Comparative and International Education Society
Council for Exceptional Children
Council for Learning Disabilities
Home Economics Association
International Reading Association
International Society for Technology in Education
Kappa Delta Pi
Lutheran Education Association
National Alliance of Black School Educators
National Art Education Association
National Association for Bilingual Education
National Association for Gifted Children
National Association for Teachers of Hospitalized/Homebound
National Association of Biology Teachers
National Association of Elementary School Principals
National Association of School Nurses
National Association of Secondary School Principals
National Business Education Association
National Catholic Education Association
National Council for the Social Studies
National Council of Teachers of English
National Council of Teachers of Mathematics
National Rural Education Association
National Science Teachers Association
Phi Delta Kappa
Society for Music Teacher Education

Each publishes a journal and holds meetings. Many have state and local branches. Consult with your mentor for addresses.

Student Teaching Will Not Have Prepared You

Student teaching rarely includes any training in what to do on the first day of school. First day? You probably did not receive any training for the first minutes of class when the students walk in and decide whether they are going to be with you or against you.

Your master teacher is not to be blamed. No one ever trained your master teacher in what to teach you. Few teachers took over a class on the first day of school when they were student teaching. Few student teachers enter teaching with any experience in what to do on the first day of school. Typically, the master teacher started the class and then turned the class over to the student teacher. Or the student teacher came to teach for a period of time during the school year.

Thus most student teachers enter the teaching profession with no training and no experience in what to do on the first day of school.

> I do not remember this teacher's name, but had it not been for her, I never would have made it this far. Bless her! Something happened to me before the first day of school when I began teaching 26 years ago in Los Angeles.
>
> I was standing in the teachers' lounge when this experienced teacher came to me and said, "You don't know how to start, eh?"
>
> I said, "How can you tell? If you can only start my classes for me and get them rolling, I'll be able to carry on."
>
> No one had taught me how to start the first day of school.
>
> Gail Sutton
> Portland, Oregon

The District May Not Have Prepared You

In teaching, entry into the profession is sudden. Unlike the business world, where the newcomer goes through a training or apprenticeship period, gradually gaining knowledge, experience, and responsibility, this may not happen in the teaching profession. Newly hired teachers, not just neophyte teachers, are given a key to a room and told to go teach. What are you to do?

Figure it out yourself.
Do it yourself.
Keep it to yourself.

> **The beginning teacher is expected to assume the same tasks and responsibilities as the most seasoned teacher on the staff.**

In the trades, plumbers and electricians go into an apprenticeship program, first working as an apprentice, then laboring as a journeyman, and finally qualifying as a licensed tradesman or craftsman. In sports, you begin as a rookie on the bench, slowly gathering knowledge and experience as you work toward a starting position and a higher league.

Have you ever wondered why your seemingly problem students do so well at a fast-food restaurant? Restaurants like McDonald's and Domino's Pizza have sophisticated training programs to prepare workers before they face the public. Go behind the scenes at one of these places, and you will see workers studying videos, learning and reviewing aspects of their jobs. **Effective schools and teachers, likewise, have an induction program for all newly hired teachers.**

Induction Can Help Beginning Teachers

Induction has three purposes:

1. To **reduce** the **intensity** of transition into teaching

2. To help you **improve** your **teaching** effectiveness

3. To **increase** the **retention** of greater numbers of highly qualified teachers

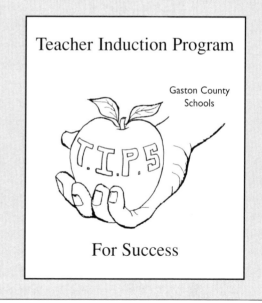

Teacher Induction Program

Gaston County Schools

T.I.P.S

For Success

The Gaston County schools received the North Carolina Governor's Award for Excellence for their new teacher induction program.

You Will Be Expected to Perform Immediately

Do not sign a contract until you ask a district if it has a new teacher induction program.** Effective districts want to help their newly hired teachers succeed. They offer induction programs that begin before the first day of school and may extend for several years thereafter. Induction is not orientation, mentoring, or evaluation. (See pages v and xiv.)

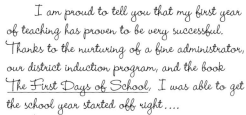

I am proud to tell you that my first year of teaching has proven to be very successful. Thanks to the nurturing of a fine administrator, our district induction program, and the book The First Days of School, *I was able to get the school year started off right....*

Together, we completed a year that proved to be rewarding to both me and my students.

Marita Lacey
Oklahoma City, Oklahoma

Marita Lacey is now working with fifth graders in her seventh year of teaching and is still very successful.

You will be expected to perform your full complement of duties immediately while learning them at the same time.

Yes, you will be expected to be perfect on the first day of school and then get better each year. You can do it, but you will be able to do it better if your district puts you through an induction program and then partners you with a mentor. Welcome to the teaching profession!

Some school districts have model classrooms that are prepared before the first day of school. Induction program teachers visit these classrooms to see how a classroom can be set up for the start of school.

17

Your First Year of Teaching Can Be a Happy Experience

> **Here's the biggest secret to teaching success:**
>
> **Beg, Borrow, and Steal!**

It's really called research and learning, but you walk into the classrooms of effective teachers, look around, and if you see something that you think might help you, you say, "Gimme, gimme, gimme." There are many veteran teachers who will be happy to share with you and help you.

Your whole life is ahead of you, and it can be filled with happiness and success. **If you want positive results from your life, you must keep certain responsibilities in focus:**

✔ **Work** in a collegial manner with your colleagues.

✔ **Associate** with and learn from positive mentors.

✔ **Join** a professional organization.

✔ **Continue to learn** through classes, workshops, conferences, in-service meetings, books, journals, tapes, and advanced degrees.

Avoid teachers who constantly complain and make excuses. Do not allow people who cannot control their own behavior to be in control of your behavior. The only limitations are those you place on yourself and those you allow other people to place on you. **You are the only person on the face of the earth who can use your abilities. It is an awesome responsibility.**

Seen on a third-grade teacher's bulletin board in South Chicago.

Share

what you have learned about
The First Days of School
with your colleagues

**Fastest and easiest way to order
Write or call direct**

**Harry K. Wong Publications, Inc.
943 North Shoreline Boulevard
Mountain View, CA 94043
TEL (650) 965-7896**

Share

what you have learned about
The First Days of School
with your colleagues

**Fastest and easiest way to order
Write or call direct**

**Harry K. Wong Publications, Inc.
943 North Shoreline Boulevard
Mountain View, CA 94043
TEL (650) 965-7896**

The teacher in this classroom
is a
professional
with the required training,
certification, and dedication necessary
to provide a QUALITY EDUCATION
to all students who enter.

The Subject is Success!

You Can Have Any Job in Education in Three to Five Years with a Raise in Salary of 25 Percent or More

Your future in education can be very rewarding, but only the teachers who strive for success will be rewarded. It's no different with students. Only those who work hard and have the most positive attitudes get the best grades. Here are some reasons why the future looks good for you.

- At the start of the new century, 75 to 80 percent of all teachers who were teaching in 1990 will have been replaced by more recent graduates.

- All kinds of job opportunities will be available—and not just in the classroom. Many teachers will become administrators or college professors, hold jobs in educational organizations, write software, become consultants, run educational programs for private businesses, open child-care centers, and embark on many other educationally related endeavors.

- Business will get heavily involved because it must. And companies will reeducate workers who didn't learn in the classroom. Private industry will be spending more money on education than public education.

- Although teachers are in the learning profession, they are among the worst when it comes to wanting to learn how to improve their own competencies. Most teachers do not go to conferences and deride in-service meetings.

- Because many teachers do not want to grow, those who do can have almost any position in education in three to five years at a salary 25 percent more than what they are making right now.

There is a new sense of urgency about our schools, a hopeful sign. You can play an active role during this time of urgency—and be rewarded for your contribution.

Education

And Now, a Teacher Shortage

Sunbelt school systems are caught with their rosters short

WANT TO TEACH BUT HAVE NO CREDENTIAL? asks the headline on a poster inside the Los Angeles unified school district's crash recruiting center. "Relax," continues the pitch. "We can help you get your teaching credential while you work full time as a junior or senior high school teacher . . ."

Among the remaining young people who do decide to teach, reportedly up to half quit within five to seven years.

Most threatening of all, perhaps, is the imminent prospect of numerous retirements. The average age of American teachers has risen to an estimated 40 to 43, and in the next five years, 30% to 50%

Because of the need for many more teachers in the future, there will be many opportunities for effective teachers.

The Greatest Threat

The greatest threat to a nongrowing teacher is a teacher who is growing. The stagnating teacher will do everything to discourage and prevent you from growing because your growth is perceived as a threat.

Do not listen to cynical, nongrowing teachers who try to tell you that you are no good unless you stay in the classroom, teaching at the same grade level, using the same textbook, worksheets, and tests.

These are the people who make fun of administrators, schools of education, workshop leaders, conventions, conferences, in-service meetings (if they go, they sit in the back rows), and anything and anyone else that wants to help you grow into the great teacher and person you are destined to be.

Find yourself a mentor, a fellow colleague who will serve as your role model, someone from whom you can learn and take inspiration and whom you can hold up as a symbol of the success you want to be.

The Effective Teacher

1. Works cooperatively and learns from colleagues.

2. Seeks out a mentor who serves as a role model.

3. Goes to professional meetings to learn.

4. Has a goal of striving for excellence.

KEY IDEA

The teacher is NOT in private practice.

You Are in a Helping Profession

> **Teachers are not in private practice.**
> **We are in the helping and caring profession,**
> **a service profession to help people**
> **enhance the quality of their lives.**

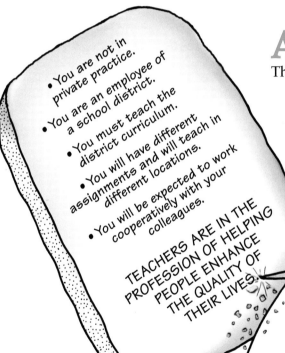

- You are not in private practice.
- You are an employee of a school district.
- You must teach the district curriculum.
- You will have different assignments and will teach in different locations.
- You will be expected to work cooperatively with your colleagues.

TEACHERS ARE IN THE PROFESSION OF HELPING PEOPLE ENHANCE THE QUALITY OF THEIR LIVES.

Anger, grief, and revenge are tiring. For happiness, sanity, and a positive outlook, it is essential that you understand your role in the teaching profession. This applies to all teachers, experienced as well as entry-level, first-year teachers.

Teaching is a craft. It is a service profession. If you want to choose your own hours, decide when and what you want to do, treat people as you please, create materials and keep them private, and avoid sharing and exchanging materials—go into private practice.

Be a brain surgeon, a self-employed cabinetmaker, or a real estate broker. Open a pizza restaurant, design and market computer software, or deal in stocks, bonds, futures, and commodities.

You Are Employed by a School District

If you choose to be a teacher, know that you will be an employee of a district or a board of education. When you sign a contract, you are agreeing to teach the district's curriculum as well as to abide by and carry out the district's policies, rules, and regulations. As a district employee, you are not allowed to teach only what you want or to do as you please.

✔ **The district is owned by the local citizens.** It has a set of policies and regulations governing the behavior of all employees and students to protect this ownership.

✔ **The district has a curriculum.** The district's curriculum has been and will be an evolving product, formulated by a district committee made up of many of your colleagues.

✔ **The district has employees, like you.** Your colleagues brought years of experience and expertise with them to formulate the district's mission, philosophy, and curriculum. The board approved their work, and it is the curriculum for the district, of which you are an employee.

For your happiness and effectiveness, accept in your own mind and heart that you can live and perform comfortably with the district's role for you. If you can't live with the district's expectations for you, perhaps you should go into private practice.

You Will Not Be in One Room Forever

Understand that your first assignment will not be your last assignment. For your sanity, accept that in a world changing at breakneck speed, you will not be allowed to stagnate in the same room teaching out of the same book forever.

> ### Palmer v. Board of Education of Chicago (1979)
>
> Probationary teacher Joethelia Palmer did not want to teach about one of the holidays. She was discharged of her duties. She took the district to court, and the district won.

The effective teacher knows the district's curriculum guide and uses materials that reflect those objectives.

Furthermore, you will be expected to do your job with the same enthusiasm that you expect from your own students. You will be expected, on your own initiative, to serve on committees, confer with parents, and attend meetings, in-service programs, conferences, college classes, and workshops to further yourself and the district's goals.

As an employee of the district, you should expect to be reassigned from time to time. Be a model of adaptability. Just as you expect your students to go into a changing world and adapt, show that you can adapt and excel in a changing world. Finally, understand that you have a role as part of a larger community and society.

Understand Your Role

1. The schools are owned and operated by the citizens of your local community.

2. Schools are the foundation for transmitting the values and traditions that ensure our life in a free society.

3. The schools are built for the STUDENTS.

Perhaps the most valuable result of all education is the ability to make yourself do the thing you have to do, when it ought to be done, whether you like it or not.

—*Thomas Huxley*

Take Responsibility for Yourself

To be an effective teacher, you need to move on to the third stage of teaching: mastery—the subject of this book. Survival, the second stage (Chapter 1), is a normal stop on your journey as a teacher, but the ideal is to get beyond it quickly. Yet on every teaching staff from kindergarten through graduate school, there are instructors who have been teaching for decades and are still at survival. Why does this happen to some teachers? They acquire ineffective teaching attitudes and techniques early on, and these become crystallized into their permanent teaching repertoire.

> *Isolation*
> *is unique to the teaching profession and,*
> *by implication,*
> *to the whole educational system.*[1]

Teacher isolation is a reality. Many teachers become comfortable in their isolation. Teachers who work in isolation cut themselves off from sources of useful information, both colleagues and professional resources. Survival mode results when teachers stay within the limitations of what they know or do not know, and the latter is always much greater.

Ineffectiveness is tiring. Working with limited information, teachers then mimic each other. They develop bad habits. They resort to busywork to keep students quiet. They develop cynical attitudes toward conferences and in-service meetings, not allowing themselves to grow. They adopt the classic stance of survival and find their life very tiring.

Good habits are easy to develop. Bad habits are difficult to break. If you are a new teacher, develop good teaching attitudes and techniques and you will be happy. If you are a veteran teacher, you can be happy and effective tomorrow. Please do the following:

- ✔ Turn to Unit E and read Chapters 25 and 26 and the Epilogue.
- ✔ Read Chapter 5 to find out how research can help you.

Then get ready for three exciting units—on positive expectations, classroom management, and lesson mastery.

What's the Difference Between an Effective Teacher and an Ineffective Teacher?

There's only one difference: The ineffective teacher is simply not doing what the effective teacher is doing. Do what the effective teacher is doing, and you will be effective—instantly.

Successful people MAKE themselves do the things that unsuccessful people will not do.

Effective teachers look at the resources available to them and then reorganize those resources to work toward a goal.

The universal mantra of all teachers is "I teach my students how to think."

Ineffective teachers look over the resources, move them aside, and rely on busywork as an excuse for learning.

Effective teachers are problem solvers. "I teach myself how to think," they tell themselves. "I analyze, synthesize, and create materials to help students learn."

Effective, problem-solving teachers do it all day long: rearrange resources and information to help students reach the goals of the class.

[1]Lortie, D. C. (1995). *Schoolteacher: A Sociological Study.* Chicago: University of Chicago Press.

If you want to become a professional educator, have a career with a future, be happy, and be recognized as a person who makes a difference in the lives of others, begin by making an impact on your own life. **A teacher cannot give what he or she is not.**

> **Some people can give thousands of reasons**
> **why they cannot succeed at something**
> **when all they need is one reason**
> **why they can succeed.**

If you do not take responsibility for yourself, no one else will. It's that simple.

Get to Know All Your Colleagues

Get to know all your colleagues. And listen to them. You will see many who are there to help enhance the lives of the students. Many know what they are doing and are happy to share with you. Learn from them. The happiest and most successful teachers, administrators, parents, and school board members are there to work WITH you to help you become an effective teacher so that you, in turn, can help and affect students.

Get to know all your colleagues. They have much to offer.

There is something inherently special about our profession that allows us to close out a previous academic year and plan for a new beginning—a sort of annual renewal, if you will.

—Lee Gray

They say that the three most important words in real estate are location, location, location. The three most important words for a teacher are **listen, listen, listen**.

If you are a beginning teacher, **listen, listen, listen**. If you are an experienced teacher, **listen, listen, listen**.

WELCOME (back) to the helping and teaching profession.

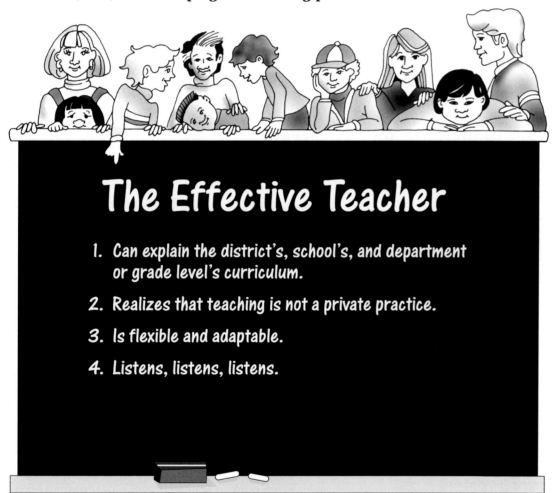

The Effective Teacher

1. Can explain the district's, school's, and department or grade level's curriculum.

2. Realizes that teaching is not a private practice.

3. Is flexible and adaptable.

4. Listens, listens, listens.

KEY IDEA

Effective teachers use proven research-based practices that are employed by thousands of other teachers.

The Research Process

> **The effective teacher understands how and why research is done.**

Research is the process of critical thinking and solving problems. It is this ability that sets humans apart from all other forms of living things. Research is simply the use of the human mind to search for and seek answers or, as some would say, to search for the "truth."

Research is what a person does to find answers. Research is not something only scientists do. Businesspeople do research; so do baseball players, knitters, plumbers, lawyers, dentists, artists, and homemakers. Students, when they do term papers, do research.

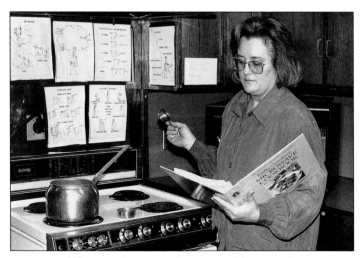

When you change a recipe, you are doing research.

Humans have always been seeking and searching. And that is what research is all about, to search. To search and search and search, over and over again. That is why it is called **re-search**.

During the Renaissance, the process for research became formalized. This process is the same basic process used by a scientist seeking an answer to cancer, a student doing a term paper, a lawyer investigating a case, or a chef trying to find a better way to make a cheesecake. It is a higher-order thinking process.

It May Be Dangerous to Teach as You Were Taught

Since the 1960s, much research has been done on education. Before that time, much about teaching, as well as much about running a school, was based on myths, hearsay, and traditions handed down from teacher to teacher or on teachers' recollections of how they were taught when they went to school.

No education professor, administrator, in-service speaker, or teacher at a workshop has ever said that the model of teaching in the illustration to the bottom right, is the way to teach.

Unfortunately and erroneously, many teachers tend to teach as they were taught. And most of us were taught by educators who either were not effective teachers or did not know the current research on effective teaching. Most teachers tend to teach as their academic college professors taught them simply because that was their last and most remembered educational experience.

✔ Academic professors are not teachers. They are researchers who are creating, seeking, and gathering new knowledge.

✔ Most academic professors do not have teaching credentials. They are not certified to teach.

Yet many teachers teach as their college professors, who are noncertified role models, taught them and think that this is teaching.

Not all research is done by college professors in an academic realm or by researchers working for a government agency. Much educational research is done by practitioners, teachers, or administrators working on a master's or doctoral thesis or by people who just like to do research.

The Research Process

Problem:	What do I want to know?
Prediction:	What do I think is the right answer?
Procedure:	How will I solve the problem?
Data:	What will I look for?
Conclusion:	What do the results tell me?

THIS MODEL OF TEACHING HAS NO RESEARCH TO SUPPORT IT

- Assign chapters to read.
- Answer the questions at the back of the chapter or on the worksheet.
- Deliver a lecture and have students take notes.
- Show a video or do an activity.
- Construct a test based on a number of points.

When Should You Ask Questions During a Video?

Educational research tells you.

Bob Wallace, a middle school teacher in Ventnor, New Jersey, reported the following as a result of his research with his students.

He divided his students into three groups and did the following:

Group 1: Showed the students a video and gave them a test.

Group 2: Briefed the group on the video to be shown, then showed the same video as shown to Group 1 and gave the same test.

Group 3: Briefed the group exactly as he had Group 2, then showed the same video. However, during the video, he stopped the tape frequently. During each stop, he asked questions and held class discussion. He then gave the same test as he had given to Groups 1 and 2.

Guess which of the three groups scored the highest on the test. Group 3, of course.

This confirms what research found to be an effective way to ask questions in the classroom.

An Example of Educational Research That Applies to Every Teacher

John P. Rickards discovered two things:[1]

1. The most ineffective place to print questions is at the end of a textbook chapter.

2. It is an ineffective method to give a student all the questions for an assignment at one time and then ask the student to answer all the questions and to turn them in all at one time.

Rickards found that if you want a student to achieve high-level comprehension, you should intersperse the questions throughout the text.

You know that this is true from having taken reading comprehension tests. Reading comprehension tests are not written with pages of text followed by a long list of questions. They constantly go back and forth, a paragraph or two of text followed by a few questions.

To put it another way, no doctor asks questions when the patient is dead. A doctor intersperses questions during the treatment of a patient.

Likewise, the effective teacher does not ask all the questions at the end of the discussion, class period, video, chapter, lecture, or meeting. **The effective teacher who wants high-level comprehension intersperses questions throughout all class activities.** This is what the research tells us.

Effective teachers do what the research tells us is most effective. Effective teachers use proven research-based practices. Why would you do otherwise?

[1]John P. Rickards. (November 1976). "Stimulating High-Level Comprehension by Interspersing Questions in Text Passages." *Educational Technology,* p. 13.

Effective Teachers Use Research-Based Practices

> **People who know what to do and people who know how to do it will always be working for those who know why it is being done.**

Educational research is not all theoretical, conducted in an ivory tower. Nearly all educational research quoted in this book was performed by researchers looking at teachers and students in functioning schools and reporting on effective and ineffective practices. The effective teacher does three things:

1. Understands how research is done.

2. Uses proven research-based practices.

3. Understands that these practices are used by thousands of other teachers and are tried-and-true methods that work.

It is one thing to know what you are doing. It is another to know how to do it. Most important, you need to know why you are doing what you are doing.

There is an extensive body of knowledge about teaching, and the effective teacher understands and uses this knowledge. Do not teach from hearsay, myths, or prevailing practices. To be an effective teacher, understand that effective school research is based on the reporting of what effective teachers do. These methods are used by hundreds of thousands of effective teachers. You can be one also!

> *Research cannot and does not identify the right or best way to teach, nor does it suggest that certain instructional practices should always or never be used. But research can illuminate which instructional practices are most likely to achieve desired results, with which kinds of learners, and under what conditions.*[2]
>
> —Myriam Met

The Four Beliefs of an Effective Teacher

1. It is the teacher who makes the difference in the classroom.

2. By far the most important factor in school learning is the ability of the teacher.

3. There is an extensive body of knowledge about teaching that must be known by the teacher.

4. The teacher must be a decision maker able to translate the body of knowledge about teaching into increased student learning.

—After Madeline Hunter

---

[2] Cawalti, Gordon (ed.). (1995). *Handbook of Research on Improving Student Achievement.* Arlington, Va.: Educational Research Service, p. 3.

Research on Improving Student Achievement

Aligned Time on Task: Students who are actively focused on educational goals do best in mastering the subject matter.

> Research findings: More than 130 studies support the obvious: The more students study, the more they learn! Time alone, however, does not suffice. The lesson criteria, learning activities, and tests must be matched and emphasized. (To see how this is implemented, refer to Chapters 22 and 23.)

Cooperative Learning: Students in small, self-instructing groups can support and increase one another's learning.

> Research findings: More than 50 studies state increased academic achievement is greater when there is frequent exchange among teachers and students. In addition, students learn teamwork skills that are essential in the workplace. Cooperative learning, however, should be only one of many different practices used by a teacher. (To see how cooperative learning is implemented, consult Chapter 24.)

Extensive Reading: Extensive reading of material of many kinds, both in school and outside, results in substantial growth in the vocabulary, comprehension abilities, and information base of students.

> Research findings: Cognitive abilities, such as comprehension and vocabulary, are enhanced with an increase in time spent reading, inside and outside of school. Studies show, however, that children spend no more than a few minutes a day reading on either assigned or independent reading. School resources need to be provided for materials and large blocks of time for students to read.

Wait Time: Pausing after asking a question in the classroom results in an increase in achievement.

> Research findings: Students are given less than one second to respond to a question. Increasing wait time from three to seven seconds, accompanied by a high-order question, results in students responding with more thoughtful answers and an increase in science achievement.

—Based on Gordon Cawalti (ed.).
Handbook of Research on Improving Student Achievement. (1995). Arlington, Va.: Educational Research Service.

The Effective Teacher

1. Understands the research process.

2. Teaches with proven research-based practices.

3. Knows the difference between an effective teacher and an ineffective one.

UNIT B

First Characteristic —
Positive Expectations

The effective teacher has positive
expectations for student success.

First Characteristic — Positive Expectations

The effective teacher has positive expectations for student success.

Unit B is correlated with **Part 2: The First Days of School** and **Part 8: Positive Expectations**
in the video series *The Effective Teacher*.

Humans Have a Success Instinct

Your expectations of your students will greatly influence their achievement in your class and in their lives.

> There is absolutely no research correlation
> between success and family background, race, national origin,
> financial status, or even educational accomplishments.
> There is but one correlation with success,
> and that is ATTITUDE.

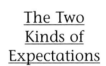

The Two
Kinds of
Expectations

• Positive
  or high
  expectations

• Negative
  or low
  expectations

All living things live to survive. They spend their entire day, instinctively, seeking food and shelter and escaping predators.

Humans have a success instinct. This is what makes humans different from all other living things. They want success, and they strive for their success potential. You can accomplish anything with students if you set high expectations for behavior and performance by which you yourself abide.

Positive and Negative Expectations

Knowing what you can or cannot achieve is called **EXPECTATION**. An expectation is what you believe will or will not happen.

Positive Expectations

An optimistic belief that whoever you teach or whatever you do will result in success or achievement. If you expect to be successful, you are constantly alert and aware of opportunities to help you be successful.

Examples of Positive Expectations

✔ "We are going to win the league championship."

✔ "I believe that every child can learn and will achieve to his or her fullest potential."

✔ "I am a good teacher, and I am proud that I am a professional educator."

✔ "I am always learning, and that is why I enjoy going to conferences, workshops, and in-service meetings."

Results of Positive Expectations

The odds are greater that what you want to happen will happen because you will be expending energy to see that this will be so. You predispose yourself to realize success both personally and with the people you deal with, such as your students.

Negative Expectations

A pessimistic belief that whoever you teach or whatever you do will not work out or will fail. For that matter, why bother to do anything or teach anyone at all? If you expect to fail, you are constantly looking for justification, proof, and demonstration of why you have failed.

Examples of Negative Expectations

✔ "We'll be lucky if we lose by only 10 points."

✔ "These kids just don't want to learn."

✔ "They can't read; they can't spell; they can't sit still; they can't behave."

✔ "In-service meetings are boring; conferences have nothing to offer to me."

Results of Negative Expectations

The odds are that what you expect to happen will not happen because you will be expending energy to see that nothing happens. You predispose yourself to realize failure both personally and with the people you deal with, such as your students.

"Look at it this way. Summer vacation is only ten months away."

A San Jose, California, shopping center ran this newspaper advertisement soon after the new school year began. Does it send a positive or a negative message to a student?

◆◆ **It takes just as much energy to achieve positive results as it does to achieve negative results. So why waste your energy on failing when that same amount of energy can help you and your students succeed?**

All Children Can Learn!

This poster was developed by the Oklahoma City Public Schools. Is the message positive or negative?

Expectations of	Negative or Low Expectations	Positive or High Expectations
Parents	I'll be happy if my children do not become involved with drugs.	I want each of my children to graduate as the class valedictorian.
Students	This class is boring. Why do we have to study this junk?	My dream and intention is to be a teacher.
Teachers	In-service meetings are so boring. Why do we have to listen to this drivel?	I learn so much and meet so many interesting people at conferences.

Expectations Are Different from Standards

Expectations should not be confused with standards. Standards are levels of achievement. Teachers who practice positive expectations will help their students reach high standards.

◆◆ **Example: "This will be an exciting class, and you are going to have the most memorable year you have ever had; as a result, you will do very well."**

Teachers who practice negative expectations will prevent students from reaching high standards.

> **Example:** **"I only give one A each year. I have very high standards"**
> **(said in aggrandizement of one's intellectual superiority).**

People are molded more by the depth of your convictions or expectations than by the height of your intelligence. Success involves converting people, not to your way of knowing, but to your way of feeling. People can refuse words, but they cannot refuse an attitude or an expectation. **Give your students more than they expect, and you will get back more than you ever expected.**

The Classic Research on Expectations

The classic research on expectations was done in the 1960s by Robert Rosenthal of Harvard University and Lenore Jacobson of the South San Francisco schools.[1] They fed erroneous information to a group of South San Francisco elementary school teachers and watched the teachers make the results come true.

In the spring of the preceding school year, the students at Oak School were pretested. When school began that fall, the researchers and the administrators told the teachers that they were special teachers who were to be part of a special experiment.

They were told, "Based on a pretest, we have identified 20 percent of your students who are special. They will be 'spurters' or 'bloomers' and are a designated group of students of whom greater intellectual growth is expected."

The names were really selected at random, but the teachers were led to believe that the status of being special children was based on scores on the pretest, the Harvard Test of Inflected Acquisition.

Each child is living the only life he has—the only one he will ever have. The least we can do is not diminish it.

—Bill Page

---

[1] Rosenthal, Robert, and Lenore Jacobson. (1968). *Pygmalion in the Classroom.* Fort Worth, Tex.: Holt, Rinehart and Winston.

"As a special reward for your teaching excellence, we are going to tell you this information, but with two conditions:

1. You must not tell the students that you know that they are special.

2. None of us are going to tell the parents that their children are special.

Thus we expect and know that you will do extremely well with these special students."

Eight months later, all the students were tested again, and a comparison was made of the designated special students and the undesignated students, as measured by IQ scores. The results showed a significant gain in intellectual growth for the 20 percent who were designated special in the primary grades but no significant gains in the intermediate grades.

The administrators brought the teachers in, showed them the growth results of their students, and congratulated them on their spectacular success with their students.

The teachers said, "Of course, we had special students to work with. It was easy, and they learned so fast."

The administrators and researcher said, "We'd like to tell you the truth. The so-called special children were picked at random. We made no selections based on IQ or aptitude."

"Then it must have been us," said the teachers, "because you said we were special teachers selected to be part of a special experiment."

"We need to tell you something else, too," replied the researcher. "All the teachers were involved in this experiment. None of you were designated special over any other teacher."

FLOWING WELLS HIGH SCHOOL

KEYS TO SUCCESS

- *Whether you think you can or think you can't—you are right.*
  Henry Ford

- *All our dreams can come true—if we have the courage to pursue them.*
  Walt Disney

- *I do the very best I know how; the very best I can; and I mean to keep on doing so until the end.*
  Abraham Lincoln

- *No legacy is so rich as honesty.*
  William Shakespeare

- *In the middle of difficulty lies opportunity.*
  Albert Einstein

- *Success is the maximum utilization of the ability that you have.*
  Zig Ziglar

The most successful schools have expectations that everyone will succeed.

This was a perfectly designed experiment. There was only one experimental variable—**EXPECTATION**.

1. The expectations of the administrators toward the teachers were stated explicitly. "You are special teachers, and these 20 percent of your students are special students who show potential for intellectual growth. Thus we expect and know that you will do extremely well with these special students."

2. The expectations of the teachers toward the students were conveyed implicitly and were unspoken. Because the teachers believed that they had some very special students in the school, their body language, personality, and attitude influenced their teaching and expectations of their students.

As the researchers stated, "The results suggest rather strongly that children who are expected by their teachers to gain intellectually in fact do show greater intellectual gains after one year than do children of whom such gains are not expected."

> **Students tend to learn as little or as much as their teachers expect. Teachers who set and communicate high expectations to all their students obtain greater academic performance from these students than do teachers who set low expectations.**[2]

---

[2]U.S. Department of Education. (1986). *What Works: Research About Teaching and Learning.* Washington, D.C.: U.S. Government Printing Office, p. 7.

The Good Ones Are Not at Home

Here they come! All precious and products of society. In September 1995, some 4.5 million youngsters entered public school, and enrollment is projected to rise to 5 million by 2005.

- On any given night, at least 100,000 children are homeless.
- 82 percent of incarcerated people are high school dropouts.
- Every year, approximately 1 million teenage girls become pregnant.
- 135,000 American students bring guns to school every day.
- Homicide is the leading cause of death among minority youth aged 15 to 19.
- Reported child abuse increased 48 percent from 1986 to 1991.

Yet schools are doing a better job of educating our children than ever before.

As Larry Lezotte said, "The parents are sending us the best kids they have. They are not keeping the good ones at home."

—Enrollment Data:
National Center for Education Statistics, 1995.

Children's Data:
National Commission on Children, 1995.

The Two Most Important Groups of People

A Tribute to My Parents

Before I was five years old, my parents said something to me over and over again. They even got my relatives to say it to me, as well as my neighbors and the local merchants.

Several times a day, I would hear, "Little Harry Wong, when you grow up, what kind of a doctor are you going to be?" This was accompanied by their pointing out to me, as positive role models, that my uncles were all doctors and that my cousins were studying to be doctors.

They told me that it was a foregone conclusion that I would be admitted to medical school, even though the competition was tough in those days. What they wanted to know was what I planned to specialize in.

Not being in kindergarten yet, I said, "I don't know."

And then came their reply, "You're going to be a brain surgeon, aren't you?" In other words, they believed that I had the intelligence to be the ultimate of all doctors, so brilliant that I could even operate on other people's brains.

My parents conveyed a message of high or positive expectations to me. For this I will be forever grateful to them, and I send them my love.

—Harry K. Wong

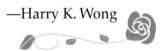

Things My Parents and Teachers Never Said to Me

You are dumb.

You are stupid.

You are no good.

You will never amount to anything.

I didn't want you; you were an accident.

You don't belong in this class; you were placed here against my wishes.

Look at it this way, summer vacation is only 10 months away.

A Tribute to My Teachers

The other reason I achieved success in school and life was because of my teachers. When I was in elementary school in the early 1940s, I remember distinctly that my teachers had a saying that they would repeat often, year after year, new teacher after new teacher. This saying became ingrained in me as a driving force or expectation in my life.

They would say, "You can be anything you want to be. You can even be president of the United States."

It is sad that the young people of today are not sent a message of becoming a leader or a hero. Rather, the heroes of today's children are a potato that sits on a couch, so lazy that a remote control is needed to change the channels on the television; crime-fighting cartoon characters; and a brat who is proud that he is an underachiever. All can be purchased as objects or dolls to serve as role models to young people.

My teachers conveyed to me a message of high or positive expectations, a powerful message that told me that I was smart and good enough to be anything I wanted to be, even to hold the highest office in the nation.

I thank my teachers for having that expectation of me.

—Harry K. Wong

The two worst things a parent can give a young person are money and wheels. The two most important things a parent can give a child are roots and wings.

—*After Hodding Carter*

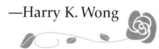

The two most important groups of people, as far as young people are concerned, are

Parents and Teachers

A preschooler was asked if he knew what he wanted to be when he grew up. He said, "A teenager."

What parents and teachers convey to young people in their formative years as expectations will influence young people to achieve accordingly.

> *. . . from conception to age 4, the individual develops 50% of his mature intelligence, from ages 4 to 8 he develops another 30%, and from ages 8 to 17 the remaining 20%. . . .*
>
> *As much of the development takes place in the first 4 years of life as in the next 13 years.*
>
> *We are inclined to believe that this is the most important growing period for academic achievement and that **all subsequent learning in the school is affected and in large part determined by what the child has learned by the age of 9 or by the end of grade 3.***
>
> *It is evident that when the school and home environments are mutually reinforcing, learning is likely to be greatest. **The nature of the learning environment is most critical during the periods of most rapid change in learning—the early years of school.**[3]*
>
> —Benjamin S. Bloom

Children are like wet cement. Whatever falls on them makes an impression.

—Haim Ginott

Who you are and what you do and say will greatly influence the young people who will be the productive citizens of tomorrow's world. **Your expectations of your students will greatly influence their achievement in your class and ultimately their lives.**

---

[3]Bloom, Benjamin S. (1964). *Stability and Change in Human Characteristics.* New York: Wiley, pp. 68, 88, 110, and 128.

The Effective Teacher

1. Has a statement of positive expectations ready for the first day of school.

2. Creates a classroom climate that communicates positive expectations.

3. Goes to professional meetings to learn.

4. Has a personal goal of high expectations.

My teacher thought I was smarter than I was; so I was.

—Six-year-old

Celebrate the First Day of School

The more the school and the family are joined as partners in educating young people, the greater the child's chances for success.

> **The most important day of a person's education is the First Day of School, not Graduation Day.**

If school does not begin with the proper, positive expectations, there may not be a Graduation Day for a student. Each year 700,000 students drop out of school, a number equal to the entire school population of Minnesota.

For some students, graduation is not a day to celebrate a joyful sense of accomplishment. Rather it is a day to mock respect, act stupid, make fun of the educational system, show disrespect to parents and teachers, and engage in wild parties that make you wonder if an education ever took place.

 The proper day to celebrate in all the schools of a country is the First Day of School.

Effective schools celebrate the First Day of School.

Celebrating the **First Day of School** must become a tradition of all educational systems. This day of celebration must include everyone associated with and interested in the education of the future citizens of the world.

45

In addition to everyone at the school site, this should include parents, the business community, and the neighborhood. It is important that students see that everyone is interested in helping them all succeed.

The more the school, the family, and the community are joined as partners in the cause of educating young people, the greater each child's chance for success.

Welcome Them to School

Just as you go on a vacation with high expectations, students come to school with high expectations also. They come to get an education, meet friends, participate, have fun, study, and learn. Their entire day revolves around school and their friends. It is an exciting time in their lives.

Therefore, the personnel of the school should extend greetings to the students before they come to school and upon their arrival. Everyone should be involved in planning the students' welcome to the school. "Everyone" means administrators, teachers, classified staff, district personnel, parents, and the business community. **The successful education of young people is an interrelated, community team effort.**

Kelly Edwards students are cordially invited to a

Celebration

of the

First Day of School

August 19th, 7:50 a.m.

Kelly Edwards Elementary School

Enter through the front doors.

This announcement appears each year in the local Williston, South Carolina, newspaper.

Schools should be built better and kept up better than banks because there's more wealth in them.

—Martin Haberman

How to Welcome Them to School

✔ Organize a **First Day of School** celebration.

✔ Stand at the bus stop and welcome them on the **First Day of School**. Wave and smile like it's Aunt Mabel who you have not seen in 14 years and her airplane has just pulled up to the Jetway.

✔ Stand at the front entrances of the school. Have all entrances covered so that no one will fail to receive a warm, friendly welcome.

✔ Bring out the school band to play at the curb or entry. If you don't have a band, have a group of students and teachers assembled to bring a welcome smile on the **First Day of School**.

✔ Hang up a computer-generated banner welcoming students to school. (What did schools ever do before software like Print Shop?)

✔ Distribute a school newspaper extolling the virtues of the school and the wonderful school spirit of the teachers and the students.

✔ Have guides in the hall. Hang up directional signs to help students get to their classrooms.

✔ Have your name and room number clearly visible on the classroom door along with your personal greeting of welcome. (See page 107.)

✔ Let the first message spoken over the public address system be one of welcome and positive expectations for the school year.

Everyone needs to be welcomed on the First Day of School.

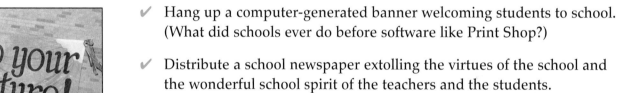

> **School is not a place; school is a concept.**

School is not a place where students come to listen to lectures, fill in worksheets, and endure boredom. Nor is it a place reserved for those who can tolerate the drab and dirty look of many schools.

School is a concept wherein students are welcome to learn and enhance the quality of their lives without fear of intimidation or harm, guided by hospitable and caring people in a clean and orderly environment.

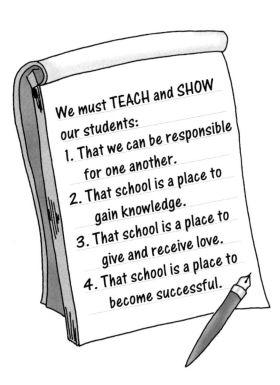

We must TEACH and SHOW our students:
1. That we can be responsible for one another.
2. That school is a place to gain knowledge.
3. That school is a place to give and receive love.
4. That school is a place to become successful.

You Will All Succeed

You will think that I'm in love with Japanese education. I'm not, but here is an anecdote that illustrates my point.

When our daughter took our granddaughter to her first day of kindergarten in Japan, she walked in casually dressed, as we might do in the United States, thinking she would drop the child off and go home. Well, not at all.

First, she discovered that all of the other parents were dressed up in their finest for a full day of ceremonies in celebration of the first day of school. They were in the room with the children, and there were speakers on the platform with a big banner that said, "Welcome to Kindergarten. ***You Will All Succeed.****"*

—Ernest L. Boyer
"On Parents, School and
the Workplace." (Fall 1988).
Kappa Delta Pi Record, p. 8.

The school, the community, and the family must all work together for student success.

Family Day

Family Day . . . We began the day by joining hands and encircling the school—parents, students, and staff—to recite our Family Day rap and sing our school song. Even the drizzling rain could not diminish the strong sense of pride and family spirit we felt that morning.

It was a glorious day. . . . Parents learned more about parenting; children learned they could say "no" to drug use and "yes" to their parents' authority. Parents and children danced together, the children mimicking the dances of yesterday and the parents struggling to do the dances of today.

Nothing else has been half as rewarding as to see more than 200 parents involved in a full day of activities with their children. On future Family Days we can continue to make positive changes toward strengthening the fiber of our society. No more lost generations at this school; **we count Family Day as an investment in our future.**

— Vernon Smith
"Family Day: An Investment in Our Future." (May 1988).
Educational Leadership, p. 56.

The students must sense that the schools are the nurturing grounds for their intellectual development in a safe, caring, positive atmosphere.

The Effective Teacher

1. Helps organize a First Day of School celebration.

2. Plans a classroom welcome for the first day.

3. Ensures the mental and physical safety of all students.

4. Creates an environment for all students to succeed.

KEY IDEA

The effective teacher dresses appropriately as a professional educator to model success.

As you are dressed, so shall you be perceived; and as you are perceived, so shall you be treated.

You Are Treated as You Are Dressed

> **You do not get a second chance at a first impression.**

Make no mistake, we judge others by their dress, and they judge us too. It may not be fair. It may not be right. But people tend to treat other people as they are dressed.

It's common sense. You will be treated as you are dressed. A salesperson sees two shoppers approaching, one appropriately dressed and the other inappropriately dressed. You know very well who will get immediate and better service.

How much credibility would a bank have if the teller who processes your paycheck was dressed in jeans and wore a T-shirt emblazoned with the slogan "Poverty Sucks"? Would you buy life insurance from a salesperson who called on the family wearing a bowling jacket with the inscription "Ma's Donuts" on the back?

In an ideal world, viewed through rose-colored glasses, it would be wonderful to be accepted for ourselves alone, not for our appearance. In the real world, however, our all-too-visible selves are under constant scrutiny.

The fact is, most people think that the cover is the book, the box front is the cereal, and the leather jacket is the person. We all make judgments. We look at someone and judge status, income, even occupation.

 It is not what is but what is perceived.

You Are a Walking, Talking Advertisement

This may be a superficial world, but it is the way the world works, so saying that something is superficial will not make it go away. **You are much better off making your dress work for you than to allow it to work against you.**

Give an elementary student three days, and the student will mirror you. Give a high school student ten days, and the student will mirror you.

—*Charles Galloway*

Teachers Are Not Downtrodden or Poor

Facts About American Teachers in 1996:

- Number of teachers in America: 3 million

- Average household income: > $53,000 a year

- Average annual salary: $36,933

- 80 percent have done postgraduate work.

- Heavy users of premium credit cards and more than twice as likely to have an American Express Gold Card than a regular card.

- Avid readers who read publications such as *Gourmet, Bon Appétit,* and *Smithsonian.*

- 99 percent have taken one or more trips outside the continental United States.

- 66 percent have a computer at home.

- 90 percent own homes or condominiums.

- 84 percent are married.

—*Market Data Retrieval* and *National Education Association*

The key is looking professional, not just looking good. **The advantage of looking professional is that it keeps you from self-destructing in the first few seconds, before the students make any hasty judgments about you.**

The effective teacher dresses appropriately as a professional educator to model success. The important word is *appropriately*. We often see signs like this one:

Successful teachers dress for success.

Yes, ties take time to tie and sometimes get uncomfortable. However, ties say, "I'm willing to take the time to show others that I respect them."

One of the reasons we have schools is for students to learn what is appropriate. Young people learn what is appropriate in society by looking at their adult role models. Your dress and your behavior are what young people will take to be appropriate.

By the end of the first or second week, the entire class will have taken signals from you as to how they should behave for the rest of the school year.

✔ We are walking, talking advertisements for who we are.

✔ We are walking, talking advertisements for who we believe we are as professional educators.

When you walk into class late, you have just made a statement. When you walk into class late with a soda can or a cup of coffee in your hand and a scowl on your face, you are making a statement.

When you walk into class early, the room and materials are ready, there is a positive classroom climate, you are standing at the door with a smile and an extended hand of welcome, and the assignments are on the chalkboard, you are making a statement.

When you allow teasing in class, you are making a statement. When you refuse to tolerate teasing in class, you are making a statement.

Every time you act, you validate who you are.

The statement that you make influences how the students will behave and achieve in class. And how students behave and achieve in class will determine your success as a teacher.

The experts tell us that teenagers get their values from their friends. That's true to the extent that there is a values vacuum to be filled. It is imperative that the parents get there first.

New teachers get their values from other teachers. It is imperative that there exist a school or district induction program coupled with a mentoring program staffed by dedicated, professional, role-model teachers.

What Is Appropriate Dress?

You expect your students to use appropriate English, write papers using an appropriate form, and display appropriate behavior and manners.

Right?

Then you understand about appropriate dress.

Dress for Respect

Clothing may not make a person, but it can be a contributing factor in unmaking a person. Whether we want to admit it, our appearance affects how we are perceived and received in definite ways. Clothing has nothing to do with students liking a teacher. But clothing definitely has an affect on students' respect for a teacher, and respect is what a teacher must have if learning is to take place.

Research reveals that the clothing worn by teachers affects the work, attitude, and discipline of students. You dress for four main effects:

1. Respect

2. Credibility

3. Acceptance

4. Authority

The effective teacher uses these four traits as assets in relating to students, peers, administrators, parents, and the community. If you have these four traits, you have a much greater chance of influencing young people to learn than someone who lacks these four traits.

You can be sure that students notice how their teachers are dressed, in the same way that they notice the appropriateness of their own and each other's dress. Furthermore, **students see how their parents go to their jobs each day and make comparisons between their parents and their teachers**.

Could Not Believe What I Saw

After Christmas vacation, one of my students left some pictures of the class holiday party on my desk. I took a look at myself and I could not believe how I looked. I looked like I didn't care about myself.

The next day I came to school more appropriately dressed, and they all noticed and commented on how nice I looked. I was so happy and they made me feel so good.

I now spend more time caring about who I am. The students care about me. I am proud of who I am. And they are also so much better behaved now as a result of who I represent.

Fifth-grade teacher
Iowa

They see their parents go to work each day, dressed in business attire or institutional uniforms. Then they come to school and observe the attire of teachers—professionals who are considered middle-class, intellectuals with college degrees, competent people with teaching credentials. You can see why the teaching profession has a difficult time gaining respect and credibility.

You can also see why some teachers have great difficulty reaching and influencing students—and if teachers cannot reach students, no teaching will take place. Not only are these teachers unable to reach students, but they also leave school at the end of the day frustrated over their own inadequacies. These inadequacies are evident in how they dress. For when you dress, you are making a statement about yourself to the world.

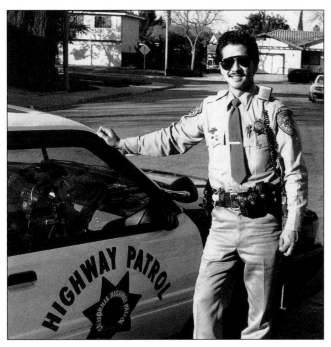

Every profession has its appropriate attire.

What I Wear for My Interviews

Bright colors convey positive, happy feelings. Children like bright colors, and when teachers wear them, they convey happiness and "aliveness." My staff likes my bright clothes; my father does too. Women must no longer try to dress like men—yea! The same rules for the business community do not always apply to the world of the school. I've worn green and black to every interview where I've been hired. When I interview teachers for job openings, I like to see some color. Conservative dressers aren't often willing to take a risk and try new approaches in the classroom. Color conveys confidence, confidence to take risks.

I think a more conservative dress is more appropriate at the high school. But remember, at the elementary level, especially K-1, teachers get down on the floor with their kids.
I would use a bright-colored pen to write a positive note to a student, but not to my principal, parents, or teachers.
At parent conferences, open houses, and the like, more conservative dress is appropriate.

—Cheryl Ralston
Redlands Unified School District, California

What's Out

Running shoes are for jogging or mall-walking.

Sweatshirts are best left for exercise.

T-shirts are for the beach.

Stretch slacks are unbecoming.

Bold prints, plaids, colors are no-no's.

Trendy clothes do not establish authority and should be left to students.

Anything in blue denim should be worn only on Saturdays.

Excessive jewelry is distracting.

What's In

Bright colors are enjoyed by elementary students.

Soft muted tones are recommended for secondary school.

Men can't miss with suits and ties or a sweater or coat and a dress shirt.

A career dress or suit is appropriate for women.

Clean clothes convey good hygiene.

Pressed clothes tell people you care.

Neat, cleanly tailored career clothes establish authority.

Career clothes prepare students for a future in the competitive global world economy.

Make no mistake about reality. Teachers have a responsibility to encourage learning, and learning begins by gaining and keeping the respect of students. Your respect begins with your appearance.

If you are appropriately dressed, students will comment when you look nice, and if something is out of place, they will tell you because they know that you are a person who cares about yourself. But if you consistently come to school inappropriately dressed, they will not say a word because they surmise that if you do not care about yourself, they need not care about you. **Dress appropriately because it is very important to know that people care about you.**

When people care about you, they will respect you, learn from you, buy from you. And as a professional educator, you are selling your students knowledge and success for the future.

Preparing Students for the World

What does it mean to dress appropriately? It is universally agreed that one major function of schools is to prepare young people for tomorrow's world. Yes, the world, not a particular city, state, or country. **We live in a competitive, global world economy where people work for companies that are international in scope.** It is likely that many of your students will work for a company that will have offices all over the world.

> **If you want to succeed in the world, you must think globally.**

If we are to prepare students for tomorrow's world, we need to know the world. If you do not know the world, ask your principal for a day off and go take a look. Stand at a major airport and watch passengers disembark from United, Lufthansa, and Japan Air Lines.

Then go downtown in the business district of a city and watch the successful people walk by—the executives, shopkeepers, salespeople, and secretaries. And speaking of secretaries, did you ever notice that the school secretary almost always comes to school more appropriately dressed than a lot of the teachers?

Having observed the world, after you have dressed in the morning, look at yourself in the mirror before you go to school to face your students who will see you as a model of success in tomorrow's competitive global world economy. Ask yourself the following three questions:

1. Would a real estate agency hire you dressed the way you are?

2. Would McDonald's allow you to hand food to a customer dressed the way you are?

3. Would you allow your loving child, grandchild, godchild, niece, or nephew to go to school and be taught by a teacher dressed the way you are?

Luisa Velasco, the school secretary at San Andreas High School, Hollister, California, conveys her competence by dressing appropriately.

Research has revealed who is more likely to be mugged on the street. Muggers were shown videotapes of people walking along the street. Overwhelmingly, muggers picked people who walked slowly, with stooped shoulders, and looked helpless and downtrodden. They rejected people who walked erect, purposefully, and confidently. These latter people conveyed the message that they were in control of their lives.

Your dress announces to the world that you care or do not care about yourself. The entire public can read this message. As a teacher, which of the two statements do you make?

1. I am one of a group of poor, underpaid, slovenly, dour, and unappreciated people.

2. I am one of a group of professional, proud, devoted, dedicated, responsible, and appreciated people.

This message is also conveyed to the students at your school, as well as to the administration and your colleagues, many of whom find the sloppy dress of many educators totally unacceptable.

People in sales, management, and leadership training will all tell you the same thing. By how you behave, you convey to the world a message of who you are and what you expect of life.

You have every right to expect the most from your life and from the lives of your students. That expectation can begin with how you dress.

You Dress Where You Want to Be

Frances Campbell, a San Francisco high school teacher, was having image problems. "I am a competent person who was coming across as kind of flaky," says Campbell. "People weren't taking me seriously." After gazing into her soul, and her mirror, she decided that her polyester baggy pants and Olympics T-shirts were to blame.

So Campbell turned to a department store shopping service for help. She spent one afternoon, and several hundred dollars, selecting a couple of outfits; she emerged with a sophisticated new look—and something more.

"Left alone in the dressing room, I saw myself for the very first time as a person who could do anything she wanted to," says Campbell. "If I had $1,000 of therapy, I wouldn't have felt anywhere near as good. It was like a religious experience.

"A professional woman should dress at least two steps above her current position," she says. "You do not dress where you are; you dress where you want to be."

— *Newsweek*
(June 25, 1984). p. 64.

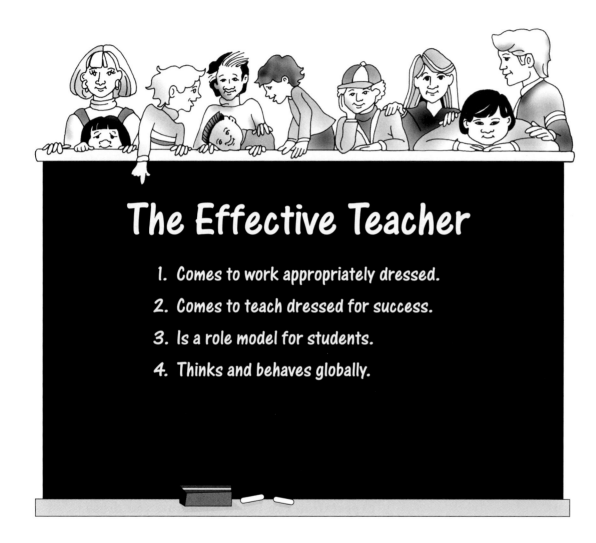

The Effective Teacher

1. Comes to work appropriately dressed.

2. Comes to teach dressed for success.

3. Is a role model for students.

4. Thinks and behaves globally.

KEY IDEA

People, places, policies, procedures, and programs must work together to invite people to realize their fullest potential.

Invitational and Disinvitational

> **Effective teachers have the power and the ability to invite students and colleagues each day and in every class to learn together.**

The parents of 25 out of 30 students came to Back-to-School Night! Cindy Wong, a teacher in San Jose, California, sent an invitation home with each of her students. She also had her students copy a letter and leave it on their desks, along with a gold-foil crane and a personal letter for their parents. They were so excited to tell their parents about a "special" surprise awaiting them. Some parents explained that their children said they just <u>had</u> to come to get their presents! This resulted in 25 out of 30 students being represented at Back-to-School Night.

Dear Parents,

Welcome to your child's classroom! I believe that what happens in this classroom will affect your child's future. Your child's time here will be well spent. He or she may even come home exhausted from all the thinking done during the day. But I will make every minute count.

We have a fantastic group of children in this class. I am looking forward to a terrific year ahead. With your help, we can make it happen.

Sincerely,
Mrs. Wong

Dear Mom,

Thank you for caring about me and taking the time to come and learn about my class. We have been learning about a young girl named Sadako who bravely fought leukemia. She believed in goodluck signs. The crane was one sign, a symbol of peace and dreams come true. Here is a crane I made especially for you. With it, I wish you love, peace, and everlasting happiness. I love you!

Love,
Emilio

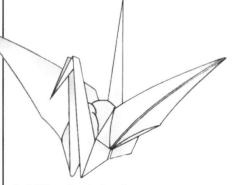

Cindy Wong then had each parent write a note to his or her child and leave it on the desk. The students couldn't wait to come to school the next day to find their surprise on their desk. What an invitation!

The person who is asked or complimented is INVITED. The person who is not asked or complimented is DISINVITED. This concept was formulated by William W. Purkey in 1978 and is known as invitational education.[1]

Invitational education is centered on the following propositions:

✔ People possess untapped potential in all areas of human development.

✔ People are able, valuable, and responsible and should be treated accordingly.

✔ People, places, policies, procedures, and programs all invite people to realize their fullest potential.

To fulfill these propositions, invitational education employs the following assumptions:

✔ Opportunities are everywhere, but little happens until invitations are sent, received, and acted on.

✔ A positive self-concept is the product of inviting acts.

✔ One inviting act can make a positive difference even if everything else is disinviting.

✔ We will always be invited if we are giving the party.

✔ Human potential is always there, waiting to be discovered and invited forth.

✔ To maintain a consistently inviting stance is the essence of an effective teacher.

Why Was I Not Invited?

It upsets me to this day. When I was in junior high school, I had straight A's and was in the honor class. One day the teacher went around the class and gave invitations to several students, but not me. They were asked to join the National Honor Society. To this day, I am still puzzled, confused, and disappointed that I was not invited.

—Rosemary Tripi Wong

---

[1]Purkey, William W., and John Novak. (1996). *Inviting School Success: A Self-Concept Approach to Teaching, Learning, and Democratic Practice.* Belmont, Calif.: Wadsworth; Purkey, William W., and John Novak. (1988). *Education: By Invitation Only.* Bloomington, Ind.: Phi Delta Kappa; Purkey, William W., and John J. Schmidt. (1996). *Invitational Counseling: A Self-Concept Approach to Professional Practice.* Pacific Grove, Calif.: Brooks/Cole; Purkey, William W., and John J. Schmidt. (1990). *Invitational Learning for Counseling and Development.* Ann Arbor, Mich.: University of Michigan, ERIC/CAS.

Are You Invitational or Disinvitational?

Even the outside of the classroom door contributes to creating a welcoming, invitational atmosphere.

Inviting Verbal Comments
"Good morning."
"Congratulations."
"I appreciate your help."
"Tell me about it."
"How can I help you?"
"Yes."

Inviting Personal Behaviors
Smiling
Listening
Holding a door
Thumbs up or high five
Sending a valentine
Waiting your turn

Inviting Physical Environment
Fresh paint
Living plants
Clean walls
Comfortable furniture
Attractively set table
Fresh air

Inviting Thoughts (Self-Talk)
"Making mistakes is all right."
"I've misplaced my keys."
"I could learn to do that."
"Sometimes I have to think what
  to say."

Disinviting Verbal Comments
"Keep out."
"It won't work."
"Not bad for a girl."
"I don't care what you do."
"You can't do that."
"Because I said so, that's why."

Disinviting Personal Behaviors
Looking at your watch
Yawning
Letting a door swing behind you
Sneering
Forgetting an important date
Shoving

Disinviting Physical Environment
Dark corridors
No plants
Graffiti
Donated, old furniture
Leftover food
Bad smells

Disinviting Thoughts (Self-Talk)
"Why am I so stupid?"
"I've lost my keys again."
"I never could do that."
"I never know what to say;
  I'm so slow to catch on."

You Are a Significant Person

An invitation is a message that states that the person being invited is responsible, able, and valuable. Conversely, a disinvitation is intended to tell people that they are irresponsible, incapable, and worthless. The critical ingredient needed for people to realize their fullest potential lies in the kinds of invitations extended to individuals by the significant people in their lives.

All individuals have significant people in their lives. These include teachers, leaders, mentors, colleagues, bosses, parents, relatives, coaches, administrators, spouses, and close friends.

> **The invitational messages that are extended to learn in school are the products of the expectancies that exist in the minds of the significant people who influence the lives of other people.**

We all like to be invited to go shopping, to go to a party, to join a group. And we all have the common courtesy to greet people at the door, to exchange courtesies when introduced to others, and to offer food or drink to a visitor. These are all obvious, expected, and practiced. These same concepts should be practiced in the classroom.

I have come to a frightening conclusion.
I am the decisive element in the classroom.
It is my personal approach that creates the climate.
It is my daily mood that makes the weather.
As a teacher I possess tremendous power to make a child's life miserable or joyous.
I can be a tool of torture or an instrument of inspiration.
I can humiliate or humor, hurt or heal.
In all situations it is my response that decides whether a crisis will be escalated or de-escalated, and a child humanized or dehumanized.

—Haim Ginott
Teacher and Child. (1976).
Avon Books.

Effective teachers have the power and the ability to invite students and colleagues each day and in every class to learn together. Attentiveness, expectancy, attitude, enthusiasm, and evaluation are the primary forces behind a teacher's being inviting or disinviting. These are the characteristics that significantly influence a student's self-concept and increase or decrease the probability of student learning.

> **All of us need to convey to our students and our colleagues every day that "you are important to me as a person."**

Every teacher, every professor, every educator ought to spend time in a kindergarten or first-grade class each year, just to look at and feel the excitement there. Children get excited about everything in the world. All the world is their stage, and there is nothing they cannot do, even though they cannot read, write, or spell. Yet they are ready to do anything you want them to do.

Then look at their teachers. They know that their charges cannot read, write, spell, or even speak correctly. Some of these students do not even know how to eat, use the bathroom, or hang up their jackets without help. Yet these teachers do not complain that they have a bunch of slow learners. Instead, their classrooms and their demeanor sparkle with an invitational attitude toward learning.

If Only the Finest Birds in the Forest Dared Sing How Quiet the Forest Would Be

If only the best readers dared read, how ignorant our country would be.
If only the best singers dared sing, how sad our country would be.
If only the best athletes engaged in sports, how weak our country would be.
If only the best lovers made love, where would you and I be?

I would be tired!

—William W. Purkey

The Four Levels of Invitational Education

There are four levels of invitations that are issued to students. These levels can determine your effectiveness as a teacher.

1. Intentionally Disinviting. This is the bottom level at which a few curmudgeonly teachers operate. They deliberately demean, discourage, defeat, and dissuade students. They use expressions like these:

"You never do your homework."
"Why do you bother to come to school?"
"I failed 12 students last term."
"I've only given one A in the 16 years that I've been teaching."
"You will never amount to anything."

And they never smile.

2. Unintentionally Disinviting. Some teachers are oblivious to the fact that they are negative people. They feel that they are well-meaning but are seen by others as chauvinistic, condescending, racist, sexist, patronizing, or thoughtless. They make comments like these:

"I teach only students who want to learn."
"If you don't want to learn, that's your problem."
"What do you want me to do? I did my job, didn't I?"
"What are they all angry at me for?"
"These people just don't have the capacity to do any better."
"I want to teach only college-bound students."
"I was hired to teach history, not do these other things."
"I believe that only students who want to come to school should be
    allowed to come to school."

And they keep their arms folded when interacting with students.

Everyone Is a VIP

Oklahoma City principal Sharon Creager keeps a "VIP book" in her office with this inscription on the inside cover:

Congratulations to these Very Important Pupils, who have distinguished themselves in various ways. These are the stars of our future.

Teachers send students to the office to have their names entered in the VIP book. The book is on permanent display in the hall and has never been vandalized. Each morning the new VIP names are read on the morning announcements.

3. Unintentionally Inviting. This is the level of the "natural-born teacher." These teachers are generally well liked and effective but are unaware of why they are effective; they do not have a consistent philosophy of education. When something does not work in the classroom, they are unable to analyze what went wrong. They are usually affable, and this characteristic often hides the fact that their students may not be learning to their fullest potential. These teachers are sincere and try very hard, and we generally like to have them on the staff and as friends. They offer remarks like these:

> "Aren't you sweet!"
> "Charge! Let's go team!"
> "That's neat."
> "Just try harder."
> "I enjoy teaching."

And they bubble with excitement.

4. Intentionally Inviting. Intentionally inviting teachers have a professional attitude, work diligently and consistently, and strive to be more effective teachers. They have a sound philosophy of education and can analyze the process of student learning. Most important, they are purposively and explicitly invitational. They know what it means to be invitational, and they work at it. They say things like this:

Eric Abrams, principal at Douglas Elementary School in Tucson, Arizona, intentionally invites his students to communicate with him.

> "Good morning. Have a great day."
> "Let me show you how to improve."
> "If you try this, you'll be sensational."
> "Please tell me about it."
> "I know that someday you will be the best at . . ."
> "Would you like to help me?"
> "Yes, I believe it is in your best interest."
> "You can do better than this; let me show you how."

They also use the proper emotion at the appropriate time.

Invitational education states that all people have limitless human potential and should be cordially summoned and invited to develop intellectually, socially, and physically. Expectation theory states that humans have a success instinct to reach their fullest potential.

When you apply the power of POSITIVE EXPECTATIONS and INVITATIONAL EDUCATION, you become a very powerful and effective teacher.

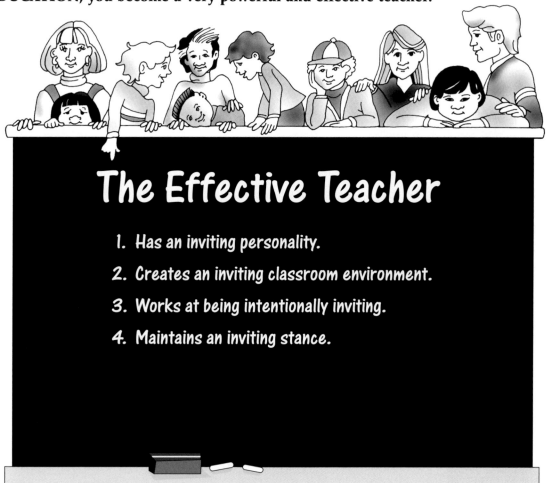

The Effective Teacher

1. Has an inviting personality.

2. Creates an inviting classroom environment.

3. Works at being intentionally inviting.

4. Maintains an inviting stance.

KEY IDEA

Significant people use significant words and actions to increase positive behaviors.

Five Significant Concepts

> **When you look at the truly effective teachers, you will also find caring, warm, lovable people.**

High expectations have nothing to do with getting A's in class, finishing college, making a lot of money, or having a great marriage. These are products or end results of life. High expectations have to do with attitude or behavior, and it is this behavior that gets us the A's in class, helps us finish college, or gets whatever else we want in life.

Life is not a destination.
Life is a journey.
As long as you continue the journey,
*   you will always be a success.*

—Albert Camus

How a person behaves in the journey of life is directly related to what a person expects to happen in life. There are five significant concepts that will help you achieve whatever it is you want in life. They are addressing a person by name, saying "please" and "thank you," smiling, and showing care and warmth.

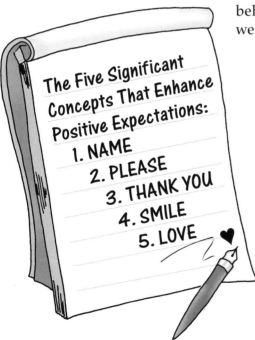

The Five Significant Concepts That Enhance Positive Expectations:
1. NAME
2. PLEASE
3. THANK YOU
4. SMILE
5. LOVE

Address a Student by Name

Effective salespeople know how to use a very simple but valuable technique. They have learned to find out your name, introduce themselves to you, and then use your name every 7 to 10 sentences when they talk with you. Why?

Your name is very important. It identifies and dignifies you. Other people in the world may have the same words as your name, but as far as you are concerned, you are the only person in the world with your name. It is a name that you can easily hear called above the din of a crowd. And when you hear your name, you pay attention. Salespeople know this when they use your name. You pay attention. You pay attention because you are important!

Effective teachers use names, especially when they want a student to do something or behave in a certain way.

✔ When you address a student, use the student's name.

✔ Use a student's name in a friendly, respectful manner. Never address a student in an angry or condescending tone. This is a put-down of a person's identity and dignity.

✔ Pronounce the student's name correctly. A person's name is precious and personal. It is that person's property. It is imperative that students hear the correct pronunciation of names. Failure to do so will tell the students that they do not have to respect each other's name and as a result can tease, mock, and make fun of each other's name.

✔ When you use a person's name, you are saying to that person, "You are important. You are important enough for me to identify you by name."

*Important people have business cards—
and who is more important than a teacher?*

Say "Please," Please

Cultured, polite people can be identified by their manners. Of course, we all like well-mannered people because we know that they will treat us politely. We like it when service-oriented people treat us kindly at the shopping center, amusement park, office, or restaurant or on public transportation. Businesspeople know that continued customer business and satisfaction is based on how the customers are treated. The customer who is treated politely will return. Just how do people learn to treat others with politeness and courtesy? From how they were treated by others primarily during their formative years, such as at school and at home.

A child's behavior is learned and modeled after the expectations of the significant people in that child's life—and the most significant people in a child's life are parents and teachers. (See Chapter 6.)

If you abuse a child, the child will grow up with the expectation of abusing others. If you treat a child with kindness, the child will grow up with the expectation of treating others with kindness.

Repetition Is the Key

For a child to learn something new, you need to repeat it on the average eight times.

For a child to unlearn an old behavior and replace it with a new behavior, you need to repeat the new behavior on the average 28 times.

Twenty of those times are used to eliminate the old behavior, and eight of the times are used to learn the new behavior.

—After Madeline Hunter

✔ Kindness begins with the word *please*.

✔ Cultured, polite, and well-mannered people automatically use the word *please*. They have learned appropriate behavior.

✔ Repetitive use of the word *please* is important if a child is to learn to use the word *please* in his or her life.

✔ *Please* is usually used when you ask someone to do something for you. Thus the most effective way to use *please* is to precede the word with the person's name to whom you are addressing the request, as in "Trevor, *please . . .*"

✔ Strongly consider adding the word *please* to your worksheets, assignments, and other papers that you distribute in class.

I Really Appreciate What You Did, "Thank You"

You really cannot use *please* without using *thank you*. The two just go together. Not using the two together would be like having a knife without a fork, a belt without a buckle, a yin without a yang.

Thank you says to others that you appreciate their effort and kindness. If you have expectations that students will work hard and will learn to be kind, saying *thank you* is your way of acknowledging that you know they have been kind and diligent and that you appreciate what they have done for you.

✔ End a statement of gratitude and appreciation for someone respecting your wishes with *thank you*.

✔ *Thank you* is the perfect transition; it paves the way to the next request, lesson, or task in class. It makes whatever you want done next much easier.

✔ The most effective way to use *thank you* is to use it with the person's name: "I truly appreciate what you did. *Thank you*, George" or "George, I truly appreciate what you did. *Thank you*."

✔ Strongly consider adding the words *thank you* to your worksheets, assignments, and other papers that you distribute in class.

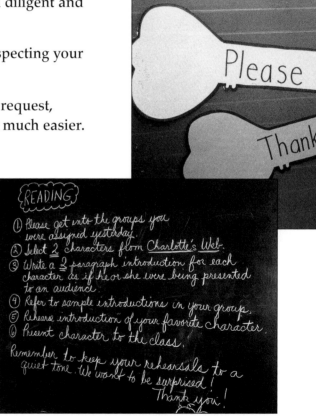

Please and thank you are used in these teachers' classrooms.

A Smile, the Frosting on the Cake

Please . . .

If you truly want to achieve maximum effectiveness when you use a person's name and say "please" and "thank you," you SMILE. It requires no effort and is even easier than frowning—smiling uses far fewer muscles than frowning and hence is less tiring to do. But like using *please* and *thank you*, smiling is a behavioral trait that is learned.

Thank you . . .

A smile is like that extra garnish on the dinner plate, the extra pat on the back when a job has been done well, or the extra hug that says "I really love you." It's the frosting on the cake, the little lagniappe (pronounced "lan-yap") that sets you apart. It communicates three things:

1. You are a person who knows the ultimate of hospitality and graciousness.

2. You have that little extra bit of polish or panache that marks you as a cultured person.

Smile!

3. You feel good about yourself and want others to feel good about themselves, too.

A smile is the universal language of understanding, peace, and harmony. If, indeed, we want the next generation to have a world of peace and understanding, we need to teach its sign, a smile.

A smile is the most effective way to create a positive climate, to disarm an angry person, and to convey the message "Do not be afraid of me; I am here to help you."

✔ There is no need for a great big smile; a controlled, slight, disarming smile is all you need.

✔ Accompany the smile with the name of the person at whom you are smiling.

✔ As you smile and speak, use momentary pauses. This is called timing. Every performer knows that the key to delivering a speech, telling a joke, or giving a performance is timing. This is the pregnant pause before speaking an important or emotional line or the punch line.

Technique for Smiling, Speaking, and Pausing

Step 1. SMILE. Smile as you approach the student, even if your first impulse is to behave harshly toward the student.

Step 2. FEEDBACK. Observe the reaction to your smile. Are you receiving a smile in return or at least a signal that the student is relaxing and receptive to your approach?

Step 3. PAUSE. (Timing, timing.)

Step 4. NAME. Say "Nathan" with a slight smile.

Step 5. PAUSE.

Step 6. PLEASE. Add *please*, followed by your request. Do this with a calm, firm voice, accompanied by a slight, nonthreatening smile.

Step 7. PAUSE.

Step 8. THANK YOU. End with "Thank you, Nathan" and a slight smile.

Love what you teach, and love whom you teach.

Example

Nathan, please stop talking to Joey and get to work on your assignment.
Thank you, Nathan. (Slight smile.)

Practice this in a mirror, over and over again.

It All Adds Up to Love

Only two things are necessary for a happy and successful life: being lovable and being capable.** The effective teacher never stops looking for ways of being more and more capable.

You may not love everyone, but you can give them unlimited positive regard.

—Source Unknown

When you look at the truly effective teachers, you will also find caring, warm, lovable people. Years later, when the students remember their most significant teachers, the ones that they will remember the most are the ones who really cared about them. Effective teachers know that they cannot get a student to learn unless that student knows that the teacher cares.

> ### The effective person offers both a product and a service.

Ineffective teachers think that all they have to do is offer a product, as in "I was hired to teach history" or "I was hired to teach third grade."

Effective teachers offer more than a product; they offer a service too. **Effective teachers can help students learn as well as enhance the quality of their lives.** They offer this service consistently because they are practicing this same belief on themselves as they increase their own effectiveness in life.

The sincerest form of service requires no money, no training, no special clothes, and no college degrees. **The sincerest form of service comes from listening, caring, and loving.**

Respect at Graduation

At our baccalaureate service, just prior to graduation, we show a videotape we make of any student who would like to say "thank you" to anyone.

Messages to parents, siblings, and teachers are touching. It could also be part of graduation.

David A. Mac Raild
Principal
Woodridge High School
Peninsula, Ohio

Beliefs of Effective Persons

I am not in the restaurant business;
I am in the hospitality business.

I do not serve food;
I nourish customers.

I do not sell clothes;
I dress successful people.

I do not sell insurance;
I help people solve problems.

I do not teach history;
I teach students.

I do not teach third grade;
I enhance the quality of lives.

People in our culture are starved for attention:

✔ The average child receives 12 minutes of attention each day from his or her parents.

✔ The average parent watches five to six hours of television each day.

✔ The number one problem reported by high school students is loneliness.

✔ Loneliness is the number one problem of the elderly, many of whom are afraid to venture out of their homes or apartments.

The Carnegie Foundation surveyed 22,000 teachers.

✔ 90 percent said that a lack of parental support was a problem at their schools.

✔ 89 percent said that there were abused or neglected children at their schools.

✔ 69 percent stated that poor health was a problem for their students.

✔ 68 percent reported that some children were undernourished.

✔ 100 percent described their students as "emotionally needy and starved for attention and affection."

You don't need to tell all the members of a class that you love them, but you certainly can show it. If you choose to be a significant and effective person in a student's life, you must demonstrate your care and love both implicitly through your body language and explicitly through what you say.

When significant people use significant words and actions, they increase the likelihood of receiving positive behaviors from other people.

Thank you.

Every day millions of students arrive at American classrooms in search of more than reading and math skills. They are looking for a light in the darkness of their lives, a Good Samaritan who will stop and bandage a burned heart or ego.

— *Jim Trelease*

Love is life . . . And if you miss love, you miss life.

— *Leo Buscaglia*

The Effective Teacher

1. Addresses people by name.

2. Says "Please" and "Thank you."

3. Has a controlled, disarming smile.

4. Is lovable and capable.

There Will Never Be a Shortage of Love

Love is the reason for teaching.
It costs nothing, yet is the most precious thing
one can possess.
The more we give, the more it is returned.
It heals and protects,
soothes and strengthens.
Love has other names such as
forgiveness . . .
tolerance . . .
mercy . . .
encouragement . . .
aid . . .
sympathy . . .
affection . . .
friendliness . . .
and cheer.
No matter how much love we give to others,
more rushes in to take its place.
It is, really, "the gift that keeps on giving."
Give love in abundance—
every day.

UNIT C

Second Characteristic —
Classroom Management

The effective teacher is an extremely good classroom manager.

Second Characteristic — Classroom Management

The effective teacher is an extremely good classroom manager.

Unit C is correlated with **Part 3: Discipline and Procedures** and **Part 4: Procedures and Routines**
in the video series *The Effective Teacher*.

You Have Arrived at Possibly the Most Important Unit in This Book

We know what the single most important factor governing student learning is. In a study reviewing 11,000 pieces of research that spanned 50 years, three researchers determined that there are 28 factors that influence student learning and these have been rank ordered. **The most important factor governing student learning is Classroom Management.**[1]

How you manage the classroom is the primary determinant of how well your students will learn. *The First Days of School* is based on the following research findings:

It is the principal who makes the difference in the school.

- ✔ The three characteristics of effective teachers:
    They have classroom management skills,
    teach for lesson mastery, and
    practice positive expectations.[2]

- ✔ Classroom management skills are of primary importance in determining teaching success.[3]

- ✔ The number one factor governing student learning is classroom management.[4]

- ✔ The first day of school is the most important day of the school year. Effective classroom management practices must begin on the first day of school.[5]

Based on these findings, this is a statement of dignity for the teaching profession.

It is the teacher who makes the difference in the classroom.

It is the teacher who makes the difference in the classroom.

---

[1]Wang, Margaret, Geneva Haertel, and Herbert Walberg. (December 1993/January 1994). "What Helps Students Learn?" *Educational Leadership*, pp. 74–79.

[2]Good, Thomas, and Jere Brophy. (1994). *Looking in Classrooms*. Harper/Collins, pp. 376–377.

[3]Emmer, Edmund, Carolyn Evertson, Barbara Clements, and Murray Worsham. (1997). *Classroom Management for Secondary Teachers* (3rd ed.). Needham Heights, Mass.: Allyn & Bacon; Carolyn Evertson, Edmund Emmer, Barbara Clements, and Murray Worsham. (1994). *Classroom Management for Elementary Teachers*. Needham Heights, Mass.: Allyn & Bacon.

[4]Wang, Margaret, Geneva Haertel, and Herbert Walberg. (December 1993/January 1994). "What Helps Students Learn?" *Educational Leadership*, pp. 74–79.

[5]Brooks, Douglas. (May 1986). "The First Day of School." *Educational Leadership*, pp. 76–79.

KEY IDEA

The teacher is responsible for organizing a well-managed classroom where the students can learn in a task-oriented environment.

The First Thing You Need to Know

> **Effective teachers MANAGE their classrooms.**
> **Ineffective teachers DISCIPLINE their classrooms.**

The fact that you know how to cook a steak does not make you a successful restaurateur. For that, you need to know about accounting procedures; federal, state, and local regulations; sanitation laws; union agreements; and worker and customer relationships. How to cook a steak is the last thing you need to know. The first thing you need to know is how to manage the restaurant.

> **Likewise, you manage a classroom;**
> **you don't discipline a classroom.**

The fact that you have a college degree in English does not make you a teacher, much less an English teacher. You need to know about academic learning time, formative and summative testing, criterion-referenced testing, discipline plans, procedures and routines, learning styles, motivation theory, record-keeping procedures, identification of learning disabilities, higher-order thinking skills, due process, privacy rights, grouping, community services, learning for mastery, remediation and correction, prescriptive learning, credibility, and a whole host of other things.

Alice Waters, who introduced California cuisine to the world, is noted not only for her skill in the kitchen but also for her skill in running her restaurant, Chez Panisse, in Berkeley, California.

A degree in English is the last thing you need. The first thing you need to know is how to manage a classroom full of students. You were not hired to teach third grade, coach football, or teach English. You were hired to take a group of students and turn them into interested and productive learners in a well-managed classroom.

Teachers almost never think about managing a classroom. They only think about presenting lessons—lectures, worksheets, videos, activities—never management. Most classrooms are nonmanaged. And any situation that is nonmanaged can easily turn chaotic.

What Is Classroom Management?

Classroom **management refers to all of the things that a teacher does to organize students, space, time, and materials so that instruction in content and student learning can take place.**

The research indicates that the amount of time that students spend actively engaged in learning activities is directly linked to their academic achievement. It also shows that teachers who are good classroom managers are able to maximize student engaged time or academic learning time. (See Chapter 21.)

Brophy and Evertson say, "Almost all surveys of teacher effectiveness report that classroom management skills are of primary importance in determining teaching success, whether it is measured by student learning or by ratings. Thus, management skills are crucial and fundamental. **A teacher who is grossly inadequate in classroom management skills is probably not going to accomplish much.**"[1]

> **Most teachers do not teach.**
>
> **Most teachers do activities. And when problems arise, they discipline.**
>
> **Most classrooms are nonmanaged.**
>
> **And because of this, little is accomplished.**

---

[1]Brophy, Jere, and Carolyn M. Evertson. (1976). *Learning from Teaching: A Developmental Perspective.* Needham Heights, Mass.: Allyn & Bacon.

Unit C will help you accomplish the dual goals of student involvement and a productive working atmosphere so that you can be a very effective teacher.

Classroom management includes all of the things a teacher must do toward two ends:

1. To foster student involvement and cooperation in all classroom activities
2. To establish a productive working environment

To foster student involvement and cooperation in all classroom activities, the effective teacher plans a variety of activities that are appropriate for learning. These activities may include reading, taking notes, participating in group work, taking part in class discussions, participating in games, and producing materials. An effective teacher has every student involved and cooperating in all of these activities.

For all students to work on their activities, the environment must be conducive to learning. Students must pay attention, be cooperative and respectful of each other, exhibit self-discipline, and remain on task. In addition, the room must have a positive climate, all materials must be ready and organized, and the furniture must be arranged for productive work.

> **The most important thing a teacher can provide a classroom the first week of school is SECURITY.**
>
> Students want a well-managed classroom more than the teachers do because a well-managed classroom gives students **SECURITY**. There are no surprises, no yelling in a classroom where everyone, teacher and students, know what is happening. It comes from installing procedures and routines.

Characteristics of a Well-Managed Classroom

You expect a department store to be well managed. When asked what that means, you would probably list some of these characteristics:

- ✔ **The store:** Its layout, organization, and cleanliness

- ✔ **The merchandise:** Its display, accessibility, and availability

- ✔ **The help:** Their management, efficiency, knowledge, and friendliness

You could probably do the same for a restaurant, an airline, or a doctor's office. In fact, you have probably said more than once, "If I ran this place, I would do things differently."

Well, if you ran a school or a classroom, which is what you do, how would you run the place? That is called classroom management, and the characteristics of a well-managed classroom are well known.

The Effective Teacher
Has a Well-Managed Classroom

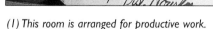

◆◆ **The Characteristics of a Well-Managed Classroom**[2]

1. Students are deeply involved with their work, especially with academic, teacher-led instruction.

2. Students know what is expected of them and are generally successful.

3. There is relatively little wasted time, confusion, or disruption.

4. The climate of the classroom is work-oriented, but relaxed and pleasant.

(1) This room is arranged for productive work.
(2) This room has a positive climate.
(3) The students are on task.
(4) The students are cooperative and respectful of one another.

[2]Emmer, Edmund, Carolyn Evertson, Barbara Clements, and Murray Worsham. (1997). *Classroom Management for Secondary Teachers* (3rd ed.). Needham Heights, Mass.: Allyn & Bacon; Carolyn Evertson, Edmund Emmer, Barbara Clements, and Murray Worsham. (1994). *Classroom Management for Elementary Teachers*. Needham Heights, Mass.: Allyn & Bacon.

Techniques to Help You Implement the Four Characteristics of a Well-Managed Classroom	**Characteristics**	**Effective Teacher**	**Ineffective Teacher**
	1. High level of student involvement with work	Students are working. (See page 200.)	Teacher is working.
	2. Clear student expectations	Students know that assignments are based on objectives. (See page 221.)	Teacher says, "Read Chapter 3 and know the material."
		Students know that tests are based on objectives. (See page 229.)	"I'll give you a test covering everything in Chapter 3."
	3. Relatively little wasted time, confusion, or disruption	Teacher has a discipline plan. (See page 141.)	Teacher makes up rules and punishes according to his or her mood.
		Teacher starts class immediately. (See page 121.)	Teacher takes roll and dallies.
		Teacher has assignments posted. (See page 121.)	Students ask for assignments repeatedly.
	4. Work-oriented but relaxed and pleasant climate	Teacher has invested time in practicing procedures until they become routines. (See page 174.)	Teacher tells but does not rehearse procedures.
		Teacher knows how to bring class to attention. (See page 181.)	Teacher yells and flicks light switch.
		Teacher knows how to praise the deed and encourage the student. (See page 183.)	Teacher uses generalized praise or none at all.

A Task-Oriented and Predictable Environment

> **A well-managed classroom is a task-oriented and predictable environment.**

A well-managed classroom is a task-oriented environment where students know what is expected of them and how to succeed. According to the research, most students will make better achievement gains in a class such as this.

A well-managed classroom is also a predictable environment. Both teacher and students know what to do and what is supposed to happen in the classroom. You should be able to close your eyes and not only envision learning taking place but also know why it is taking place because of how you have chosen to manage the classroom environment.

It is the responsibility of the teacher to manage a class to see that a task-oriented and predictable environment has been established.

Power comes when you make life predictable for people.

—Howard H. Stevenson

Aaron Rosander manages his classroom for student success.

We Even Have a Nordstrom

"We even have a Nordstrom at Tyson's Corner!" she said, with a pixieish smile of delight, as if the queen of England had just moved in next door.

Surveying my puzzled look, she said, "You mean you don't know about Nordstrom?" Her eyes conveyed a mix of astonishment and pity.

"Let me tell you about Nordstrom," she continued. "The other day, my mother came to visit me. She had never been to Nordstrom, so that's where we went. As we passed the men's clothing department, the salesman said, 'May I help you?'"

"My mother said that she was looking for some shoes. Graciously, he said, 'Please, let me show you the shoe department,' and proceeded to escort my mother and me across the store to the shoe department. He introduced my mother to one of the salesclerks, then smiled and dashed back to his department."

"She bought shoes that day but never mentioned her purchases to anyone. All she could talk about was how well she had been treated at Nordstrom."

You can have a classroom like this. For an explanation of how to have a well-managed classroom where the students are responsible, know the classroom procedures, and are on task and learning, please refer to Chapter 20.

It Works So Well, It's Scary

I start each class with a "Constitution minute" (CM). The CMs are actual transcripts from NBC Radio that were broadcast during the bicentennial of the Constitution.

Several weeks before—
- Each student is given a copy of the actual transcript.
- Each student is assigned a date of delivery in front of the class.
- Transcripts are to be memorized.
- Ideas for effective presentation are discussed.
- Procedures for the presenters' expectations are discussed.
- Procedures for the listeners' expectations are discussed.

On the day of the delivery—
- The student presenter proceeds to the front of the room ready to present his or her CM before the class begins.
- The rest of the class is seated and ready to listen and take a few brief notes.
- One minute after the bell rings, the presenter begins the CM.
- Approximately one minute later, the CM is over and the presenter sits down.
- The class checks the front board for the schedule, procedure, or assignment for the day.

Arthur Kavanaugh and his students at Wissahickon Middle School.

During this time, I sit quietly in the back of the room and listen, grading the presentation, taking the roll, and so on.

The class automatically starts itself.
- They're quiet.
- They're organized.
- They're ready to learn.
- They know what is expected.

It works so well, it's scary.

Within two minutes, the class is ready and I haven't said a word and yet we have accomplished one learning activity—all managed by procedures.

—Arthur H. Kavanaugh
Ambler, Pennsylvania

The Effective Teacher

1. Works on having a well-managed classroom.

2. Trains students to know what they are to do.

3. Has students working on task.

4. Has a classroom with little confusion or wasted time.

KEY IDEA

Teachers who are ready maximize student learning and minimize student misbehavior.

Why Effective Teachers Have a Minimum of Problems

> **The effective teacher has a minimum of student misbehavior problems to handle.**
>
> **The ineffective teacher is constantly fighting student misbehavior problems.**
>
> **Yet the situation is easy to remedy.**

Don't be ineffective—you and your students will pay for it. Ineffective teachers have classrooms that are not ready. Confusion leads to problems; problems lead to misbehavior; and misbehavior leads to constant tangling between teacher and students. The ineffective teachers, each day, become more and more stressful, burned out, negative, cynical, and angry. They quickly learn to blame everyone and everything else for their problems.

Evertson and Anderson were the first to show the importance of effective classroom management at the beginning of the school year. They did this in two articles that addressed having the room ready.[1]

Half of Your Effectiveness Is Determined Before You Leave Home

The amount of work you will accomplish will be determined before you even leave for work.

Half of what you will accomplish in a day will be determined before you even leave home.

Three-quarters of what you will accomplish in a day will be determined before you enter the school door.

You need to prepare yourself, both academically and attitudinally, before you leave home and as you travel to school.

You increase the chance of student success and decrease the chance of student disruptions if the materials, classroom climate, and teacher are ready before the students arrive.

[1]Evertson, Carolyn, and L., Anderson. (1997). "Beginning School." *Educational Horizons*, 57(4), pp. 164–168; Emmer, Edmund, Carolyn Evertson, and L. Anderson. (1980). "Effective Classroom Management at the Beginning of the School Year." *The Elementary School Journal*, 80(5), pp. 219–231.

Douglas Brooks's work, on the beginning of the school year, which is explained on page 3, supported the work of Carolyn Evertson, but it was not until the late 1980s that studies were published that had experimental findings.[2] These studies showed that for both elementary and secondary teachers, training was essential to achieve better classroom management practices.

Evertson's studies have shown that effective teachers had the classroom ready. Because they had the classroom ready, they were able to prevent many misbehaviors from occurring. The reason effective teachers are effective is that they have far fewer student problems and hence are able to get their students to work and to achieve. As such, effective teachers incur far less stress in having to deal with behavior problems and are able to leave each day feeling happy, accomplished, and proud.

> **Effective Teachers Are Ready**
>
> **Effective Teachers Have the Room Ready.**
>   Unit C: Classroom Management
>
> **Effective Teachers Have the Work Ready.**
>   Unit D: Lesson Design
>
> **Effective Teachers Have Themselves Ready.**
>   Unit A: Basic Understandings
>   Unit B: Positive Expectations

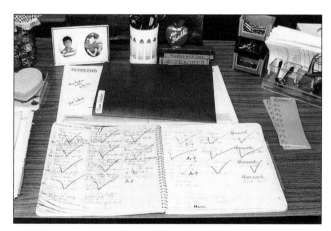

*Instead of waiting for crises to arise,
the effective teacher plans and is ready.*

---

[2]Evertson, Carolyn. (1989). "Improving Elementary Classroom Management: A School-Based Training Program for Beginning the Year." *Journal of Educational Research*, 83(2), pp. 82–90; Evertson, Carolyn. (1985). "Training Teachers in Classroom Management: An Experiment in Secondary Classrooms." *Journal of Educational Research*, 79, pp. 51–58.

A Successful Restaurant Is Ready

The Table Is Ready. The table is set and waiting when you arrive at your reservation time.

The Dining Room Is Ready. The atmosphere or ambiance is conducive to a pleasant dining experience.

The Staff Is Ready. You can expect fine service because the staff has high expectations that you will enjoy your dinner.

A Successful Teacher Is Ready

The Work Is Ready. The desks, books, papers, assignments, and materials are ready when the bell rings.

The Room Is Ready. The classroom has a positive climate that is work-oriented.

The Teacher Is Ready. The teacher has a warm, positive attitude and has positive expectations that all students will succeed.

Have your classroom ready, every single day, especially the first days of school. This is obvious. When you walk into a restaurant, an office, or a store, you expect it to be ready—for YOU. You become upset if things aren't ready.

When people come to your home for a dinner party, you increase the possibility of having a successful dinner if your table is ready. When your team or group goes out to compete or perform, you increase the chances of winning if your team or group is ready. When the students come to the student council meeting, you will probably have a successful meeting if the agenda has been well thought out.

The Perfect Tribute, The Imperfect Film

This is a true story.

In haste, a teacher whipped out her film library catalog and ordered the perfect film for her U.S. history class lesson on the Civil War. The film was **The Perfect Tribute (Abraham Lincoln)**.

She told the clerk the name of the film and the catalog number, inadvertently giving the clerk the catalog number of the next film, also called **The Perfect Tribute**.

Without previewing the film, she ran it for the class. It was a film made for morticians on how to sell caskets—**The Perfect Tribute**.

All battles are won before they are fought.

— Sun Tzu

93

You know very well that if a client calls and you are not ready, you will lose the sale. If you are not prepared for your interview, you may not have another one. If you are not ready when the teacher calls on you, you may receive a poor grade.

In the real world, you would be fired if you were not ready. In the competitive world economy, our students must be ready. We teach readiness by modeling readiness: in our work, in our class environment, in ourselves. People who are not organized and not ready suffer the consequences.

> **Readiness is the primary determinant of teacher effectiveness.**

Before You Move a Single Desk ...

Before you move any furniture or put anything on the walls, here are some truisms:

1. A climate of work is what you want to establish during the first week of school.

2. The first week of school should stress large group organization and student procedures.

3. Spend your time on classroom management of student procedures rather than making your classroom look like a showcase. A few bare but clean bulletin boards, shelves, and flowerpots won't disturb anyone.

4. Do not overarrange or overdecorate your room for the opening of school.

5. Your room should be neat and pleasant, but don't spend time making it the ultimate room you want by Back-to-School Night.

6. Don't bother having the learning center, classroom library, or resource center complete. (*You don't need a learning center on the first day of school. Wait a week or so after the students have the classroom rules and procedures and routines down pat before you allow them to work at the learning center.*)

The three most important words to a painter, pilot, or chef are **preparation, preparation, preparation**.

The three most important words to a teacher are **preparation, preparation, preparation**.

A cluttered or barren room sends a negative message to your pupils. A well-organized, attractive room gives an "in control" image that students respect. It is imperative that you have your room ready and inviting before the students come on the first day of school.

Strategic Locations for Students with Behavioral Problems

Behavioral problems will occur from time to time. They come with the turf, just like infractions in hockey. And when an infraction occurs in hockey, there is an area, or strategic location, set aside for the offender.

The effective teacher states to the class that behavioral problems will be handled promptly and competently. This conveys the message that you are in control and ready.

An axiom of handling behavior problems is that little or no instructional time should be lost (Chapter 19). Time is wasted when you stop to find a place or move furniture around for the offender. The good students resent this waste of time just as much as you resent the troublemaker.

Types of Students
Who Cause Behavioral Problems

Aggressive—the hyperactive, agitated, unruly student
Resistant—the student who won't work
Distractible—the student who can't concentrate
Dependent—the student who wants help all the time

Locations for Students
Causing the Problems

Separate—Disruptive students must be separated from the class or at least from other problem students. This is appropriate for aggressive and resistant students.

Nearby—Disruptive students must be placed close to the teacher. This is appropriate for distractible, dependent, and occasionally resistant students.

The following examples, like most examples in this book, are generalized and conceptual. Apply and adapt the examples to your situation.

Prepare the Floor Space

✔ Count the number of desks and chairs needed. Arrange to have damaged furniture replaced and sufficient furniture brought in. Ask for needed items well ahead of time. Do not be hostile if things are not as you want them, especially if your requests are made at the last minute.

✔ Administrators and custodians are truly helpful people and want quality education for the children as much as you do. Get to know them and you'll discover that they are competent, cooperative, compassionate, and helpful. They are not the ogres the negative teachers would want you to believe they are.

✔ Even if you plan to change your room arrangement during the school year, it is wise to begin the year with the desks in rows facing the teacher. This minimizes distractions, allows you to monitor behavior more readily, and helps you become familiar with the students in your class.

✔ Desks do not have to be in traditional rows, but all chairs should face forward so that all eyes are focused on you.

✔ Place students' desks where students can easily see the teacher during whole class or small group instruction.

✔ Keep high-traffic areas clear. Don't put desks, chairs, or tables in front of doors, water fountains, sinks, pencil sharpeners, or your desk.

✔ Have a strategic location ready for students who need to be isolated from the rest of the class.

Prepare the Work Area

✔ Arrange work areas and desks so that you can easily see and monitor all the students and areas no matter where you are in the room.

✔ Students should be able to see you as well as frequently used chalkboards, bulletin boards, screens, demonstration areas, and displays.

✔ Keep traffic areas clear. Allow enough clearance to move up and down and around the last seat in the row.

✔ Keep access to storage areas, bookcases, cabinets, and doors clear.

✔ Learn the regulations regarding fire, earthquakes, tornadoes, hurricanes, and other natural disasters, and have the classroom ready for such emergencies.

✔ Make sure that you have enough chairs for the work areas.

✔ Be sure that you have all necessary materials for your work areas, such as books, laboratory supplies, media, activity cards, tools, and instruments.

✔ Test any equipment to make sure that it works before you intend to use it.

✔ Use tote trays, boxes, coffee cans, dishpans, or whatever to store the materials students will need. Arrange your room for these to be readily accessible to the students.

✔ Arrange work areas where students can go for reading and math groups, science laboratory areas, project work, learning centers, and independent study. (Remember, you may not need these areas on the first days of school.)

Prepare the Student Area

✔ Save yourself many a headache! Plan areas for student belongings now. Provide space for their binders, backpacks, books, lunchboxes, umbrellas, shoes, show-and-tell items, lost-and-found items, skateboards, and projects.

✔ Provide a coatrack for the students to hang their coats.

Prepare the Wall Space

The most effective classes are those where the students are self-disciplined, self-motivated, and self-responsible learners. Teach your students to consult the bulletin boards for information on what to do and how to do it. You do this by teaching procedures and routines (Chapter 20). Also, consult Chapter 15 on posting your assignments.

- ✔ Cover one or more bulletin boards with colored paper and trim, and leave it bare. The purpose of this bulletin board is to display student work, not to be decorated by a teacher to look like a department store show window.

- ✔ Display your discipline plan in a prominent place. You can relocate it after the first week. (See Chapter 18.)

- ✔ Post procedures, assigned duties, calendar, clock, emergency information, schedules, menus, charts, maps, decorations, birthdays, and student work.

- ✔ Have a consistent place for listing the day's or week's assignments.

- ✔ Post a large example of the proper heading or style for papers to be done in class.

- ✔ Post examples of tests students will take, assignments they will turn in, and papers they will write.

- ✔ Display the feature topic, theme, chapter, or skill for the day or the current unit.

When to Prepare

You don't build your football team on game day.

You don't drill a well when you get thirsty.

And you don't discuss procedures once an emergency has begun. That's not the time to discuss what should be done. Preparation is the key for teacher success.

Prepare the Bookcases

- ✔ Do not place the bookcases or display walls where they obstruct any lines of vision.

- ✔ Rotate materials on the shelves, and leave out only those items you are willing to allow students to handle.

- ✔ Do not place books or other loose materials near an exit where they can easily disappear or where they may hide emergency information.

Prepare the Teacher Area

aximize your proximity to students and frequently used materials and equipment. Time is lost when teachers and students waste steps to reach each other, gather materials, or use classroom equipment.

The closer you are to your students, the more you will minimize your classroom behavior problems. When the teacher is physically close to the students and can get to them quickly, their on-task behavior increases. When the teacher is far from a student and cannot get to a student quickly, the student is more likely to stop working and disrupt others. **Maximize your proximity to minimize your problems.**

> **A teacher's discipline problems are directly proportional to the distance from the students.**

✔ Place the teacher's desk, file, and other equipment so that they do not interfere with the flow of traffic. Do not create a barrier between yourself and your students. Place your desk so that you can move quickly to a student to assist, reinforce, or discipline.

✔ Place the teacher's desk so that you can easily monitor the classroom while at your desk or working with individual students.

✔ Place the teacher's desk away from the door so that no one can take things from your desk and quickly walk out.

✔ If you choose to have everything on and in your desk treated as personal property, make this clear during your teaching of classroom procedures and routines.

A teacher's problems are directly proportional to the amount of distance between the teacher and the students.

Prepare the Teaching Materials

✔ Have a letter ready with the materials you want your students to bring from home. Have a place and a procedure ready for the storage of these materials.

✔ Have a method ready for matching students to a desk. Have name cards ready and on the students' desks. Or use an overhead transparency correlating desk arrangement with the student's name.

✔ Have your basic materials ready for the first week of school. These include books, papers, pencils, rulers, glue, chalk, felt pens, stapler, tape, clipboard, crayons, felt-tip markers, construction paper, instruments, calculators, laboratory supplies, manipulatives, playground equipment, and computer software. Buy a bell or a timer if you wish to use either as a signal.

✔ Find and organize containers for your materials. Use copy paper boxes, dishpans, coffee cans, milk cartons, and shoeboxes to store materials. Label your containers, and place in each an inventory card listing everything that should be in the container.

✔ Store seldom-used materials out of the way, but be sure they are inventoried and ready for immediate use.

✔ Place electronic media where there are electrical outlets and where the students will not trip over the wires. Have an extension cord and an adapter plug handy.

✔ Organize and file your masters, stencils, and computer disks. Do likewise with your extra worksheets so that they are immediately ready for any students who were absent or who need extra help.

Finally, Prepare Yourself

✔ Keep your briefcase, purse, keys, and other valuables in a safe location.

✔ Have emergency materials handy, such as tissue, rags, paper towels, soap, first-aid kit, and extra lunch money. Store these for your use, not the students'.

✔ Obtain a teacher's manual for each textbook you will use in your class.

✔ Obtain a supply of the forms that are used for daily school routines, such as attendance forms, tardy slips, hall passes, and referral forms. Since you will use these forms each day, place them where you can find them immediately.

To be an effective teacher, be prepared. **Teachers who are ready maximize student learning and minimize student misbehavior.**

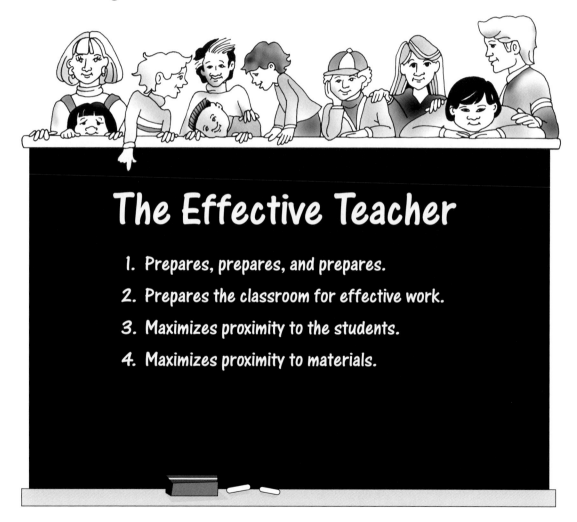

The Effective Teacher

1. Prepares, prepares, and prepares.

2. Prepares the classroom for effective work.

3. Maximizes proximity to the students.

4. Maximizes proximity to materials.

KEY IDEA

How you introduce yourself on the first day may determine how much respect and success you will have for the rest of the school year.

Your Reputation Precedes You

> **Right or wrong, accurate or not, your reputation will precede you.**

People have reputations. You know of people who are sweet, kind, honest, industrious, and dependable and others who are sleazy, curmudgeonly, arrogant, lazy, and undependable.

Businesses have reputations. Some have terrible service, sell shoddy merchandise, and do not guarantee their products. Other businesses you can trust implicitly.

Companies with good images, such as IBM, Coca-Cola, Sony, Hallmark, Nordstrom, and Hewlett-Packard, enhance their sales. Companies with poor images, try as they may to change them, suffer in their sales. This is why companies spend billions to create a corporate image—because they know that people buy from companies they trust. Their image precedes a sale.

Your Image Enhances Sales

HALLMARK: "When you care enough to send the very best"

LEXUS: "The relentless pursuit of perfection"

KODAK: "Depend on us"

WATERFORD: "Worthy of the moment for over two centuries"

TIMEX: "It takes a licking and keeps on ticking"

Even before you first see your students, your success at winning their respect and attention may have already been predetermined by your reputation. **Right or wrong, accurate or not, your reputation will precede you.**

✔ If you have a good reputation, the students will enter your classroom with high expectations, and this will be to your benefit.

✔ If you have a poor reputation, the students will enter with low expectations, and this will be to your detriment.

Whether you like it or not, the students will talk about you, the parents will talk about you, the administration will talk about you, and your colleagues will talk about you.

Everyone likes and supports a winner. Parents want their children in the classes of the teachers with the outstanding reputations. Teachers with poor reputations often get what's left after all the sifting and shuffling of students and teachers has been done.

You will attract better students, have a minimum of problems on the first day of school, and generally be much happier with your job if you have students who want to be in your class. It makes no sense to be a teacher that no one wants to have as a teacher.

Protect your reputation and create a positive image. You have nothing to lose and everything to gain.

She Got the Leftovers

I am sure that many of your readers after reading your article would feel that Mrs. T was treated unfairly when relieved of her teaching duties. I taught in the same school for 25 years so I'm aware of what was happening in the years that she taught.

Many parents and teachers would agree that junior high students in the last 10 or 15 years have become more difficult to handle and that discipline of the age group is more and more of a problem. Mrs. T's inability to handle her class was common knowledge.

It took real courage for the school board and administration to say, "For the good of the children this teacher has to go."

As to the claim that her classes were packed with problem children: The policy in our school at the time was that parents could request a certain teacher or ask that a child be reassigned. Many parents, knowing of the problems, asked that their children not be in Mrs. T's room.

Those who were left were often the most difficult discipline problems and Mrs. T got them.

—Letter to the Editor
San Jose Mercury News.
November 13, 1988.

Preschool Invitation or Visit

Here are some welcoming techniques used by effective teachers. Apply and adapt the examples to your situation.

1. Send a letter home to the parents BEFORE school begins.

> **The Importance of Parents**
>
> Parents are their children's first and most influential teachers. What parents do to help their children is more important to academic success than how well off the family is.[1]

✔ Tell the parents that you are looking forward to having their child in your class.

✔ Ask them to put the dates of the school's open house on their calendar, and explain why it is important for them to attend. You will be explaining homework, grading, discipline, and classroom procedures.

✔ Include information on what materials you want the students to have ready for school.

2. Send a letter home to each student BEFORE school begins.

✔ Include a message of welcome.

✔ Tell the students who you are.

✔ Invite them to call you if they have questions.

✔ Help them prepare by listing the materials they should have with them. They will be ready if you are ready. Do not surprise your students.

✔ Tell them your, not their, expectations.

3. Visit the home of each student BEFORE school begins (check to be sure that this is an appropriate thing to do).

✔ Introduce yourself.

✔ Bring the letters just described with you.

✔ Share with the parents how they can help.

---

[1] U.S. Department of Education. (1986). *What Works: Research About Teaching and Learning.* Washington, D.C.: U.S. Government Printing Office, p. 7.

In Awe and Admiration

Dear Mr. Mundy,

My daughter, Angela, attended Longfellow School last year. Her teacher's name was Miss Sather. The reason for this letter is to officially give a parent's commendation of the performance of Miss Sather.

First of all we moved to Minot just weeks before the school year was to begin. After I registered my daughter for school I did not expect any communication from the teacher until after the first day of school. However, Miss Sather came to our house a few days before school began to welcome Angela to her class. That may seem like a small factor, but it made a big impression on me and it helped my daughter in adjusting to a new school.

Never, in my life, have I known any other teacher who cared so much as to do this for a student. Later I learned that this is a common practice for Miss Sather.

Additionally, her classroom was always orderly, well organized and disciplined. She involved the parents in the students' learning by sending home parent-child homework assignments and notes of problems or progress frequently. She used positive methods of discipline and gained the respect and love of her pupils.

Other parents, my husband and myself included, were in awe and admiration of her. She is an extremely talented and outstanding teacher. I would like to ask that she be recognized for her efforts.

Sincerly,
Mrs. JKM

Sherry Sather Braaten

Am I in the Right Room?

Douglas Brooks discovered that the very first thing a student wants to know on the first day of school is, "Am I in the right room?"[2] **Finding the correct room on the first day of school can be one of the most frightening experiences for a student.** There is nothing more embarrassing than to discover that you are in the wrong room—15 minutes after class has begun.

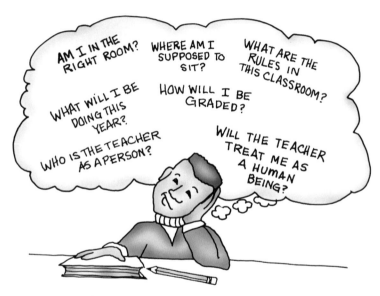

These are the seven things students want to know on the first day of school.

Dear Dr. Wong,

When I came home from your in-service meeting, I asked my 13-year-old son the following question: "What's the most frightening thing about the first day of school?"

After thinking for a moment, he said, "Two things—having the teacher mispronounce your name and walking into the wrong classroom."

> —Classroom teacher
> Garland, Texas

How to Greet Them on Day 1

Stand at the classroom door with a big smile and a ready handshake. You do this when company comes or when meeting people. Airline, restaurant, and auto dealership personnel do it. Effective teachers do what is obvious—not what everyone else is doing at school. If you're the only one standing at the door with a smile, does that make you wrong and the others right? Of course not! It makes you more effective at what you do.

---

[2]Brooks, Douglas. (May 1985). "The First Day of School." *Educational Leadership*, pp. 76–78.

Here is a successful technique used by many effective teachers for greeting students on the first day of school.

Step 1. Post the following information next to the classroom door:

✔ Your name
✔ Room number
✔ Section or period, if appropriate
✔ Grade level or subject
✔ An appropriate welcome or greeting

The students can see the information on the wall and can compare it to the correct information on their registration form.

This is no different from finding flight information posted at each gate at an airport, a doctor's name on the office door, or movie information, times, and prices at a theater box office.

Step 2. Stand at the door on the first day of school. Have a smile on your face, hands ready to shake the students' hands, and a look that says you can't wait to meet them.

Step 3. As they stand there, wondering if you are the right teacher and this is the correct room, welcome them to a new school year and tell them the following information:

✔ Your name
✔ Room number
✔ Section or period, if appropriate
✔ Anything else appropriate, such as seating assignment

I love to stand at the door on the first day with a giant smile on my face, hand stuck out in an invitational pose, waiting for those "little darlings" to come down the hall.

Help your students find your room by posting information at the door as well as inside the classroom.

Step 4. Check each student's registration card, and if the student is in the wrong place or is lost, help the student or find a guide who will.

Step 5. After you greet a student, the student should be able to enter the classroom and see the same information written or posted in the room:

✔ Your name
✔ Room number
✔ Section or period, if appropriate
✔ Grade level or subject
✔ An appropriate welcome or greeting

Because the students are exposed to the same information three times, it is highly unlikely that any students will be in the wrong place on the first day of school. Their anxiety level and their tendency to be confrontational are reduced, and they will feel welcome and at ease.

What has just been suggested as an effective and cordial way to start a new year should be obvious. Have you ever gone somewhere on an errand or for an appointment and been unable to find the right address, building, or office? You know how frustrating that can be.

Perhaps you have driven to a strange place and wished the streets were better marked. Or you were in an unfamiliar store and wished there was someone around to help you find what you were looking for.

Everything possible should be done to welcome the students and to make sure that they know where to go and how to get there on time.

Seating Chart and First Assignment

If you choose to have assigned seats, tell each student this fact upon entering the door. Do not rearrange the seating after the class is all seated. The students will moan and groan over why they have to move and why they can't sit near someone.

How to Help Students Find Their Assigned Seats

✔ Have their names on place cards on the desks.

✔ Have their names written on a seating chart transparency that is projected onto a screen.

✔ Give them an index card with a letter and a number on it, such as B5, A8, C3, and ask them to find their seats based on the seating chart that is projected. Do not use this method if you feel it will be too difficult for your students to figure out two coordinates. You want them in their seats when the bell rings, not running around confused.

As the students go to their assigned seats, inform them that they will find their first assignment at their seat. **Tell them to start to work on it immediately!**

The first assignment should be short, maybe interesting, easy to complete, and successful for all students. It may simply be an alphabet or number sheet or an information form that will not be graded.

How NOT to Start the First Day of School

The ineffective teacher suddenly appears through the door just as the bell rings. The teacher's name and the room number are nowhere to be found. The teacher regards the class with an icy stare. The first day of school goes like this:

1. The teacher stands behind the desk, glaring over eyeglasses, inspecting everyone walking in with a look that says, "You're infringing on my space."

2. The teacher never mentions a name, the room number, the class, the grade level, or the period.

3. The teacher announces that he or she will call the roll.

4. The teacher also announces that as the roll is called, the seating assignments will be changed so that everyone is seated in alphabetical order. A collective groan arises. (See "Succeeding with Your First Request," page 114.)

5. The teacher calls the first student and points to the student sitting in the first chair and demands, "Up." That student rolls his eyes and goes and leans against the wall.

6. The teacher then points to the first student and says, "You, sit there."

7. As each student is dislodged from his or her chair, students lounge along the wall.

8. The students are all looking at each other, shaking their heads, "Who is this disorganized person? Our teacher? It's going to be a long year!"

You greatly increase the probability that school will start successfully for both you and your students when these four points are true:

1. You have your room ready.
2. You are at the door.
3. You have assigned seats.
4. You have the first assignment ready.

The important thing is to make a statement to your students about your efficiency and competence as a classroom manager and teacher. **What you do on the first day may determine how much respect and success you will have for the rest of the school year.**

Are You and Your Students Enigmas?

Display some information about yourself. Post your diploma. Graphically describe your personality and expectations. As soon as possible, make every student a welcome part of the class. Put something on a bulletin board from each student, with the student's name on it. Putting something up from each student makes each feel a part of the class.

The more that students know about you, the more likely they are to respect you. And the same can be said about the students—the more they know about one another, the more likely they are to respect one another.

Let your students know who you are.

How Students Are to Enter the Room

Observe how your students enter the classroom. You need to begin teaching procedures and routines (Chapter 20) the moment you meet them at the door on the first day of school.

✔ Ask any student who enters the room inappropriately to return to the door and enter appropriately. You do not send the student out of the room but rather to the door. You do not want to send anyone "out of the room" in the very first minute, as "out of the room" has a negative connotation.

✔ Do not make dubious remarks like these:
"Try coming in again correctly."
"We walk into this room like ladies and gentlemen."
"You walk in properly, understand?"

✔ Rather, calmly but firmly, do the following:
1. Ask the student to return to the door.
2. Tell the student why.
3. Give directions for correctly entering the room.
4. Check for understanding.
5. Acknowledge the understanding.

Example

Todd, please come back to the door. I am sorry, but that is not the way you enter our classroom. You were noisy, you did not go to your seat, and you pushed Ann.

When you enter this classroom, you walk in quietly, go directly to your seat, and get to work immediately on the assignment that is posted. Are there any questions?

Thank you, Todd. Now show me that you can go to your seat properly.

Don't forget the importance of using the student's name, please, and thank you. (See Chapter 11.)

Your manner and voice should be gentle and calm, even with a smile, but firm. Your voice should communicate that you are not the least bit flustered or angry. You are simply in control and know what you expect from your students, and you are communicating this expectation.

It is a mistake to let any misbehavior, such as entering a room inappropriately, go unchallenged under the rationale that you will have time to deal with this later. Effective teachers know that it will be much more difficult to correct misbehavior at a later date.

Ineffective teachers bark and yell, have no guidelines or expectations, and assume that misbehavior will correct itself. Asking students to enter the classroom according to a set of procedures indicates that there are definite boundaries to what they can and cannot do in your room.

It is important that you state the correct procedure for entering the room at any time of the day. Rehearse this procedure until it becomes automatic. Praise the students when it is done properly, and encourage them to make it a routine every day. It is best to save what has been explained in this paragraph until after you have introduced yourself as suggested in the next section.

Master teacher, Jim Heintz.

How to Speak to the Class

Stand up when you address the class, and speak in short, clear sentences or phrases. Students have a way of turning off long, complex sentences. Your purpose is to establish authority and understanding, not to impress with your intelligence. Most important, students will gauge their confidence in you by how you say what you want to say.

You do not need to speak loudly. The most effective teachers have a firm but gentle voice. Learn to "speak loudly" with your tone, not your volume. When you speak softly, the class listens carefully. You modulate the noise level of the class by the loudness of your voice. And on those rare occasions when you would need to raise your voice, you will have twice as much impact.

Learn to use nonverbal language. A nod, a smile, a stare, a frown, a raised eyebrow, or a gesture is often all that is needed, and it does not even disturb the class at work. Body language can speak volumes. Use it to manage the classroom and minimize disruptions.

Your Important First Words

There are two major things you want to state at the outset on the first day of school: your name and your expectations. It behooves you not only to tell the class your name but to pronounce it so that they will call you by the name you want.

Students want to know who you are as a person and if you will treat them as a person. (See "Seven Things Students Want to Know," page 105.) It is important that you allay any fears they may have about being in your class. The best way to do this is to smile, exude care, and communicate positive expectations.

You Will . . .

On the first days of school, learn to begin many of your sentences with "You will . . ." The first few days are critical. This cannot be stressed enough.

Your mission is to establish student habits, called procedures in this book, or routines. If not, **students will develop their own habit patterns in classes where teachers do not teach procedures and communicate expectations.** These habit patterns spread, and soon the entire class develops its own agenda, its own curriculum, and its own set of procedures. It's the third day of school, perhaps, and you have just lost your class.

The effective teacher establishes control right from the start to prevent the classroom from becoming a breeding ground of confusion and discontent. You can ease up after you have control of your class.

Example

Welcome. Welcome to another school year.

My name is Mr. Wong. There it is on the chalkboard. It is spelled W-O-N-G and is pronounced "wong." I would like to be addressed as Mr. Wong, please. Thank you. I am looking forward to being your teacher this year. Relax. I have over 30 years' experience as a teacher. I am what is called an experienced teacher, a veteran teacher.

Outside of class, I go to workshops, conferences, in-service meetings, college classes, and seminars. I also read the professional journals and work together with my fellow teachers. So you know I am up-to-date in my professional knowledge and my teaching skills. And I love to teach! I enjoy teaching, and I am proud that I am a teacher. So you can relax. You are in good hands this year with me, Mr. Wong.

You are going to have one of the greatest educational experiences of your life. We will not only study (subject), but I will also share with you some life-skill traits that will help you to be successful in tomorrow's world. I can assure you that if you should run into me at the shopping mall 25 years from now, you will say, "You were right, Mr. Wong. That was the most memorable, exciting, and fascinating class I ever had."

So welcome!

Your Room Is an Introduction to Yourself

✔ Have a spot ready with schedule, rules, procedures, calendar, and a big welcome.

✔ Have an assignment posted before the students walk in. Post the assignment in the same consistent location every day.

The students now know what to expect from you the rest of the year.

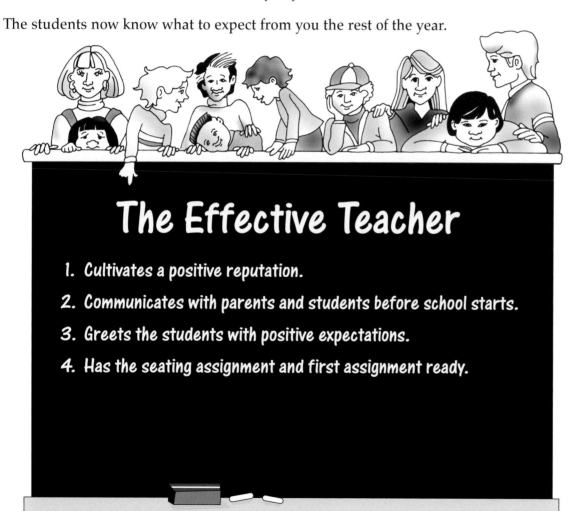

The Effective Teacher

1. Cultivates a positive reputation.

2. Communicates with parents and students before school starts.

3. Greets the students with positive expectations.

4. Has the seating assignment and first assignment ready.

KEY IDEA

The students must sit in such a way as to accomplish what you want them to accomplish.

Your Very First Set of Directions to Your Class

The Success of Your First Request

How the class reacts to your first directions will be an indication of how they will react to your directions for the remainder of the year.

Y ou can tell right away how successful you will be in giving directions by the success of your first request. Your very first request of your students will probably be to tell each one of them where to sit.

They will react in one of two ways:

"Good morning. Here's your seating assignment."

1. They will follow your orders promptly and courteously.

2. They will grumble and argue over everything you want them to do for the rest of the year.

Yes, the rest of the year! Here's why.

Succeeding with Your First Request

The Effective Teacher

✔ Is present in the room or at the door when the students arrive.

✔ Assigns seating to everyone as they enter the room.

✔ Has an assignment ready for the students on each desk.

What you do the instant the student enters the school, the library, the office, or the classroom communicates immediately if the student is welcome there.

The teacher is standing at the door with a smile and an extended hand to shake. The teacher bids everyone to enter, and each student gets a safe, nonthreatening smile. The welcome mat or red carpet is at the door for the class. This conveys a positive message to the students.

People welcome people. Textbooks, chalkboards, lectures, worksheets, and examinations do not welcome students to school. Teachers, bus drivers, administrators, secretaries, aides, and counselors invite students to have a successful experience at school.

Upon entering the classroom, the students find a pleasant environment. Your name, the room number, the period, and the class are on the chalkboard. Directions for seating (whether assigned or open) are reiterated. Information about the first assignment, which is on the desks, is clearly stated and tells the students to get to work even before the bell rings. The message you are relating to these students is that the classroom is a safe, positive, work-oriented environment where every second will be devoted to success and learning.

If students are invited to have successful experiences in the classroom, they will know that they are welcome, appreciated, cared for, and wanted. **And if the students feel wanted, they will be more likely to accede to your directions and requests.**

How to Make Your First Request Effective

Step 1. Check each registration at the door.

Step 2. Put a firm but friendly smile on your face.

Step 3. Look the student in the face and communicate understanding and acknowledgment.

Step 4. Verbally welcome and acknowledge each student.

Step 5. Then lower your voice to a firm but soft tone. Speak slowly and communicate understanding and acknowledgment.

Step 6. Then tell the student if seating is open or assigned. (See page 119.)

Step 7. Follow this with "And when you sit down, you will find an activity on your desk. I think you will enjoy doing it. Please begin working on it right away. Thank you." (See page 108.)

Failing with Your First Request

The Ineffective Teacher

✔ Is nowhere in sight when students arrive.

✔ Reshuffles the whole class after everyone has found a seat.

✔ Grumbles about all the administrative details that must be done before class can begin.

The students walk into the classroom, and no teacher is in sight. Some students find a chair; others wander around. But they all ask, "Who's the teacher? Is this the right room? Is this history?" And they all respond, "I don't know."

The bell rings, and suddenly a teacher appears from an office or from around a corner, like a monster from a dungeon. It is Cold Start Charlie, the perennial ineffective teacher. He can always be found in the faculty lounge, gulping coffee and puffing away on his cigarettes. On this day, the first day of school hasn't even begun yet, and he's already griping about the same thing he's been griping about for years.

Hurrying down to his classroom, he arrives just as the bell rings. The students immediately read the growl and the menacing look that dares anyone to breathe out of unison. He never introduces himself and may or may not identify the class or period. Standing in front of the class with the posture of a drill sergeant, he says, "When I call your name, come up and bring your registration card for me to sign."

When seemingly everyone has been registered, he looks up and asks if everyone has been called. One hand goes up. Discovering that the student is in the wrong classroom, Cold Start Charlie tells him where he should be. As the student leaves the room, all eyes are focused on him, with two

messages behind the stares: "Dummy. How can you be so stupid as to be in the wrong room?" and "Isn't he lucky not having to to put up with this jerk of a teacher for the rest of the year!"

A student has just been humiliated because a teacher was not prepared and acted in a noninvitational manner. And the students' first impression about Charlie will be reflected in their work for the rest of the year.

Your First Request Will Be Ineffective . . .

1. If you are not in the room when the students enter.

2. If you do not check any of the registration cards before the students enter the room.

3. If you do not tell the students your name, the room number, the period or grade level, and the class.

4. If you do not welcome the students.

5. If you reshuffle the class after everyone has taken a seat.

6. If you grumble that you have to do administrative work.

7. If you have provided no assignment and the students have nothing to do while you register the class.

Seating Arrangements or Seating Assignments?

Should I assign seats or allow students to sit wherever they choose? That question is germane only after you decide what you want the students to do. Seating assignments is not the issue. Seating assignments come after seating arrangements are determined. **Seating arrangements take priority.**

> **The purpose of arranging seats is to accomplish classroom tasks.**

The teacher must know what the students are to accomplish. Then the desks are arranged to maximize the accomplishment of the tasks and to minimize behavior problems. After the seats are arranged, students may be assigned seating in whatever order is desired.

Seating Arrangements	Seating Assignments
Are arranged to coincide with the task you have designed.	Are assigned to maximize learning and classroom management and minimize behavioral problems.
Examples	
First-day registration and procedures	**Examples**
Cooperative learning	By height or age
Listening to a lecture	In alphabetical order
Sitting to hear a story	For peer-group tutoring
Class discussion and interaction	For paired problem solving
Small-group activity	Placing lower-ability students at the front of the room
Taking a test	
Individual research or deskwork	

Seating Arrangements

To determine seating arrangements for the accomplishment of classroom tasks, you need to ask, in order, the following questions:

1. **What do I want to do?**
   Do I want to read a story, do small-group activities, teach discipline, procedures and routines, lecture, show a video, conduct a chorus, lead exercises, have individual study?

2. **What kind of seating arrangements are possible?**
   These photos show some possible seating arrangements.

Performing arts

Test, movie, or lecture

Group activity

Discussion or demonstration

Story time

117

3. **Which seating arrangement will I use?**

    Different seating arrangements need to be used to accomplish tasks efficiently. The students must sit in such a way as to accomplish what you want them to accomplish.

    There is no one form of seating that should be permanently used the entire school year. Change may be as frequent as furniture is moved in a living room, changed in the ballroom of a hotel, or rearranged in a store window display.

The only way for the students to learn discipline rules and procedures and routines is to have the seats arranged so that every pair of eyes will be looking at you. Assuming that you want to teach your rules and procedures and routines, do not arrange the room in a series of centers or circles in which half the students have their backs to you. Discipline rules and procedures and routines are explained in Chapters 18 to 20. Teaching these is best done with the chairs arranged in columns and rows.

Whatever the classroom arrangement, do not seat students with their backs to you or to the front of the classroom on the first day of school. If you are their focus of attention, as you should be at the start of school, the students will acknowledge your importance and listen to what you are communicating to them.

Problems When Students Have Their Backs to You

1. You explain a rule of discipline, and the students sitting in a small group look at each other and roll their eyes toward the sky. They have just invalidated the rule by their actions.

2. You explain a procedure, and half the students must turn around and write it down, then turn around again. You have invalidated the procedure for teaching procedures.

3. You explain another procedure, and you cannot tell if half the students understand because you cannot see them practicing the procedure with their backs to you.

Seating Assignments

The effective teacher assigns students to their seats on the first day of school. Don't make finding a seating assignment on the first day of school a frustrating treasure hunt. The task should be over within a matter of seconds. It is not a topic for class discussion. It should then be a dead issue because you are the teacher in charge of the instructional program. When you wish to rearrange the room or the seating, deal with the change in the same expedient way.

You will have a much more effective class, most of the time, if you assign students to their seats. For group work, you should assign students to their groups and then assign the groups to their workstations or seating arrangements. For instance, you are hosting a dinner party with guests at three separate tables. You don't ask your guests to get their own utensils out of the drawer and sit wherever they please. If you are a gracious host, you tell your guests where you'd like them to sit.

Airlines, theaters, and restaurants—the good ones—will designate a seat or seat you in a chair of mutual choice. Do likewise in the classroom. You are the teacher, the conductor, the facilitator.

Seating assignments are sometimes made for social and behavioral reasons. When you do not want certain students to sit together, separate them. Before going to an assembly, you say, "Please wait for me to place you before you take your seat."

There are times when seating assignments are not important—for instance, when the whole class sings, you read a story, or students are doing individual research.

Seating assignments should not become an issue in the classroom. Student success and the instructional program are your major focus.

Reasons for a Seating Chart

1. Facilitates roll taking

2. Aids name memorization

3. Separates potential problem students

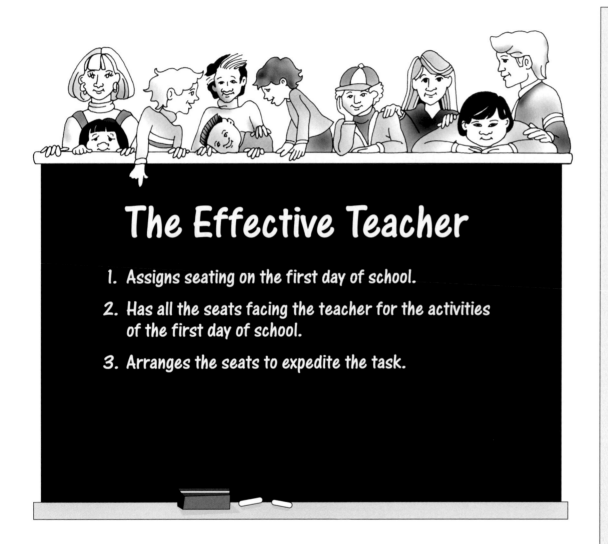

The Effective Teacher

1. Assigns seating on the first day of school.

2. Has all the seats facing the teacher for the activities of the first day of school.

3. Arranges the seats to expedite the task.

What If the Chairs Cannot Be Moved?

If the chairs are bolted in place, you are restricted to that arrangement and must adapt your activities to that seating plan.

For instance, you would not play football in the bathroom, cook in the bedroom, or take a shower in the kitchen sink. Similarly, you cannot effectively have small-group activities or have eye-to-eye class interaction and discussion if you have to teach a class in the school auditorium.

For your own sanity, adjust your classroom instruction and teaching techniques. This is life. You have been in situations before where the circumstances and the budget dictated the terms—for example, you could invite only 75 guests to a wedding reception and it had to be held in your home and not the ballroom of the Ritz.

Accept that all things are not the way you want them, so stop beating yourself over the head.

Learn to nourish your body and go on with improving the quality of your life.

KEY IDEA

Post your assignments if you want your students to do them.

Your First Priority When Class Starts

> **Your very first priority when the class starts is to get the students to work.**

Your first priority is not to take roll; it is to get the students to work immediately. It is no different in the private sector. When your students go to work, as in a part-time job, they are expected to begin working at the appointed hour.

At the appointed hour, the part-time workers also know what to do. They do not stand around waiting for directions or ask questions like "What do you want me to do today?"

When class begins, you can easily get students to work if three criteria have been met:

1. The students have an assignment.
2. They know where to find the assignment.
3. They know why they are to do the assignment.

Daily and in the Same Place

Common sense and research on the effective classroom emphatically tell you to POST YOUR ASSIGNMENTS EVERY DAY!

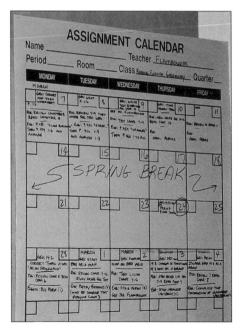

Assignments should be posted daily, always in the same place.

Post the assignments in the same place every day. Even if it is the same assignment, post it. There is no need for students to ask, "What is the assignment?" or "What am I supposed to do?" if they know that the assignment is in the same place every day.

Assignments can be posted on the chalkboard or on a bulletin board, handed out at the door, or displayed from a transparency. Just make sure that the assignments are displayed in the same place so that the students know exactly and consistently where to look for them.

Assignments Must Be Posted Daily and Consistently

1. An assignment must be posted before the students enter the room.

2. The assignment must be posted in the same location every day.

Sample Assignments

For the students to get to work immediately, an assignment must be posted.

Sample Elementary Assignment

SPELLING:

1. Number your paper from 1–15.
2. Take practice spelling test.
3. Change papers with spelling partner.
4. Correct tests.
5. Write words missed five times each.

Sample Secondary Assignment

- Review criteria for haiku. Use chart on board or see page 76 in text.
- Compose haiku about winter.
- Give it a <u>one-word</u> title. Title cannot be used in the body of the haiku.

Are We Doing Anything Today?

The ineffective teacher keeps the assignment a mystery until it is announced, and it may be announced in different ways and posted in different places each day. Sometimes there may be no assignment, even though the students ask for one. This may be because the teacher does not know what should be done, what the student is to learn, or how to teach it.

You can always tell classes where no assignments are posted. Ineffective teachers say things like this:

"Where did we leave off yesterday?" (I have no control.)
"Open your books so that we can take turns reading."
   (For what reason?)
"Sit quietly and do the worksheet." (To master what?)
"Let's watch this movie." (To learn what?)
"You can have a free study period." (To do what? I do not have an assignment for you. I am unprepared.)

The textbook is not the curriculum. Having students fill in worksheets to keep them busy and quiet is not the curriculum. Teachers who have no curriculum follow the textbook, page by page, cover to cover, and look for busywork for the students. When this happens, you have students who walk into the classroom and say things like this:

"Are you going to show us a movie?"
"Are you going to read to us?"
"Are you going to lecture to us?"
"Are you going to let us have a study period?"

Or worse yet,

"Are we going to do anything today?"
"Are we going to do anything important today?"
"Did I miss anything important while I was absent?"

The Fatal Fallacy of Textbooks

- A committee's or teacher's choice of a textbook is the single most important decision in establishing the curriculum.

- The curriculum is a set of knowledge and skills packaged in textbooks.

- Most teachers base their instruction on covering—and hence being imprisoned by—a single textbook.

- Teachers have faith in the textbook. (Some lament, "If only the right one could be found!")

- Students are trained to seek the "right" answer from the textbook.

- All supplementary activities add to the textbook.

Although teachers express concern for student attitudes, they continue to be imprisoned by the traditional teaching model—assign, recite, and test—all based on the textbook.

A teacher's reliance on the textbook may reflect an inability to conceptualize the dynamic nature of the curriculum, the purpose of education, and the practices and procedures associated with student learning.

In classes where students make comments like these, they take no responsibility for their work. The teacher is the only responsible person in the classroom. That's why they ask the teacher what is going to happen. They look to the teacher for direction, for entertainment, and for work.

Assignments Teach Students Responsibility

 The student must be responsible for classwork. The direction and responsibility for a student's classwork, however, are based on the teacher's having a daily schedule and an assignment ready.

> **Post your assignments if you want the students to do them.**

The effective teacher teaches RESPONSIBILITY. This is because effective teachers have their schedules and assignments posted. It is a joy to watch such teachers and such classes in action. The students in these classes know what to expect during the day and where to look for their assignments. They can now go about doing the work on their own. You cannot teach students to be responsible unless they know what you want them to do.

Post your schedule if you want your students ready to learn.

You Start the Class, Not the Bell

Shirley Bert Lee is a California mentor teacher. This means that she has been recognized for her excellence in the classroom. In addition, students want to be in her class, and parents pressure administrators to have their children in her class.

You can understand why Shirley's fifth- and sixth-grade classes are so effective when you see how efficiently she opens each day of her class.

- She has a posted morning routine, which is followed.

- She posts her assignments every day.

- She knows how to develop routines with her students.

On the first day of school, this is what she tells her students:

Mrs. Lee does not start the class. The bell does not start the class. YOU start the class.

This is what will happen when you come to class, each day. There is a morning routine you are to follow. You immediately go to your seat, you get out your materials for work, and you get to work on the assignment.

The assignment will be posted on the chalkboard in the same place every day. For instance, you may be given the following seven questions and these new vocabulary words.

Please get to work on these new vocabulary words when you come in. Do not wait for the bell to ring or for the teacher to signal you to get to work.

You will have 10 minutes after the bell rings to get the assignment done. (See Chapter 20 for how routines like these are implemented.)

Shirley Bert Lee
from Roseville, California.

Shirley Lee's class is a joy to behold. She doesn't even have to open her mouth when the bell rings. She may say "Good morning" or compliment the class on their appropriate behavior, but while the students are quickly and quietly at work, she completes her chores, which typically must be done by all teachers, like taking roll.

Yes, she takes roll *after* the students are at work. The first priority of a teacher is to get the students to work, not to take roll.

The Effective Teacher

1. Has a posted morning or class-opening routine.

2. Has the assignment posted daily.

3. Posts the assignment in a consistent location.

4. Teaches the class where to find the assignment.

Do not involve the class in the roll-taking process.

The Results of Ineffective Roll Taking

> **The effective teacher starts the class immediately with an assignment, not roll taking.**

Y ou can't imagine how many veteran teachers are still taking roll at the beginning of each day or period, wasting five or more minutes of student learning time, and arguing with the class as to who is absent.

Please do not take roll at the very beginning of the class.

Typical Ineffective Roll Takers

1. The Drill Sergeant or Camp Counselor

These people ask the class to answer by signifying "present" when their names are called. This is what actually happens.

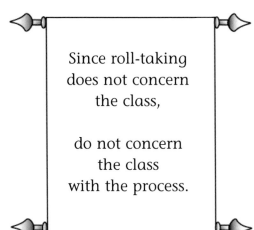

Since roll-taking does not concern the class,

do not concern the class with the process.

"Justin." "Present."
"Kimberley." "Present."
"Mario." "Present."
"Kenny." "Here." Several students look at Kenny for his cute, unauthorized answer. The teacher blithely continues, despite the inappropriate answer.

"Maria." "Present."
"Irwin." "Present."

"Tanya." "Yep." More students now look at Tanya, some giving her positive signals for her inappropriate answer. But the teacher just goes on. And the class noise level is now higher.

"Tran." "Present."
"Susan." "Present."
"Marvin." "Yo." The whole class breaks up. But the teacher, glancing up for a second, goes right on.

The students quickly learn that the teacher does not mean what is said. Worse yet, the teacher does nothing whenever inappropriate behavior occurs.

During the prep period, you can find this teacher in the lounge, one of the lounge lizards, complaining about the noise level in his class. The problem is not the students. The problem is the teacher who wants his class to bark out responses like they were at a military camp or summer camp.

2. The Grade-Book Mumbler

This is the teacher who says, "All right, everyone, I want it quiet while I take roll." Translated, this means, "I want you hyperactive, psychosexual, pubescent junior high school students to sit still, without talking or doing anything for the next four to five minutes (that'll be the day!) while I take roll."

This ineffective teacher stands in front of the room and reads the roll, just as she has been doing for decades. She is totally oblivious to the fact that the class couldn't care less about taking attendance, not to mention that the noise level is slowly increasing.

The problem begins because students have a strange sense of attendance. They believe that if they are anywhere on campus, or even within a mile of the school site, they are present, whereas most teachers consider a student absent if a warm body is not in an appropriate seat.

They Know You Are Taking Roll

Even when you do not involve the class in the roll-taking process, some of the students are so astute in the teaching process that they will offer attendance information without your even asking for it.

For instance, you are quietly taking roll. They see you with the grade book in your hand. And as you scan the class, someone says, "Mrs. Prasad, Joey is not absent. He's at the counselor's office. I saw him."

Isn't it wonderful that the students know how to run a class? Many of them could possibly run a more effective classroom than many of the teachers—unless the teachers themselves continually work at excellence.

Excellence is the process of constantly working at making a process operate better and better.

To achieve excellence, teachers must always be willing to work on methods that improve classroom operations.

When this teacher comes to a name in the roll book that gets no response or sees that a seat is empty, the teacher says, "Ah, Ernie is absent," and is about to mark Ernie absent. Then a voice, maybe more than one, shouts out—without permission—"Ernie is not absent. He's coming down the hall. He'll be here." Or, "I saw him in the library. There's a long line. He'll be here."

Now what is this teacher going to do? It's the teacher against the class. The class says that Ernie is present on the campus, but the teacher does not see Ernie in his seat. She marks Ernie absent nonetheless.

And with four absences in the class, the scene repeats itself four times. Each time, the noise level rises and more on-task time is wasted.

The Outcomes of Ineffective Roll Taking

✔ Each time the class yells out a response, the noise level gets higher.

✔ Confrontation builds up between the class and the teacher as to whether or not a student is absent.

✔ Valuable minutes are wasted.

✔ Many students sit there bored while precious study time is wasted on a bookkeeping chore that really does not concern the class.

The old way of taking roll that you saw your teachers use 10 to 15 years ago is really quite inefficient. The effective teacher is constantly evaluating how the teaching process can be improved.

Effective Roll Taking in an Effective Class

The effective teacher starts the class immediately with an assignment, not roll taking. The effective teacher not only starts the class but has trained the class to start working on its own. (See Chapter 20 on procedures and routines.)

> ### Students That Have Been Effectively Taught Know . . .
>
> ✔ How to enter the room quickly and courteously.
>
> ✔ How to go to their seats and take out their materials.
>
> ✔ Where to look for their assignment.
>
> ✔ To begin their work immediately.

There are many ways to take roll; however, your first priority is to get the students on task.

✔ As soon as the tardy bell rings, your first task is to scan the room, not to take roll but to look for students who are not at work.

✔ You quietly signal these students to get to work immediately. Use a firm smile and a hand gesture that clearly indicates that you want them to work.

✔ They know where the assignment is located, and they know what to do. You are maximizing academic learning time. (See Chapter 21.)

✔ As soon as the class is at work, proceed to do whatever administrative chores are necessary. Taking roll is usually one of these.

WHEN should you take roll? After the students are on task.
HOW should you take roll? Without involving the students.

The Student Who Is Absent

I have a procedure for roll taking and for students who are absent. I have three students trained to take the roll on a rotating basis. They do this while the students are completing their opening assignment.

If a student is absent, they complete a form that says, "Makeup work for Mr. Hockenberry," clip it to the work for the day that has already been prepared, and place it in an envelope along one of the walls marked with the appropriate period.

A returning absent student does not come to see me. The procedure is that when absent students return, they obtain their work from the envelope and ask one of the three students if something is not understood before coming to me for help. They seldom do, and class proceeds quickly with the lesson for the day.

—Ed Hockenberry
Midlothian Middle School,
Virginia

Three Ways to Take Roll Efficiently and Effectively

1. Look at your class and refer to your seating chart. Mark whoever is absent.

2. Have folders or something personal in a box at the door. When the students come in, they are to take their folders, go to their seats, and get to work on the posted assignment. After the students are at work, you look in the box. You see three folders left, note the names, and mark these students absent.

3. Have each student's name on a clothespin. Clip these pins to a cutout, such as an animal or a seasonal object like a jack-o-lantern or heart. When the students come in, they move their clothespin to a cutout indicating they are in attendance. After the students are at work, you note which pins have not been moved and mark these students absent. Assign a student the task of transferring the clothespins to the original cutout at an appropriate time.

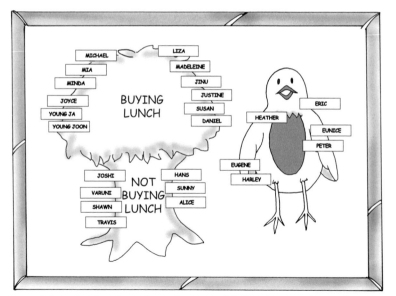

Other administrative tasks can be accomplished at the same time, such as indicating whether or not lunch will be purchased.

There are many other ways to take roll. **Regardless of which method you use to take roll, you are to take roll quickly and quietly without disturbing the class.** There is no need to involve the class in the roll-taking process.

131

The Effective Teacher

1. Has a posted assignment ready for the students.

2. Takes roll after the students are on task.

3. Does not disturb the class during roll taking.

4. Takes roll quickly and quietly.

KEY IDEA

A grade record book must show the results and progress of each student at all times.

It's Prime Time

> **Prime time in school is the first few moments in a class.**
> If you blow these moments, you blow the impression,
> the sale, and the success of a class.

The term *prime time* was invented by the television industry to denote the time when the audience is potentially at its largest. It is the most important time during the broadcast day; thus shows and sponsors jockey for position. That is why it is called *prime* time.

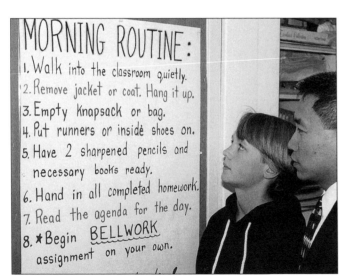

MORNING ROUTINE:
1. Walk into the classroom quietly.
2. Remove jacket or coat. Hang it up.
3. Empty Knapsack or bag.
4. Put runners or inside shoes on.
5. Have 2 sharpened pencils and necessary books ready.
6. Hand in all completed homework.
7. Read the agenda for the day.
8. ★ Begin BELLWORK assignment on your own.

Posted morning routines allow students to get on-task immediately.

> **Student on-task work is the major activity during academic prime time. The students must immediately get to work when they enter the room.**

An assignment must be available, and the students must know the procedure for getting to work immediately. (See Chapter 20.) Do not destroy prime time with non-prime-time activities such as taking roll, announcements, or paper shuffling.

An organized grade record book keeps time spent on roll taking and other record-keeping activities to a minimum. This is another practice of the efficient and effective teacher.

It's Really a Grade Record Book

From Day 1, you will need a book in which to keep student records. It must be ready before you see a single class. This book is typically called a "grade book," and it comes in all different sizes, shapes, and configurations. **A grade book should more correctly be called a student record book or a grade record book.** A grade record book contains far more than grades. It is used to keep various records about each student.

Typically, schools or school systems buy one kind of grade book and give it to all of their teachers. This assumes that if you are an elementary school teacher, you will keep records the same way whether you teach kindergarten or sixth grade. Likewise, if you are a secondary school teacher, the physical education teacher or the English composition teacher, you will all keep records identically. Ridiculous, yet this is what is assumed when all the teachers get the same grade record book!

The Problems with Most Grade Record Books

The problem with many grade books is that they have only one line, or perhaps two lines, on which to record information for a student. Thus you have these problems:

✔ You have only enough space to show one record, such as attendance.

✔ To record additional information, you have to turn to another page and possibly write all the names again. You are constantly flipping pages.

✔ If the number of students in your class exceeds the number of lines on a page, you have to repeat the information, at the top of every page.

✔ The major problem comes when you need a progress report or a summary for report-card grades. Because there is only one line to record all information for each student, you must sift through attendance, homework, projects, tests, and anything else you may record for the student to determine the student's progress. Progress is not readily apparent at a glance.

Because of the inadequacies of most grade books, the correct title for this chapter should be "How to Prepare Your Own Grade Record Book." Or, if you are planning to buy your own grade record book, you must first determine how you will be grading and what records you will be keeping so that you will know what to look for when you shop.

It is imperative that you decide before you begin the school year just what you want to record. People in other professions do the same thing:

✔ An accountant sets up the categories on a ledger before entering numbers.

✔ A businessperson names the columns on a spreadsheet before entering data.

✔ A statistician names the columns in a baseball box score so that the results can be entered in the right places as the game progresses.

✔ A bride-to-be designs a chart to record information about the people coming to the wedding.

Designed properly, a grade book should let you see each student's RESULTS and PROGRESS immediately.

You must determine what you want for each student, for example:

Attendance	Project grades
Homework assignments	Extra-credit work
Classroom work	Class participation
Test grades	Classroom behavior
Skills mastered	Cumulative progress

Subject **CORE B**		1st Week					2nd Week				
Indicate Calendar Date →		8/27	28	29	30	31	9/3	4	5	6	7
Grade **ATTENDANCE**		M	T	W	T	F	M	T	W	T	F
The Blank Columns at the Right May Be Used to Indicate Assignments	Text Book No.						H O L I D A Y				
ANDRIANO, LEO ₁						✗					
AQUINO, JODY ₂											
CASTRO, RHONDA ₃					✗		T				
COLLINS, JOEL ₄				⊼			⊼				
DOAN, DUC ₅											
ELDER, SCOTT ₆											
FLYNN, SANDI ₇											
GILBERTSON, ERIC ₈					✗						
HARRIS, ELIZABETH ₉											
HUNG, VINCENT ₁₀											
JAEHNICHEN, TONY ₁₁							✗	✗	✗		
KIM, PETER ₁₂											
KWONG, MAY ₁₃							T				
LEVINE, SALLY ₁₄											
McBIRNEY, NANCY ₁₅			⊼								
POLOMSKI, ROBYN ₁₆											

Grade books with one or two lines per student may not have enough space for all the information you wish to record.

Keeping the Three Basic Records

To keep good student records, you probably need three or even four lines after each student's name. Because most commercial grade books have only one or two lines after each name, you may have record-keeping problems if you are given an inadequate grade book.

 The **three basic records** in a grade record book each require a separate line:

1. Attendance
2. Scores
3. Running Total

First Line: Attendance

An attendance record is probably mandated by the administration, if not by the school board. Attendance is a fact of life in most of our everyday endeavors. Schools are paid, people are paid, and students are graded by their presence on a job or in school. So make the recording of attendance as efficient and painless as possible. (See Chapter 16.)

The four common attendance records you need to keep are *present, absent, unexcused absence,* **and** *tardy.*

1. **Present.** Typically, nothing is noted in the space. This tells you that the student was in class on this day.

2. **Absent.** Typically, an **A** is noted in the space, telling you that the student was absent on this date. If the student brings a note that excuses the absence, you may want to draw a diagonal line through the **A**. This tells you that you have seen a note or received authorization from the office, excusing the absence. If you do not see a diagonal line, it means that you are still waiting to see the excuse.

Neat Shelves Were More Important than School Effectiveness

Mr. Fussy was the most appropriate name for the registrar at our school. His dress, his office, and his record keeping were immaculate, to the point where Felix Unger of *The Odd Couple* would have been Oscar Madison in his office.

For nearly two decades at this high school, he was the sole determiner as to what grade book we were to use. He ordered the grade books, distributed them during preschool orientation, collected them on the last day of school, and checked them to be sure that the grades were recorded properly. You did not get signed out until you got his seal of approval.

Why did he use the same grade book for decades? Because all the grade books were the same size, so they fit on the shelves in his record-keeping room!

After all, he would tell us, he needed to be able to find and interpret a student's records, if needed, years after we may be gone. No argument there.

However, the fact that the grade books were outdated in their design was immaterial. What mattered to Mr. Fussy was that they all fit neatly on his shelves.

For a stress-free way to take care of assignments missed during absences, refer to Ed Hockenberry's procedures on page 131.

3. **Unexcused Absence.** If no note is presented explaining the absence, place a check or a breve (‿), the mark used to indicate a short vowel sound, above the **A**.

An unexcused absence is simply one for which the student does not have a note of explanation, typically from a parent, a doctor, or another teacher. In some schools, you will determine if the absence is excused or not. In other schools, an attendance office will process this beforehand.

How you treat an unexcused absence may be determined by school policy. Ask. A school may allow only so many unexcused absences before administrative action is taken. A good school will notify the home at once if an unexcused absence or cut has been determined. You should make it your responsibility to work with the administration and the home to curtail the cutting of school or classes as quickly as possible. The main advantages of this action will be the preservation of your sanity and the lessening of stress in the classroom.

Also, ask other teachers how they treat unexcused absences. **In most cases, an unexcused absence does not release a student from responsibility for missed work or assignments.** The student must make up the work.

What an unexcused absence may mean is that the teacher may not be obligated to help the student make up the work; for instance, the teacher may have to explain to the student:

> *You cut the class, so you must accept the responsibility for having missed the lecture, movie, or activity. You must find the material you missed on your own. That is the price you must pay when you do not show up for class.*

4. **Tardy.** This is typically denoted with a **T**. If the student has a pass excusing the tardiness, erase the **A**. If the student does not have a pass, the student is tardy. Erase the **A** and write a **T**, or just write a **T** over the **A**. Find out what the school policy is concerning tardiness. You may be asked to refer the student to the office after a certain number of tardies.

Second Line: Scores

You really need a second line to record the results of individual assignments, such as tests, projects, papers, worksheets, and homework. You can show results using whatever system you choose, in letter grade or numerical form. However, a numerical system is much better if you want to weight each score differently or if you want a running progress report.

Third Line: Running Total

Teachers are bombarded with requests for results on students' progress. You will get calls from parents, requests from the counseling department or the main office, forms to complete for determining extracurricular activity eligibility, and students' questions about their own progress. **An up-to-date overview of the progress of each student must be available at all times.**

With a three-line grade record book, as each score is entered on line 2, add it to the previous score on line 3. The progress report or running total allows immediate access to any student's cumulative grade. A student's progress is then available at any time.

You will appreciate having a three-line grade record book when it is time to turn in grades at the end of the grading period. Because you have a running progress report, you will not need to ask someone to summarize weeks of grades, wait in line to share a calculator or a computer, or waste valuable time determining a cumulative record.

While all others are gnashing their teeth, "trying to get their grades in," you can have time to pursue other interests, visit a health club, have a candlelight dinner, or rest with a good book because you planned the records you wanted to keep for each student and then constructed a grade record book to keep them.

You now have a grade record book that shows the results and progress of each student at all times.

"The Three-Line Attendance and Grade Record Book"

Merle Whaley is a teacher who was frustrated with the one-line grade book supplied by his district. So he told his wife, "I want to make a grade book anyone could understand that would also show each student's progress immediately." After two years and many changes, *The Three-Line Attendance and Grade Record Book* became more than a dream.

He says, "I finally had a book and a method of doing grades that easily displayed a student's records and progress in seconds. With three lines per student, I could now have attendance or essential skills on the first line. The second line could be used for all of the student's scores, such as daily work, quizzes, projects, and test scores. The very important third line would show a running total for each student. Now when parents call or visit the school, the progress is available in seconds."

Whaley's grade record book also has a tear-off top to each page. You only need to record the date or assignment ONCE, at the top of one of the pages, for all the students having the same activity. All unused tops are torn off and index tabs are applied so that you can have fast access to any class. For instance, in a large class such as a band with 100 students, the band teacher writes the student's name once and the dates, activities, and scores just once for all 100 students. The tops of the five unused pages are torn off, saving a tremendous amount of time on grade record book work.

Whaley has developed a program which will print the parent, student, phone, and ID data on his continuous-form loose-leaf version of the three-line grade book pages. He then inserts the pages into his six-ring loose-leaf binder, creating a flexible hard copy use for the three-line loose-leaf pages without first typing or handwriting the names each grading period.

The grade record book is available from

Merle J. Whaley
2941 B 1/2 Road
Grand Junction, CO 81503
TEL (970) 241-7777   FAX (970) 241-0016

With a three-line grade book, you can show each student's attendance, score, and running total.

PERIOD: Core A COURSE: HISTORY TIME TEACHER	© MERLE J. WHALEY 1996	p.70 1-20 evens	p.73 6-11	p.78 1-20 odd Quiz	p.80 Review	CH. 10 TEST
ABSENT SYMBOL	DATE / DAY	11/6 M	7 T	8 W	9 T	10 F
TARDY SYMBOL	DAILY TOTAL	10	10	10/20	10	60
	CUM. TOTAL	10	20	30	60	120
Mrs. Young 935-7998 11-3-86 A/92						
1 Anderson, Jill		10	8	10/16	7	51
		10	18	44		102
Mr. Spor 938-7271 12-2-86 B/85				A^u		
2 Barnes, Karl		10	7	8/15	7	48
		10	17	40		95
M/M Carter 935-7220 9-9-86 C/78			Ⓧ			
3 Carter, Liz		9	6	7/15	7	45
		9	15	37		89
M/M Durfee 938-1962 9-29-86 C/75			Ⓧ		Ⓧ	
4 Durfee, Nan		10	7	7/14	6	45
		10		38		89
Mrs. Feller 938-0645 1-5-87 A/94		Ⓧ				
5 Feller, Tammy		7	10	10/19	8	55
		7				109
M/M Floyd 938-3601 12-20-86 A/93						
6 Floyd, Riley		10	9	9/18	8	52
		10				106
Mr. Frische 938-3601 12-5-86 B/87						
7 Frische, Sidnee		10	9	8/14	9	55
		10				105
Mrs. Anton 935-9544 10-15-86 B/89						
8 Howell, Shawn		10	8	8/14	10	53
		10				103

The Effective Teacher

1. Knows what results should be recorded.

2. Designs or modifies a grade record book to record these results.

3. Keeps a running progress of student work.

Discipline with a Plan

Effective teachers present their rules clearly and provide reasonable explanations of the need for them.

The three most important student behaviors that must be taught the first days of school are these:

1. **Discipline**
2. **Procedures**
3. **Routines**

I Did Not Even Have a System

I was going insane and then I realized that I did not have a fair system or even any system. . . .

My students, after we had the plan in effect, commented on how quiet the room was and how easily they could do their work. The principal commented about the plan and said how pleased he was to see quiet, working, behaved students!

As for me, I was thinking of quitting teaching because I was so uptight—until you shared a plan with me.

Sheila
Lethbridge, Alberta,
Canada

Effective teachers introduce rules, procedures, and routines on the very first day of school and continue to teach them the first week of school. During the first week of school, rules, procedures, and routines take precedence over lessons. The ineffective teacher is too eager to present lessons; consequently, when disruptive behavior occurs, they discipline—often without a plan.

Many teachers complain that their students will not behave and that they get no backing from the administration. There is a reason. The administration cannot back up a nonexistent plan; nor can students guide their behavior when a plan does not exist. If a student were to ask, could you produce a copy of your discipline plan? Teachers who do not have a plan resort to disciplining by yelling, screaming, scolding, and demeaning. **If you do not have a plan, you are planning to fail.**

Continuum of Discipline Plans

There are many discipline plans. They all have their good and bad points, but they are all plans. Plans are not charters, laws, or theorems. You have plans for vacations, parties, and weddings.

If you are looking for a foolproof discipline system that works automatically, you will never find one. What you need to do is to develop a plan of your own, based on what you want to accomplish with your students.

It is imperative that you have a hard copy of a plan and that you follow that plan.

Discipline plans range from those where the student is in charge to those where the teacher is in charge. You will behave differently as you move through the different plans. These plans form a continuum. The method suggested in this book falls more toward the teacher-in-charge end of the spectrum.

Who's in Charge?
— *Teacher Behaviors When* —

Student in Charge	Both Student and Teacher	Teacher in Charge
Teacher silently looks on.	Teacher questions.	Teacher provides reinforcement.
Teacher uses nondirective statements.	Teacher uses directive statements.	Teacher uses physical intervention and isolation.
Teacher accepts excuses.	Teacher models proper behavior.	Teacher accepts no excuses.
Teacher listens.	**Teacher confronts and agreements are reached.**	**Teacher tells what is to be done.**

Books to Support Plans

Thomas Gordon, *Teacher Effectiveness Training*	William Glasser, *Schools Without Failure*	Saul Axelrod, *Behavior Modification for Teachers*
Louis Rath, Merrill Harmin, and Sid Simon, *Values and Teaching*	Linda Albert, *Cooperative Discipline*	Lee Canter, *Assertive Discipline*
	Richard Curwin, *Discipline with Dignity*	
	Barbara Coloroso, *Nonviolent Conflict Resolution*	

Why You Should Have Rules

The effective teacher invests time in teaching discipline and procedures, knowing that this will be repaid multifold in the effective use of class time. The key word is ***invests.***

You, not the administration or the counselors, are primarily responsible for communicating and maintaining behavior. **The most successful classes are those in which the teacher has a clear idea of what is expected from the students and the students have a clear idea of what the teacher expects from them.** Expectations can be stated as rules.

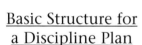

Basic Structure for
a Discipline Plan

- **Rules:** What the expected behaviors are. (Chapter 18)
- **Consequences:** What the student chooses to accept if a rule is broken. (Chapter 19)
- **Rewards:** What the student receives for appropriate behavior. (Chapter 19)

✔ Rules are expectations of appropriate student behavior.

✔ After thorough deliberation, decide on your rules and write them down or post them **before the first day of school**.

✔ Clearly communicate in both verbal and written form to your students what you expect as appropriate behavior.

✔ It is easier to maintain good behavior than to change inappropriate behavior that has become established.

✔ You will have firm confidence in your ability to manage a class if you have a clear idea of what you expect from your students and they know that that is what you expect from them.

✔ Rules immediately create a work-oriented atmosphere.

The research shows that the most effective schools are those with a well-ordered environment and high academic expectations.

✔ Rules create a strong expectation about the things that are important to you.

Schoolwide Discipline Plan

The most effective discipline plans are applied universally so that no matter where the students go, they encounter the same plan. **The key to a good discipline plan is schoolwide consistency.** This is why there are many schools where the students are all busily working and the teachers are all busily teaching—and everyone is happy and succeeding.

The best discipline plan is a schoolwide discipline plan. In a schoolwide discipline plan, all persons in authority are trained in an agreed-on discipline plan, support the plan, and continuously work together to refine it. As a result, the students acknowledge and are familiar with the discipline plan. **The key to an effective schoolwide discipline plan is that everyone uses it with consistency!**

A schoolwide discipline plan is like the speed-limit law. We know that there are speed limits; however, the limits differ from one neighborhood, community, or state to another. The acceptable speed is posted for all to see and abide by.

Likewise, under a schoolwide discipline plan, everyone does not necessarily have the same set of rules. The bus drivers may have different rules from the teachers, food-service personnel, nurses, librarians, paraprofessionals, and counselors. Each person in authority can have a separate set of rules.

- A schoolwide discipline plan is posted in every room, bus (yes, bus), office, gymnasium, cafeteria, library, hall, and other locations where there is an employee responsible for the safety and education of the students.

- The plan has the same basic design so that when a student goes from room to room or to the office, cafeteria, bus, library, or recess, it is the same basic plan.

- Since everyone at the school uses the same plan with consistency, the students know what is expected of them and all members of the staff support one another. This also makes life much easier for new employees, because a plan is already in effect.

- Introducing a discipline plan to each new class of students is easy because a plan, rooted in a prevailing culture, already exists at the school.

The best discipline plan is an industrywide or schoolwide discipline plan.

The Two Kinds of Rules

The function of a rule is to prevent or encourage behavior by clearly stating student expectations.** The two kinds of rules are general and specific.

General Rules. General rules are the more encompassing and may cover a plethora of behaviors. Here are some examples:

> Respect others.
> Take care of your school.
> Be polite and helpful.
> Keep the room (or cafeteria) clean.
> Behave in the library.

The advantage of general rules is that they offer flexibility in that a great deal of behavior can be covered by a few general rules.

The disadvantage of general rules is that they must be explained; otherwise students will not know exactly what behaviors are acceptable and not acceptable in the classroom. For instance, students must be told that respecting others includes no hitting, no stealing, no tattling, no name-calling, and so on.

Specific Rules. Specific rules are to the point and clearly cover one behavior. Here are examples:

> Be in class on time.
> Keep your hands, feet, and objects to yourself.
> Listen to instructions the first time they are given.
> Do not use vulgar or offensive language.
> Have all materials ready to use when the bell rings.

The advantage of specific rules is that they clearly state the expected student behavior.

The disadvantage of specific rules is that you are limited to no more than five rules. (See page 147.) Therefore, you must have good classroom management skills and know exactly what behaviors are important to you.

General or Specific Rules?

General rules are more successful when used by effective veteran teachers who have learned how to encourage good classroom behavior over the years. These teachers never raise their voices; they seldom get angry; they don't get flustered. All they do is give the student a signal, a wave of the hand, or a stare (See page 164.), and the student behaves.

Specific rules are probably better for the newer teacher or the experienced teacher looking for a better discipline system. You can always move from specific rules to general rules during the school year as the students learn about your expectations of their behavior.

What Should My Rules Be?

Refrain from copying and using other people's rules. You cannot expect your students to behave if you do not know how you want them to behave. **It is essential that you state your specific behavior expectations.**

Here are some examples of specific rules that you may want to consider for your discipline plan.

Universal Specific Rules

1. Follow directions the first time they are given.
2. Raise your hand and wait for permission to speak.
3. Stay in your seat unless you have permission to do otherwise.
4. Keep hands, feet, and objects to yourself.
5. No cursing or teasing.

Specific Rules for Elementary Grades

1. Wait for directions with no talking.
2. Eyes front when the teacher is talking.
3. Change tasks quickly and quietly.
4. Complete the morning routine.
5. Report directly to the assigned area.

Specific Rules for High School

1. Be in your seat when the bell rings.
2. Bring all books and materials to class.
3. No personal grooming during class time.
4. Sit in your assigned seat daily.
5. Follow directions the first time they are given.

Specific Rules for the Playground

1. Swing only forward and backward on the swings.
2. Do not throw ice or snow at anyone.
3. Sliding paths must be clear before you start your slide.
4. Only two on the seesaw or teeter-totter at a time.

Specific Rules for the Cafeteria

1. Follow correct traffic flow from serving counter to table and from table to trash to exit.
2. Make your seating choice and remain there.
3. All food is to be eaten in the cafeteria.
4. Raise your hand to be excused when finished eating.
5. Scrape food into bins with a rubber spatula and put utensils in the water.

These Are Not Good Rules

- Academic behavior should not appear on your list of rules. Such things as doing homework, writing in ink or typing, and turning in assignments fall into the realm of procedures (Chapter 20) and academic performance (Unit D). Your discipline plan should be concerned with behavior, not academic work.

- If possible, state rules positively. But recognize that sometimes a negative rule can be more direct, understandable, and incontestable:

  No cursing or swearing.
  No smoking.
  No fighting on the playground.

How to Introduce Your Rules

Why You Should Have Only Three to Five Rules

Have you ever noticed that your phone number, credit card, social security number, auto license number, and zip code are written in groups of five numbers or less? That is because people find it easier to remember numbers in groups of three to five.

- Limit rules to a number that you and the students can readily remember—never more than five.

- If you need more than five rules, do not post more than five at any one time.

- The rules need not cover all aspects of behavior in the classroom.

- You have the right to replace a rule with another.

- As a new rule becomes necessary, replace an older one with it. The rule you replace can be retained as an "unwritten rule," which the students have learned. The students are still responsible for the one you have replaced.

It is important to introduce the discipline plan on the first day of school. Before you do so, check to see that the following things have been done:

✔ You have carefully planned for what you want to accomplish.

✔ You have written the rules to help you accomplish those goals.

✔ You have posted the rules, along with the consequences and rewards. (See Chapter 19.)

✔ You have welcomed the class (Unit B), introduced yourself (Chapter 13), and taken care of administrative duties (Chapter 16).

To introduce your discipline plan this is what you might say:

Step 1. "We are all here for **YOU**—for you to succeed and to enjoy this class. Because I care about each of you, I am here to help you. So I will not allow you to do anything that will interfere with your success in this class."

Step 2. "We will be working together this year. We need to have a class where you can come without fear of being ridiculed or threatened. Because I care about **ALL** of you, I will not allow you to do anything that will interfere with someone else who is trying to learn."

Numbers in groups of three to five are easy to remember.

Step 3. "I am the teacher, and I am looking forward to being your teacher this year. I have an exciting year of learning planned for you, and I will not allow you to do anything to interfere with my desire to teach you. Nor will I allow you to do anything that will interfere with all of us having an enjoyable year."

Step 4. "So that **YOU** can learn, so that **WE** can all learn, so that I can teach, I have a set of rules to ensure that we will have an orderly classroom."

The rules should be written and permanently posted in the classroom and given to students on paper or copied by students into their notebook.

Should You Involve Students in Forming Rules?

You can involve the students in forming rules, but their role will necessarily be limited, for two reasons:

1. Schoolwide and district rules must be accepted as they are. These generally refer to such things as attendance, substance abuse, smoking, profanity, hitting, use of the facilities, and fund-raising activities. These and many more are in a policy book.

2. Classroom policies essential to managing instruction cannot be left to student discretion—for example, attentiveness, homework, and care of the classroom and equipment.

What is left is rather limited: gum chewing, eating, talking during seat work, and pencil sharpening. Most of these are not rules anyway and should be treated as procedures (Chapter 20).

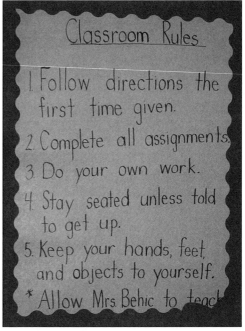

The discipline plan should be posted for the first day of school, with a copy ready for distribution to each student.

Read Chapter 20 before working on your discipline plan. What you think is a rule may be a procedure. Know the difference between a rule and a procedure.

Rather than spend too much time with the whole class forming rules, it may be better to involve the class in discussing matters such as these:

✔ Why rules are needed

✔ Why a particular rule will help students succeed

✔ Specific examples of general rules, such as "What does it mean to 'respect others'?"

What should my rules be?

Just close your eyes and say to yourself . . .

This is what I want to accomplish. Now, if the students will only do these three things, I'd be the happiest...

District and School Rules

Many schools have rules prohibiting or requiring certain behaviors, and the teachers are expected to enforce these rules. It is to everyone's advantage to do so! A set of rules enforced consistently acquires greater legitimacy because the rules are everyone's rules. You must know the school rules.

- You can be sued for negligence if you allow a behavior that is forbidden and a student is injured.

- Find the rules in the teachers' handbook.

- Listen carefully at orientation, faculty, and department meetings.

- Ask your administrators, department head, another teacher, or the secretary about school and district rules.

The Effective Teacher

1. Has the discipline plan posted when the students arrive on the first day of school.

2. Posts a maximum of three to five rules or responsibilities.

3. Explains the posted rules and is willing to make changes as the class situation requires.

KEY IDEA

Rules are most effective when there are consequences to enforce them and reward them.

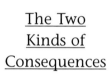

The Two Kinds of Consequences

- Positive consequences with REWARDS

- Negative consequences with PENALTIES

Why Rules Are Necessary

> **School must be a safe and protected environment, where a student can come to learn without fear.**

Rules are used to set limits. Setting limits helps students behave better. Limits tell students how far they can go. Limits are important in school because different kinds of behavior are expected or tolerated by different teachers. For example, wandering around the room may be permitted by some teachers but not others.

Effective teachers use rules as a way of setting limits. Teachers who set limits are not ogres; rather, they give students a sense of security as to how far they can go. This is like a parent who builds a railing around a patio deck.

Students need to feel that someone is in control and responsible for their environment and not only sets limits but maintains them. School must be a safe and protected environment where students can come to learn without fear.

Discipline Plans Have Consequences

When dealing with students, rules must have consequences. Some students know that they can break certain rules because the aftermath is consistent and predictable: Nothing will happen to the violator. The responsible adult may find this hard to accept, but many people—children and adults—believe that nothing is wrong until they are caught.

Imagine this typical classroom setting. A teacher is speaking at the front of the room. The students are in their seats facing the teacher. The teacher is explaining a diagram on the chalkboard.

Student A, without permission, goes to the pencil sharpener.

Student B walks over to another student to ask to borrow a pencil.

Student C abruptly speaks up to ask the teacher a question not relevant to the topic.

Student D leans over to say something to student E.

Students F through Z look on.

Students are aware of a teacher's enforcement or nonenforcement of the rules.

✔ Students will test the rules to find the limits of their behavior and to determine whether a rule will be enforced or not.

✔ Students will swiftly violate a rule that others are violating if the rule is not enforced.

✔ Students often observe that teachers do not mean what they say.

All discipline plans have consequences. **POST YOUR CONSEQUENCES.**

Consequences Can Be Positive or Negative

Consequences are what result when a person abides by or breaks the rules. Some people philosophically believe that students should be involved in the making of rules, which is fine. However, it may be better if less time is spent discussing rules and more time is spent discussing consequences **because a person's life, at any given point, is the result of that person's actions.**

> **Continue to do what you are doing, and you will continue to get what you are getting.**

Many teachers, especially at the elementary level, prefer to use the simpler word *penalty* on their posted discipline plan. Whether you call them consequences or penalties, they are the result of choices that people make. Through discussion the students understand that their actions or choices result in consequences and that they will responsibly accept these consequences throughout life. So it is advisable to spend more time discussing consequences than discussing rules.

> **Positive consequences:**
> **REWARDS** that result when people abide by the rules are positive consequences.
>
> **Negative consequences:**
> **PENALTIES** that result when people break the rules are negative consequences.

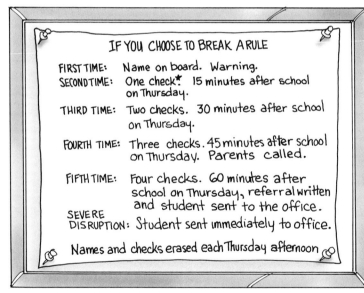

IF YOU CHOOSE TO BREAK A RULE

FIRST TIME: Name on board. Warning.
SECOND TIME: One check.★ 15 minutes after school on Thursday.
THIRD TIME: Two checks. 30 minutes after school on Thursday.
FOURTH TIME: Three checks. 45 minutes after school on Thursday. Parents called.
FIFTH TIME: Four checks. 60 minutes after school on Thursday, referral written and student sent to the office.
SEVERE DISRUPTION: Student sent immediately to office.

Names and checks erased each Thursday afternoon

A typical set of negative consequences posted by a teacher.

★**Secondary school classroom:**
Erase names once a week if students meet one period a day. This is why Thursday was used in the example.

Elementary school classroom:
Erase names at the end of each day if the teacher has the same students all day.

153

Example of Negative Consequences

Classroom Rules

1. Follow rules the first time they are given.
2. Raise your hand for permission to speak.
3. Raise your hand for permission to leave your seat.
4. Do not touch anyone else with your hands, your feet, or any object.
5. No cursing or profanity.

Consequences or Penalties

Dana   Your name on the board =
            10 minutes detention at lunch hour

Dana ✓   One check mark =
            20 minutes detention at lunch hour

Dana ✓✓   Two check marks =
            30 minutes detention at lunch hour
            and your home will be called

Dana ✓✓✓   Three check marks =
            Entire lunch hour detention,
            your home will be called,
            and you will be sent to the office

The consequences shown here are examples only. They are not to be used universally. Lunch hour detention may be illegal in your district, as board policy may state that you cannot deprive anyone of lunch. Lunch hour detention is also not recommended for students in the primary grades. Having lunch in the room with the teacher may be considered a reward rather than a penalty by many children.

Rules must have consequences.

Reasonable and Logical Consequences

The best consequences are reasonable and logical. Students will rebel only
when the consequences do not make sense.

✔ A reasonable consequence is one that follows logically from the behavior
rather than one that is arbitrarily imposed.

✔ The best logical consequences teach the students to choose between
acceptable and unacceptable actions.

Logical and Illogical Consequences

Student Behavior	Logical Consequence	Illogical Consequence
Chews gum	Disposes of gum; writes paragraph on how to prevent infraction from occurring again	Teacher sends student to office
Turns in sloppy paper	Redoes the paper	Teacher refuses the paper
Walks in noisily	Walks in again	Teacher ignores behavior
Passes paper in incorrectly	Passes paper in properly 10 times	Teacher deducts 10 points
Arrives late	Misses instruction and suffers consequences	Teacher ignores behavior
Does not bring textbook	Does without it for the period	Teacher supplies textbook
Does not bring pencil or pen	Teacher has a box full (why fight it?) and has student borrow and sign for the pencil or pen	Student sits without one

✔ Avoid consequences that are related to the academic grade, such as deducting a grade or points for that day. (This may not always be possible, however.)

✔ Most students will accept reasonable consequences because they recognize the need for teachers to maintain an orderly classroom to help them learn.

✔ A consequence is reasonable when the student sees that it is reasonable and logical and in the student's best interest.

✔ When students see the logical connection between what they do and what happens to them, it helps them learn to choose what is appropriate and what is inappropriate behavior.

✔ Students will cooperate more readily when they understand how consequences follow logically from their behavior.

✔ Explain consequences ahead of time, when the rules they accompany are presented. The subsequent use of the penalty will be more acceptable to the students.

✔ The consequence should be suitable and proportional to the violation; in other words, the penalty should fit the crime.

✔ Choose consequences that are uncomfortable for the student.

✔ Tell the student that the consequence was the result of his or her choice. (See "What Are You Picking on Me For?" on page 158.)

✔ When delivering the consequence, encourage the student to use appropriate behavior in the future.

Reasonable and Logical Consequences
Time out
Demerit or fine
Detention
Assignment to write six ways to correct the problem
Being the last to leave
Deprivation of some reward
Exclusion from class participation

Do Not Stop the Lesson

If you stop a lesson to penalize a student, you disrupt the lesson, interrupt an important point you are making, or disturb people while they are working. **DO NOT STOP THE LESSON.**

Cardinal Principle

Do not stop instruction when giving out the consequence.

When you see a violation of one of the rules, immediately give out the penalty.

Give out the penalty quietly as you continue with the lesson or classwork.

Here are some suggested ways for giving out penalties.

1. **Chalkboard.** Do not stop the lecture, discussion, or movie. Just go to the designated area on the chalkboard and write the student's name or place a check mark after the student's name.

   You may need to take a few seconds at the end of the period or day to remind those students of their penalty.

   Failure to work off the penalty automatically moves the student up to the next level of the consequences or doubles the penalty.

2. **Transparency.** This is similar to the chalkboard method except an overhead projector is used. This method is especially useful for floating teachers, who must move from room to room. You can take the transparency with you and have a record for each of your classes.

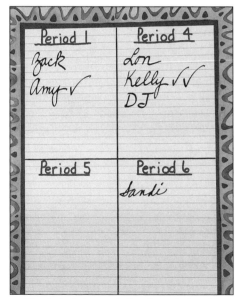

If a student chooses to break a rule, put the student's name or a check mark on the board or in a special location without interrupting the lesson.

3. **Ticket.** This is the same concept as receiving a traffic ticket. Develop a method for giving the student a ticket. There is no need for a fancy form. A piece of paper with the **student's name** and the **number of the rule broken** is all that is needed.

This method is ideal for circumstances where you do not have a chalkboard or transparency projector, such as physical education classes, an assembly, or a field trip.

You will need to keep a record of who has been given a ticket. This can be done in your grade record book, with a carbon, or with carbonless forms.

4. **Pattern.** Have students make patterns or cutouts to represent themselves for the bulletin board. When you see a rule violation, go to this board and "flag" the student's pattern. A flag could be the addition of a self-adhesive note, removing the pattern, or turning the pattern over. If the pattern has been laminated, a felt pen mark may suffice.

5. **Heart.** Have the students make a pattern with their name on it. Place all the patterns inside a heart—your heart—on the bulletin board. If there is a violation of a rule, kindly remove the pattern and place it outside your heart. Encourage the student to return to your heart.

What Are You Picking on Me For?

What do you say to the following three major questions asked by students worldwide?

> *What are you picking on me for?*
> *What did I do?*
> *Everyone else is doing it.*
>   *Why me?*

Stand in front of a mirror and practice the following 100 times until you can say it calmly and automatically every time one of these questions is asked:

> *Because you CHOSE to break the rule.*
> *Because you CHOSE to break rule*
>   *number x.*

Do not argue. Do not ask the student if he or she is questioning your authority. Do not yell, scream, or raise your voice. Just calmly say every time:

> *Because you CHOSE to break*
>   *the rule.*

After a few days, no one will ever ask, "Why are you picking on me?" because everyone will know exactly what you will say.

The key word in the phrase is *CHOSE*. *Chose* means that one is responsible and accountable for one's actions. You are teaching your students responsibility and accountability.

> *The teacher is not picking on you.*
> *There are five rules in the classroom.*
> *The rules were discussed, agreed on,*
>   *and signed. So when you CHOOSE to*
>   *break one of the rules, you must accept*
>   *the consequence.*

After a few weeks or months, if someone should ask you, "Why are you picking on me?" all you have to do is stand and smile at the student. The entire class will respond for you:

> *Because you CHOSE to break*
>   *the rule!*

Getting Administrative Support

You will be fortunate indeed if you are hired as a new teacher and find yourself at a school with a schoolwide discipline plan. That is like getting hired to work at Nordstrom (page 88). Successful businesses and schools have an established culture. You can fit into the culture and devote more time to student achievement.

Have high expectations that the administration wants to help. They want to help and cooperate with you, as they want a disciplined situation as much as you do, maybe even more so. You need to approach them in the same way you would approach your students, in a nonconfrontational, friendly, cooperative manner.

✔ If there is no schoolwide discipline plan, go to your administrator with your plan. It is imperative that you have thought out your plan. You need to know what you want to accomplish.

✔ Present your plan, in writing, with your rules, consequences, and rewards. Most administrators know this system, so it will not be a surprise to any of them.

✔ Check that your plan does not violate any board policy and can be supported by the administration.

✔ Show the administrator what YOU plan to do if the students violate the rules.

✔ Show the administrator that you plan to refer the student to the office after a certain number of violations.

✔ Ask the administrators what they plan to do when you refer students to the office. It is only consistent and fair that the office knows what you plan to do, that you know what the office will do, and that both the students and their parents know what you and the office will do.

Getting Parental Support

Your objective is to acquire parental support to work cooperatively with you in correcting a student's misbehavior. Your purpose should not be to humiliate the student, "get the student into trouble," aggravate the parents, or have the parents "do something to the kid."

To assist in acquiring parental support, give the parents a copy of the discipline plan to use as a basis for home-school cooperation.

Parents need to see your discipline plan, discuss it with the child, and sign it. You will, of course, want the students to sign it also as an indication that they understand and accept the plan as discussed in class and at home.

The form should be simple and easy to understand. Don't forget to give the parents and the student an extra copy to keep on hand. The form can be as simple as the one shown here.

How to Call the Home

Effective teachers communicate and work cooperatively with students' homes. However, calling the home is not something most teachers like to do. This is because most teachers do not know how to call the home. They are as scared to call the home as the people at home are to hear from the school. Such a call usually brings bad news. But it need not be that way, even if it is the third violation and you need to call the home to have a misbehavior corrected.

Here is a wonderful system that not only works but also teaches the student at the same time **problem solving, responsibility, and self-discipline**.

Note on your discipline plan that you will be calling the home during one of the consequences. At this consequence, have the student complete the form shown on the following page, "My Action Plan."

Discipline Plan for Room 16
Classroom Rules

1. Have all appropriate materials and supplies at your table and be seated when the bell rings.
2. Respect the people, equipment, and furnishings of Room 16.
3. Adjust your voice level to suit the activity.
4. Follow directions the first time they are given.
5. Observe all rules in the student handbook.

If You Choose to Break a Rule

First Time: Name on board. Warning
Second Time: One check. 15 minutes after school on Thursday.
Third Time: Two checks. 30 minutes after school on Thursday.
Fourth Time: Three checks. 45 minutes after school on Thursday and parents called.
Fifth Time: Four checks. 60 minutes after school on Thursday, referral written, and student sent to the office.

Severe disruptions: Student sent immediately to the office.

Names and checks erased each Thursday afternoon.

Rewards

Praise (daily)
Positive notes home (random)
Whole-class radio time or free time (weekly)
"Raise a Grade" certificate (monthly)
Movie and popcorn party for class (every 9 weeks)
Various other positive perks (throughout the school year)
The joy of learning (each day of the school year)

STUDENTS: I have read this classroom discipline plan and understand it. I will honor it while in Room 16.

Signature_____ Date_____

PARENTS: My child has discuss the classroom discipline plan with me. I understand it and will support it.

Signature_____ Date_____

TEACHER: I will be fair and consistent in administering the discipline plan for Room 16.

Signature_____

******IMPORTANT******
PLEASE KEEP THIS SHEET IN YOUR BINDER AT ALL TIMES.
Thank you

My Action Plan

1. What's the problem?

2. What's causing the problem? (Please list the factors.)

3. What plan will you use to solve the problem?

_____
Student's Signature

_____
Date

My Action Plan

1. What's the problem?
I have too many tardies.

2. What's causing the problem? (Please list the factors.)
I can't make it here in 7 minutes from P.E.
It's to far away.
I have to shower.
I have to return the towel.
I have to get a drink.
I have to go to the bathroom.
I have to go to my locker.
The lock is hard to open.
I have to return my library book.
I have to see my girlfriend.
I have to see the counselor.
I have to check and see if I have made the team.

3. What plan will you use to solve the problem?
I will shower.
I will return the towel.
I will see my girlfriend quickly.
I will go to my locker.
I will get a new lock for my locker.
I will move faster.
Will Watson
Student's Signature

Thurs. October 3
Date

Step 1. Give the student a copy of "My Action Plan" and be prepared to work with the student on answering the three questions:

What's the problem?
What's causing the problem?
What plan will you use to solve the problem?

What's the problem? Indicate the rule or rules the student has violated.

What's causing the problem? The student is to list all the factors that are causing the problem to occur.

Work with the student in a **PROBLEM-SOLVING** mode here. Share with the student that the only way a person can solve a problem is first to isolate and identify it. You are not interested in degrading or scolding the student. You want to teach the student how to solve a problem, a technique that the student can use in future life.

What plan will you use to solve the problem? The student is to write the action plan needed to solve the problem.

Have the student look at the factors causing the problem. Show the student that the way to solve a problem is to change, eliminate, or correct the factors causing the problem. Help the student see the logic of this.

Have the student write a plan based on the causative factors listed under the second question. The student now takes **RESPONSIBILITY** for the plan. You did not tell the student what to do. The student, through problem solving, devised his or her own plan to correct the problem. You are teaching responsibility.

Now, for the student to carry through with his or her responsibility, encouragement is needed from the home and the school to get the student to achieve **SELF-DISCIPLINE**.

Step 2. Have the student indicate responsibility by signing the action plan.

If the problem is not corrected, go back and modify the third part of the action plan. It is much better to teach problem solving, responsibility, and self-discipline than to yell, scream, and flunk. Yelling, screaming, and flunking benefit no one. Learning to be responsible and self-disciplined benefits all of society. Through persistence, have the student work on the action plan over and over until the problem is corrected.

Commend the student when that occurs.

Step 3. Tell the student to show the action plan to a parent. Inform the student that when you call tonight, you will not call to cause trouble. **You will be calling to discuss the action plan and the behavior, not the person.**

> **Always deal with the behavior, not the person.**
> **You leave a person's dignity intact when**
> **you deal only with the behavior or the issue.**

Step 4. Call the home in a pleasant, friendly, but businesslike manner. Explain that you are happy to have the student in your class and that the purpose of tonight's call is to discuss the action plan.

The beauty of the action plan system is that there is no argument, confrontation, or aggravation with the parents. Neither party wants that. You did not call to degrade the child, because no parent likes to hear, "You have a no good, rotten kid who can't come to class on time." Tell parents this and they will say, "The schools are doing a terrible job." No one wins, and the child is not helped, defeating the purpose of your call.

Note the three key concepts in the value of using "My Action Plan":

✔ Problem solving
✔ Responsibility
✔ Self-discipline

Step 5. Explain to the parent that the child has come up with a plan. Impress the parent by explaining that this is something the student has done as a result of problem solving and the use of higher-order thinking skills.

Step 6. The reason you are calling is simple:

Mrs. Watson, I am calling to see if I can enlist the cooperation of the adults at home, working together with the school, to see if we can encourage Will to follow through with what he said he would be RESPONSIBLE for doing.

If the parent refuses, go on with your life. You tried. But most parents will not say no because the one thing that both parents and teachers want is to instill RESPONSIBILITY. They can't say no to that.

The parents will think the world of you. So will the student. This was all possible because you operated in a responsible, problem-solving, self-disciplined way yourself.

Rewards or Positive Consequences

REWARDS!

Daily: Sunshine notes
       Table Points

Weekly: Class free-time
       (no detentions issued)

Monthly: Video*
       Field trip or Activity*
       * 80% or higher citizenship

Marking period: Ice cream party
       (100% citizenship)

Semester: 6th Grade Reward party
       (no office referrals or
       bus slips)

A typical set of rewards posted by a teacher.

Everyone likes and expects special recognition, rewards, or incentives when good work is done. Perks, rewards, honors, prizes, and awards are commonplace.

Although rewards are a fact of life, the time has come in education when the wholesale bribery system of giving out endless supplies of stickers, candies, and other tangibles has got to come to a halt. Let's stop the "what's in it for me?" welfare and bribery system.

> **The best reward is the satisfaction of a job well done.**

That is self-discipline—and self-discipline is what discipline is all about. You can't teach self-discipline if the students are always looking for more "goodies."

One of us has operated very successfully during our years of teaching with only one reward: **30 minutes of free time on Friday.** This was also a classwide reward. Everyone had to work together cooperatively the entire week for the reward.

The 30 minutes of free time on Friday was effective because it was not a thing. The time was used, mostly, for schoolwork. There were no popcorn parties, pizza parties, or movies to plan for and clean up after, just free time to work!

✔ Like rules and consequences, post your rewards.

✔ Indicate the time factor associated with the reward. Will the reward be given daily, weekly, when?

✔ Explain the system by which the reward is to be earned. That is, you do not *give* rewards; the students *earn* rewards.

✔ The most common way of earning rewards, on a class basis, is to put a tally mark somewhere when you catch someone following directions or doing good. When the class has earned a predetermined number of tally marks, it can have the reward.

✔ If you don't like tally marks, use marbles in a jar, raffle tickets, or red indicators on a drawing of a thermometer.

Suggestions for Rewards

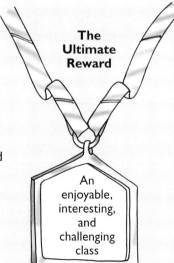

The Logical Reward
- Earned good grades
- Made the honor roll
- Was tapped for honor society
- Received a scholarship
- Got extra credit
- Had good work posted
- Was first to be dismissed for lunch, recess, etc.
- Participated in a special event
- Was chosen as student of day, week, month, etc.
- Was awarded a VIP certificate

The Ultimate Reward

An enjoyable, interesting, and challenging class

The Simplest yet Best Reward
- A smile
- A high five
- A pat or handshake
- A word of encouragement
- Praise for the deed, encouragement for the person (see page 183)
- A note or "Warm Fuzzy"
- A note home
- A phone call home

Discipline with Your Body, Not Your Mouth

Calm is strength; upset is weakness. The effective teacher knows what to do to get a student calmly back on task. Practice these steps in front of a mirror.

1. EXCUSE yourself from what you are doing.

2. RELAX. Take a slow relaxing breath and CALMLY approach the student with a meaningful business look.

3. FACE the student directly and CALMLY wait for a response.

4. If there is no response, WHISPER the student's first name and follow with what you want the student to do, ending with "please." Relax and wait.

5. If the student does not get to work, RELAX and WAIT. Repeat Step 4, if necessary.

6. If backtalk occurs, relax, wait, and KEEP QUIET. If the student wants to talk back, keep the first principle of dealing with backtalk in mind:

   IT TAKES ONE FOOL TO TALK BACK.
   IT TAKES TWO FOOLS
   TO MAKE A CONVERSATION OUT OF IT.

7. When the student responds with the appropriate behavior say, "Thank you," and leave with an affirmative SMILE. If a student goes so far as to earn an office referral, you can deliver it just as well relaxed. After all, **ruining your composure and peace of mind does not enhance classroom management.**

— Adapted from Fred Jones, *Positive Classroom Discipline* and *Positive Classroom Instruction*.

Effective Communication of Your Discipline Plan

Now that you have thought out, constructed, and posted your discipline plan, all that is left is to communicate this plan to your students on the first day of school. How you communicate your plan will determine its success or failure.

The Ineffective Teacher

✔ May have no clearly defined rules.

✔ Communicates rules sporadically and as they are suddenly needed to stifle a situation.

✔ Conveys rules in a gruff, angry, and condescending manner.

✔ Winces, shrugs, or conveys with facial or body motion disbelief in what is being said.

✔ Conveys that "I'm only doing this because the administration wants me to do it."

✔ Implies that "I was hired to teach world literature, not to maintain discipline."

✔ Tells the students, "If you don't want to learn, that's not my problem."

✔ Berates students with meaningless phrases to convey expectations of appropriate behavior, such as "Don't you know any better?" or "How many times do I have to tell you?"

The Effective Teacher

✔ Has a discipline plan that does not degrade students.

✔ Communicates the plan at the start of school in a firm but controlled and friendly manner.

✔ Does not wince or convey disbelief in what is being said.

✔ Makes eye contact with each student while presenting the plan.

✔ Provides an understandable reason for the plan.

✔ Provides a copy of the plan for each student.

✔ Sends home a copy of the plan.

✔ Enforces the rules consistently.

✔ Tells the students that the administration supports the plan.

✔ Reviews the plan with new students.

✔ Has learned how to discipline with the body, not with the mouth.

✔ Has positive expectations that all of the students will abide by the rules.

✔ Are confident in themselves and their capabilities.

✔ Teaches students the concept of consequences and responsibility.

Activate Your Discipline Plan

Now that you have a discipline plan, **work your plan**. Put your plan into practice daily, and make your behavior predictable and consistent. This is the attribute of an effective teacher.

To be an effective teacher:

1. Post your rules.
2. Post your consequences and rewards.
3. Immediately enact the consequence when a rule is broken.
4. Give positive feedback to individuals as well as to the class.
5. Make your behavior predictable and consistent.

The Effective Teacher

1. Thinks through a discipline plan before school begins and conveys the plan to the students when school begins.

2. Discusses the plan so that students understand the logic of it and consider it reasonable.

3. Involves the administration to help guarantee and enforce the plan.

4. Has high expectations and confidence in his or her capacity to teach young people self-discipline.

KEY IDEA

A smooth-running class is based on the teacher's ability to teach procedures.

The Problem Is Not Discipline

> **The number one problem in the classroom is not discipline; it is the lack of procedures and routines.**

You have now arrived at the most important chapter in this book. What you are about to read will determine whether you will succeed or fail, have a classroom that is chaotic or a well-oiled learning environment, whether you will leave school at the end of the day frazzled and angry or happy and successful. Why?

Most teachers do not teach.
They "cover" or "do" activities.
Then when things go wrong, they discipline.
In short, most classrooms are nonmanaged.

A vast majority of the behavior problems in the classroom are caused by the failure of students to follow procedures and routines. These are the main reasons why students do not follow procedures:

1. The teacher has not thought out what happens in the classroom.
2. The students have not been trained to follow the procedures.
3. The teacher spends no time managing the classroom.

Thus the students do not know the procedures.

The Person Who Works Learns

Do not blame the students if a classroom is chaotic when there are no operating procedures to govern how the class is to function. **Students readily accept the idea of having a uniform set of classroom procedures because it simplifies their task of succeeding in school.** Procedures allow a wide variety of activities to take place during the school day, often simultaneously, with a minimum of confusion and wasted time. If there are no procedures, much time is wasted organizing and explaining each activity, even for recurring activities. The lack of procedures also leads to students' acquiring undesirable work habits and behaviors that are subsequently hard to correct.

No learning takes place when you discipline. Learning takes place only when a student is at work. All discipline does is stop misbehavior. The reason parents have their children practice the piano is that the more they practice, the better they play. The reason coaches have their teams run the plays over and over again is that the more they run the plays, the better they will be able to execute the plays during the game. Effective teachers know that the more time on task, also called academic learning time, spent by the student, the more the student learns. Who is working and learning in your classroom?

Comparison of an Effective and an Ineffective Classroom

Effective Classroom:
The students are actively involved in meaningful work. The procedures govern what they do and they understand how the class functions. The teacher is moving around the room, also at work, helping, correcting, answering, disciplining, smiling, and caring.

Ineffective Classroom:
The students are in their seats doing busywork or nothing. The only person who is observed working is the teacher. The teacher is in control of the class.

Learning occurs only when a person is actively involved. Are the students working in your classroom?

The Difference Between Discipline and Procedures

Classroom management should not be equated with discipline. Discipline is but a very small part of classroom management. Procedures are not found in a discipline plan; nor should a procedure be a threat, a rule, or an order. **A procedure is simply a method or process for how things are to be done in a classroom.**

Procedures and routines are different from a discipline plan. Do not confuse procedures with discipline. There are two major differences.

A rule is a **DARE** to be broken, whereas a procedure is not.
A procedure is a **DO**, a step to be learned.

✔ **DISCIPLINE:** Concerns how students **BEHAVE**.
✔ **PROCEDURES:** Concern how things are **DONE**.

✔ **DISCIPLINE:** *HAS* penalties and rewards.
✔ **PROCEDURES:** Have *NO* penalties or rewards.

A student is generally not penalized for not following a procedure nor rewarded if a procedure is followed.

Example of a Procedure

There is a procedure for opening a lock on a locker. It's usually two turns to the right, one turn to the left, and a final turn to the right.

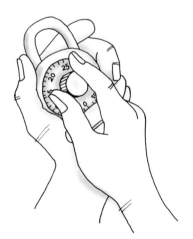

There is no penalty if the procedure is not followed. The lock just does not open. Likewise, there is no reward if the procedure is followed. The lock simply opens. **To do anything in life successfully, you simply follow the procedures.**

Student success or achievement at the end of the school year is directly related to the degree to which the teacher establishes good control of the classroom procedures in the very first week of the school year. **It is the procedures that set the class up for achievement to take place.**

Why Procedures Are Important

Students must know from the very beginning how they are expected to behave and work in a classroom work environment. Discipline dictates how they are to behave, and procedures and routines dictate how they are to work. Procedures and routines, especially, offer security. Students cannot get down to the serious business of learning unless they feel secure in the classroom. They want instruction and guidance on all the how-to's in class—how to head a paper, how to ask for help, how to sharpen a pencil, how to get to work, how to turn on the computer, how to . . .

> **PROCEDURE:**
> What the teacher wants done.
>
> **ROUTINE:**
> What the students do automatically.

Since a **PROCEDURE** is how you want something done, it is the responsibility of the teacher to have procedures clearly stated. A **ROUTINE** is what the student does automatically without prompting or supervision. Thus a routine becomes a habit, practice, or custom for the student.

Procedures are necessary for an effective classroom for several reasons.

✔ Classroom procedures are statements of student expectations necessary to participate successfully in classroom activities, to learn, and to function effectively in the school environment.

✔ Classroom procedures allow many different activities to take place efficiently during the school day, often several at the same time, with a minimum of wasted time and confusion.

✔ Classroom procedures increase on-task time and greatly reduce classroom disruptions.

✔ Classroom procedures tell a student how things operate in a classroom, thus reducing discipline problems.

Students are less likely to act up in frustration, trying to figure out what the teacher wants, if the classroom procedures are clearly stated.

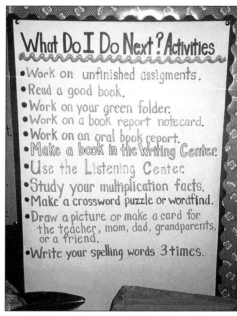

Students will cooperate if they know what it is that you want them to do.

Students Accept and Want Procedures

Effective teachers manage with procedures. **Every time the teacher wants something done, there must be a procedure or a set of procedures.** For instance, have procedures for taking roll, exchanging papers, registering the students on the first day, collecting lunch money, and moving from task to task. If you don't, time that should be spent on learning will be wasted getting these tasks done.

Classroom procedures answer such questions as these:

> **A smooth-running class is the responsibility of the teacher, and it is the result of the teacher's ability to teach procedures.**

What to do when the bell rings
What to do when the pencil breaks
What to do when you hear an emergency alert signal
What to do when you finish your work early
What to do when you have a question
What to do when you need to go to the rest room

Tell your students that classroom procedures are for their benefit. Following procedures will help them do their work with less confusion and thus help them succeed. Knowledge of classroom procedures tells your students such things as these:

How to enter the classroom
What to do when they enter the classroom
Where to find the assignment
What to do when you want their attention
How a paper is to be done
Where you want the paper placed
What to do if they want to sharpen a pencil
Where to find assignments if they have been absent
What to do at dismissal of class

My daughter hated school until this year. She loves school now.

Why? Because of the way her teacher has organized the class.

—A parent

Every class needs to have a set of procedures. Procedures allow the class to operate smoothly. A smooth-running, effective class is free of confusion and is a pleasure to teach and learn in.

Procedures Are a Part of Life

Procedures are important in society so that people can function in an acceptable and organized manner. Real life is full of procedures—for instance:

Telephone Book. At the front of a telephone book are procedures on how to make a long-distance call, make a foreign call, contact directory assistance, get emergency help, and contact the business office.

Airplane. After the "discipline plan" is stated at the beginning of the flight, the flight attendants explain the procedures. These procedures include how to use the seat belt, how to use the oxygen mask, where to find the life vest, and how to find the aisle in case the cabin is filled with smoke.

Traffic Light. There are procedures at an intersection with a traffic light. The light governs who will turn, who will stop, and who will go. A procedure also determines when and how to make a right turn if the light is red.

Wedding. At the conclusion of a wedding ceremony, a procedure is followed. The bride, groom, and wedding party leave. They are followed by the parents in the first row, followed by each row from the front of the seating area.

Procedures demonstrate how people are to function in an acceptable and organized manner. When we say that someone is ill-mannered, it is because that person doesn't know or doesn't care what the local customs or procedures are. To function successfully with other people, the best guideline is "When in Rome, do as the Romans do."

Judie Gustafson of Manor, Texas, is a high school math teacher. On the first days of school she gives her class an eight-page paper, "Procedures." It begins:

Procedures are a part of life. We follow procedures for using a telephone book, boarding an airplane, approaching a traffic light, and attending a wedding. The reason we have procedures in life is so that people can function in society knowing the acceptable and efficient ways other people do things.

There are also procedures in this classroom. These procedures establish our classroom culture.

This is followed by procedures for use in the following situations:

Entering the classroom	Responding to my request for attention
When you are tardy	When you are absent
Leaving the classroom	When someone knocks
End-of-period class dismissal	If the phone should ring
Asking a question	Working cooperatively
Listening to and responding to questions	Changing groups
When you need a pencil or paper	An emergency alert
Sharpening your pencil	Keeping your notebook
Turning in papers	When you need help or a conference
Indicating whether you understand	Progress reports

Procedures Are a Part of School Life

As in real life, procedures must be followed in the classroom. Here are some that nearly every teacher must teach.

> **The first few days of school, teach only procedures necessary for the smooth opening of class.**
>
> Delay the other procedures until the appropriate activity arises.

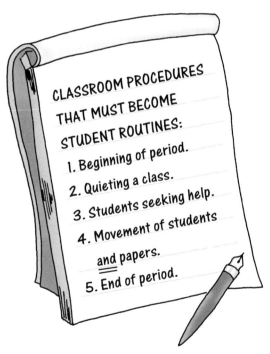

CLASSROOM PROCEDURES
THAT MUST BECOME
STUDENT ROUTINES:

1. Beginning of period.
2. Quieting a class.
3. Students seeking help.
4. Movement of students and papers.
5. End of period.

Procedure for Dismissal at the End of the Period or Day. When the dismissal bell rings, are the students already standing at the door waiting to leave, or do they just get up and leave, even if you are in the middle of a sentence? You can always tell who is running the class, the students or the teacher, by how the students behave at the end of the period or day. (See page 177.)

Procedure for Quieting a Class. Do you know how to quiet a class in 15 seconds or less? It can be done easily! Do you yell, scream, and flick the lights—all to no avail? Or if you do succeed, does it take a long time to get the students' attention, not to mention years on your life span from stress? (See page 181.)

Procedure for the Start of the Period or Day. When the students enter, do they know what to do, where to sit, and what materials to have ready? Or do they sit and wait for the teacher to tell them what to do? (See page 185.)

Procedure for Students Seeking Help. Do your students raise their hands when they want your help, wigwagging their hands to attract your attention, calling your name at the same time, stopping work in the process accompanied by muttering and complaining to their classmates because you do not respond instantly? (See page 186.)

Procedure for the Movement of Students and Papers. Do your students take forever to pass their papers in and even longer to change from group to group or task to task? And when they turn their papers in, do they throw them in a pile on your desk or punch each other in the back as the papers are passed forward? (See page 189.)

There are also procedures to follow on the school bus and in the cafeteria, library, and attendance office. And if these locales are run effectively, you can be sure that the bus driver, food server, librarian, and secretary have taught the students the correct procedures in their area of authority.

The Three-Step Approach to Teaching Classroom Procedures

 Most behavior problems in the classroom are caused by the teacher's failure to teach students how to follow procedures.

The Three Steps to Teaching Procedures

1. **Explain.** State, explain, model, and demonstrate the procedure.

2. **Rehearse.** Rehearse and practice the procedure under your supervision.

3. **Reinforce.** Reteach, rehearse, practice, and reinforce the classroom procedure until it becomes a student habit or routine.

Step 1. Explain Classroom Procedures Clearly

Effective teachers know what activities need to be done and have worked out the procedures for each of them. These procedures are posted or distributed to the students early in the school year or when the activity surfaces in class. Unless the students read well, primary grade teachers should teach the procedures verbally rather than post them.

Explain

✔ Define the procedure in concrete terms.

✔ Demonstrate the procedure; don't just tell.

✔ Demonstrate a complex procedure step by step.

It is essential that you have the procedures for each opening-of-school activity ready on the first day of school. Revise and hone these procedures year after year until they become models of efficiency.

Step 2. Rehearse Classroom Procedures Until They Become Routines

 All procedures must be rehearsed!

Run the Play, Sing the Song

The reason that many teachers cannot get students to do things, is that they just tell the students what to do.

You must do what all coaches do, what all music teachers do, and what all effective second-grade teachers do: Have your students run the plays, sing the songs, and spell the words over and over again **until the procedures become routines.**

Effective teachers spend a good deal of time during the first weeks of school introducing, teaching, modeling, and rehearsing procedures. Do not expect the students to learn all the procedures in one day, especially at the elementary school level. Behaviors must be taught, modeled, practiced, monitored, and retaught.

Watch a good music, drama, athletic, or foreign-language coach. Such people are masters at the rehearsal technique. They tell and show you a technique, even have you watch a video of the technique. Then they have you do it repeatedly while they watch you. Some people call this technique "guided practice."

 Rehearse

✔ Have students practice the procedure, step by step, under your supervision. After each step, make sure that the students have performed the step correctly.

✔ Have the students repeat the procedure until it becomes a routine. The students should be able to perform the procedure automatically without teacher supervision.

Step 3. Reinforce a Correct Procedure and Reteach an Incorrect One

Again, watch a coach because good coaches are the best teachers. As the coach guides a team, class, or student through practice, corrections are made instantly. The coach tells, shows, demonstrates, cajoles, and even loudly calls out commands until the task is done right.

And when it is done right, the coach responds with words of praise, hugs, pats, and smiles. But good coaches don't stop there. They reinforce the correct technique by having the student do the acquired technique over and over again, each time exhorting the student to do it better.

Reinforce

✔ Determine whether students have learned the procedure or whether they need further explanation, demonstration, or practice.

✔ Reteach the correct procedure if rehearsal is unacceptable, and give corrective feedback.

✔ Praise the students when the rehearsal is acceptable.

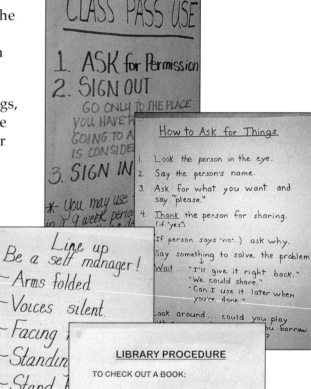

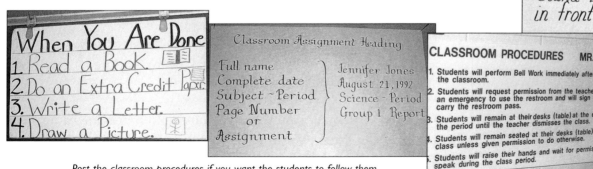

Post the classroom procedures if you want the students to follow them.

Using the Three-Step Approach to Teach Procedures

The following are examples of how some procedures are taught. You may not need or want them, but note how each procedure is taught. Then substitute your own procedure, using the **explain**, **rehearse**, **reinforce** technique just described.

<table>
<tr><td>✔</td><td>How to dismiss a class</td></tr>
<tr><td>✔</td><td>How to quiet a class and have the students' attention</td></tr>
<tr><td>✔</td><td>How to have a class working when the bell rings</td></tr>
<tr><td>✔</td><td>How students are to ask you for help</td></tr>
<tr><td>✔</td><td>How students are to pass in papers</td></tr>
</table>

For Whom Does the Bell Toll?

The bell, buzzer, or chime at the end of the period or day is a signal for teachers notifying them that instructional time has come to an end. The bell is of no concern to the students. The bell does not dismiss the class. You dismiss the class with a pleasant greeting of farewell.

Procedure for Dismissal at the End of the Period or Day

Explain

Students, there is a procedure at the end of the period. You are to remain in your seat (or at your desks with the chairs pushed in) until I dismiss the class. The bell does not dismiss the class. You do not dismiss the class. The teacher dismisses the class. Thank you.

You will want to explain the criteria for dismissal, such as how clean you want the desk or work area and where and how you want the chairs and equipment to be positioned.

Show and demonstrate this procedure. Have several students (never one, as it makes a show-off example of one) demonstrate the procedure. Praise each so that the students know that you are validating the correct procedure.

The ineffective teacher has students standing at the door waiting to leave before the bell rings.

Rehearse

Be alert a few seconds before the bell rings on the first day of school. Anticipate that you will need to make an immediate correction if the procedure is not followed. If the class starts to file out, it is too late to correct the procedure. The failure to correct a procedure will only escalate the problem until it is the students who dismiss themselves and are really the ones in control of the class.

On the first day of school, remind the class of the dismissal procedure a few seconds before the bell rings at the end of the period or day. This will reduce the hassle of correcting the class; however, if any students begin to leave at the bell, you simply say,

> *No, no, no. Tom, Joel, Anne, please return to your desks.*

Do not scold, yell, or demean. And do not use meaningless phrases or questions like "Listen to me" or "What did I say the dismissal procedure was?" You do not want a discussion, an argument, or a response. You want all students at their desks. Calmly, but in a voice of authority, tell the students who began to leave to return to their desks.

Reinforce

| **Every time a procedure needs to be corrected:** |
| 1. **REMIND** the class of the procedure. |
| 2. Have the class **EXPERIENCE** the procedure. |

Remind: *Class, I would like to remind you of the procedure at the end of the period. You are to remain at your desks until I dismiss the class.*

Experience: *Look around the room. You are all at your desks (and your chairs are pushed in). This is the correct procedure, and I thank you for doing it correctly.*

> *Well done. Please do it again tomorrow. Have a nice day!*

One of the greatest gifts a caring teacher can contribute to children is to help them learn to sit when they feel like running, to raise their hand when they feel like talking, to be polite to their neighbor, to stand in line without pushing, and to do their homework when they feel like playing. By introducing procedures in the classroom, you are also introducing procedures as a way of living a happy and successful life.

Effective teachers have the students see, feel, and experience the procedure. The students see one another in their seats and experience the procedure correctly. Ineffective teachers only tell students what to do. The students do not experience what should be done. That is why many teachers fail when they want students to follow procedures.

Repeat the procedure every day until the procedure becomes a routine. By the end of the third or fourth day, the procedure will have become automatic.

Thereafter, all you need to do a few seconds after the bell rings is smile and say, "It's been nice seeing all of you. See you tomorrow. Have a nice day." This is much better than "You're dismissed."

Technique for
Teaching Procedures

1. Explain
2. Rehearse
3. Reinforce
   - Remind
   - Experience

Why Children Never Tell Mom They Are Going Out

So many parents shake their heads in frustration when their children leave the house and never say, "I'm going out, Mom." They just leave, showing no respect or manners.

If, every day, for 180 days, when the class is seated and ready for dismissal at the end of the period or the day, the teacher says, "Have a nice day" to dismiss the class, **the teacher is modeling respect and manners**.

The students may not realize it, but they are getting a lesson in the appropriate behavior of well-mannered people. People acknowledge people as they leave a setting. Perhaps students too will learn to tell parents that they will be gone for awhile.

An adult should repeatedly model appropriate behavior so that a student may experience how to behave in society.

How to Teach a New Student All the Class Procedures

You have invested a few weeks of practice and rehearsal of the classroom procedures. Your class is now a smooth-running, humming learning environment.

Suddenly, a new student joins the class. What do you do? No problem! First, understand that you cannot tell a new student the classroom procedures if you haven't first told your existing class. If your class is never sure what to do, there is no way you can ever orient and teach a new student. Second, if you have a class where the students have learned the routines, you have developed a classroom culture. A culture is the prevailing way a group functions—for instance:

- When people stand before an elevator, they know to let people off before they get on.

- On an airplane, people lower the window shades when the movie begins.

- At a wedding, people stand when the bride walks down the aisle.

- At a Chinese family dinner table, the prevailing culture is never to help yourself first. That would be considered selfish and uncouth. You always say, "You first, please."

You create a culture when students perform in a manner understood to be appropriate in your classroom.

- When a new student joins the class, give the student a copy of the classroom procedures.

- Explain to the student what the procedures are and why you have them.

- Tell the student that you will help with the procedures but that the student will probably be able to learn them by observing how the rest of the class functions.

For example, the bell rings at the end of the period and the new student begins to leave. Suddenly the student notices that everyone is in their seats. The student says mentally, "Oh, oh, I'd better stay seated, too, like the rest of the class." The student has just learned the class procedure.

Procedure for Quieting a Class

Explain

Students, I have a procedure when I want your undivided attention. You will see me stand here with my hand up. Or I may tap a bell because some of you will not be able to see my hand while you are working in a group. When you see my hand or hear a bell, the procedure is as follows:

1. *Freeze.*
2. *Turn and face me; pay attention and keep your eyes on me.*
3. *Be ready for instruction. I will have something to say.*

Let me repeat and demonstrate what I said.

Repeat and look for class understanding.

Byron, please tell me the procedure when you see my hand or hear a bell.

Byron does so.

Yes, yes, yes. Thank you, Byron.

Repeat this with several more students.

Is there anyone who does not understand or know what to do if you see my hand or hear a bell?

Rehearse

Good, let's rehearse the procedure. We will be working together this year, so let's get to know one another. Please look at the person to the right of you. You may have two minutes to introduce yourself and get acquainted.

Calmly and without saying anything, raise your hand when you want the class quiet.

At two minutes, hold up your hand or ring the bell, perhaps doing both this first time. Do not say a word when you raise your hand. Do the demonstration exactly as you will be doing it for the rest of the year. Be patient and wait until the class does the three steps and pays attention.

Do not give up as you wait for the students to give you their undivided attention. Compliment them when you have their attention.

No matter what grade level you teach, **all procedures must be rehearsed**.

> *Thank you. You practiced the procedure correctly.*

> *Now please look at the person to the left of you. You may have two minutes to introduce yourself and get acquainted.*

At two minutes hold up your hand or ring the bell. Compliment them.

> *Thank you. You followed the procedure correctly.*

> *We are not finished with the rehearsal. You will often find yourself out of your seat—working in groups or alone somewhere in the room away from your seat. So let's try a different scenario.*

> *I would like two of you to stand by the pencil sharpener, two of you at the sink, two of you at the bookcase, and one of you at the computer.*

You then hold up your hand and watch for the seven students to pay attention.

Reinforce

> *Thank you. That was the correct procedure when you see my hand or hear a bell. Please do the same thing each time you see my hand or hear a bell.*

You keep using the same language because you must use the same procedure if you want the students to exhibit the same routine. You can also use a technique called "Praise the Deed, Encourage the Student," described on the next page.

Praise the Deed, Encourage the Student

An effective way to praise is to praise what the person did, rather than the person, and then encourage the person to do the achievement or deed again. The technique is called specific praise, or "praise the deed, encourage the student." Praise is nice, but it is not tangible or meaningful—for instance:

> *Amber, you are a bright child.*

For a more effective kind of praise, point to something the student did well. Then encourage the student to do it again—for instance:

> *Amber, please get your last spelling test out. What did you get? Right, 19 out of 20 correct. Great! Pat yourself on the back. Shake your own hand. Congratulate yourself. DO IT AGAIN ON THE NEXT TEST.*

Here are some other examples:

> *Thank you, class. That was the correct procedure when you see my hand or hear a bell. Please do the same thing each time you see my hand or hear a bell.*

> *Heidi, thank you for the excellent report at the faculty meeting. The next time I need assistance, I would truly appreciate your help again.*

> *Wayne, thanks for helping with the dishes tonight. Mom had a meeting to go to, and you helped out. The next time Mom needs assistance, I would be glad to have you help out again.*

The reason people are more likely to do well again is that they know that you saw them do something specific. They believe, "You were paying attention to me. You noticed me! And you thanked me for doing something I did personally."

Pep talks are invigorating but hollow. They become meaningless quickly because no one is sure to whom the message is directed. When you praise the deed and encourage the student, you help the student do two things:

1. Accept *responsibility* for having done the task

2. Develop a sense of *accomplishment*

The key words are *responsibility* and *accomplishment*, two things that all people must develop to be successful in life.

We are grateful to Barbara Colorosa, author of *Kids Are Worth It*, for suggesting this technique.

She Quieted 100 People in Five Seconds

We were invited to our daughter-in-law's class to attend the annual International Day celebration. Students from three sixth-grade classes were gathered in a large room for the culmination of their study of the country of their ancestry or choice. The students were dressed in native attire and had information and food samples typical of their selected countries.

The three classes and an assortment of guests—parents, teachers, administrators, school board members, and friends—numbered about 100 people. As we were walking from display to display, talking with the students and tasting food, we suddenly heard the students call out, "... 3, 4, 5."

Then there was silence in the room. Everyone faced the teacher, Cindy Wong, and she spoke. Then everyone went back to what they were doing.

Later I asked Cindy what she did to quiet the room so quickly. She said, "Dad, it's a variation on your three-step technique. I have a five-step procedure because I teach younger students than you do, so I wanted to be more specific as to what I wanted."

"My five steps are these:

1. Eyes on speaker
2. Quiet
3. Be still
4. Hands free (put things down)
5. Listen

"The way it works is, I say, 'Give me five.' They go through each of the five steps in their mind.

"I have rehearsed them in this procedure, so when I say, 'Give me five,' it takes them no more than five seconds before I have their attention."

I asked, "Do all three sixth-grade classes know this routine?"

"Yes," she said.

I replied, "Wow. This has now become the culture for all the sixth graders."

Cindy Wong and the Give Me Five plan as posted in her classroom.

184

Three more examples of classroom procedures will be presented; however, the technique of explain, rehearse, and reinforce will not be illustrated. Refer to the two previous procedures for the technique.

Procedure for the Start of the Period or Day

An effective teacher always has the procedure or schedule posted or ready for distribution when the students arrive. For previous examples of how efficiently this is done, see pages 121, 122, and 124.

Here is another example of a procedure for the beginning of the school day.

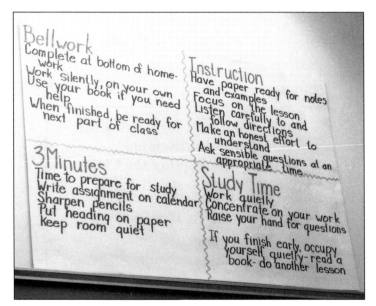

Routines are the hallmark of an effective classroom.

Morning Routine

Remove jacket.
Empty backpack or bag.
Get core folder.
Sharpen pencil.

Check for the following:
    Books for core
    Assignment
    Binder
    Pencils and pens
    Paper

Begin start of class sponge activities:
    Grammar and punctuation
    Word of the day
    Morning message
    Overhead

Please turn to page 203 for an example of a teacher with no opening morning routine and the subsequent disaster in the classroom.

Procedure for Students Seeking Help

Hand raising is not effective when students want your attention. There are better methods for students to use to get your attention.

The class is at work and you are walking around the room helping. You see a hand up and say, "Pam." The whole class stops to look at you and Pam.

Pam says, "May I sharpen my pencil?"—a reasonable request.

You say yes or no, and the class goes back to work.

A few seconds later, you see another hand up. You say, "Carlos," and the whole class stops to look at you and Carlos.

Carlos says, "I need your help"—an appropriate request.

You say, "Wait a minute," and the class goes back to work.

Every time you speak, you interrupt the class. These interruptions occur frequently, often two or three times a minute.

You would be distracted if the principal came over the loudspeaker two or three times a day, no less two or three times a minute. Before you complain that the principal makes a few announcements during the day over the intercom system, consider how many times a teacher interrupts a class when the students are concentrating on their work.

Student Methods for Getting the Teacher's Attention Without Interrupting the Class

Hand signal: The student signals with different number of fingers.

Toilet tissue tube: The student signals with a colored tube.

Styrofoam cup: The student signals with the position of a cup.

Index card: The student signals with a message on an index card.

Textbook: The student signals with an upright textbook.

Hand Signal

In this system, the students signal the teacher with a predetermined number of fingers. The number of fingers raised corresponds to a predetermined request established by the teacher.

Post a sign on the wall with your hand signal chart. Then train your students to use the system.

✔ If they wish to speak, they are to raise the index finger.

✔ If they wish to leave their seat, they are to raise two fingers.

✔ If they need your help, they are to raise three fingers.

✔ When you see a signal, silently respond to the signal with a nod of the head or a gesture of the hand.

The important thing is that the class is not disturbed.

To Obtain the Teacher's Attention, Raise—

One Finger:
"I wish to speak."

Two Fingers:
"I wish to leave my seat."

Three Fingers:
"I need your help."

A Difference in the Noise Level Alone

Dear Rosemary,

We really enjoyed seeing you again at our symposia. The wonderfully creative and practical ideas you gave us will be put to good use. My husband is already using your hand signals in his grade 5/6 classroom, and he can't believe the difference it has made in the noise level alone.

Thanks again for all of the above, and so much more.

Debbie Fraser
Kinburn, Ontario

Toilet Tissue Tube

Take an empty toilet tissue tube and wrap one end with red construction paper and the other end with green construction paper. The tube is placed with the green end up on the student's desk.

The procedure when the student wants the teacher's attention is to turn the tube so that the red end is up and to **continue to work**. When the teacher comes to help the student, the green end is turned back up.

Styrofoam Cup

Tape a short length of string to the bottom of a Styrofoam cup. (Styrofoam cups are suggested because they are noiseless.) Tape the other end of the string near the edge of the desktop, and leave the cup dangling off the table.

The procedure when the student wants the teacher's attention is to place the cup on the desk and to **continue to work**.

Index Card

(faces teacher)

Fold and tape an index card into a three-sided pyramid. On one side write, "Please help me." On another side write, "Please keep working." Leave the third side blank. Place the card on the table so that the blank side is facing the student.

(faces student)

The procedure when the student wants the teacher's attention is to turn the card so that "Please help me" is facing forward. The student sees "Please keep working" and is reminded to **continue to work**.

Textbook

High school teachers may appreciate this simple system. The procedure when the student wants the teacher's attention is to take a textbook and place it in an upright position and to **continue to work**.

Procedure for the Movement of Paper

If your students are sitting in columns and rows, it is more effective to have them pass their papers across the rows to the side of the room rather than up the row to the front of the room.

 Students should pass their papers across the rows, not up the rows.

Why? Here are the problems with passing papers up to the front of the room.

1. If papers are passed up the row, you cannot see what is happening behind each student's back as you stand at the front of the room waiting for the papers.

2. Some students tap, poke, shove, and hit the back of the student in front to announce that the papers are coming up the row. Others wave the papers in the face of the student in front. No matter what is done, the student in front is irritated, words are spoken, and the disturbance in the class increases.

3. When papers are passed from hand to hand, some papers may fall to the floor.

4. There are frequently more students up a row than across rows.

5. Thus passing papers up a row takes longer to accomplish and is frequently accompanied by student agitation.

There are advantages to passing papers across the rows to the side of the room. The procedure is as follows:

Step 1. Have the students place their papers on the desk next to theirs, starting with the student at one end of the row.

Step 2. The next student is to add his or her paper to the stack and place the papers on the next desk. Do not have the students pass the papers from hand to hand. This will eliminate flicking of papers as papers are passed.

Step 3. As the students pass the papers from desk to desk, monitor the procedure, making adjustments and corrections when necessary and praising when appropriate.

Step 4. Walk to the side of the room and look across all the rows to monitor the procedure. This tactic allows you to see across the rows, whereas you cannot see behind the backs of students when you stand in front of the room and they are passing papers forward.

Step 5. Pick up the papers, or ask a student to pick up all the papers. If the students are sitting at tables instead of chairs in a row:

> ✔ Have the students place their paper at the head of the table (point to the designated spot).

> ✔ Have students or an aide pick up the papers, or do so yourself.

It is not a good procedure to have the students place their papers in a basket on the teacher's desk. This procedure involves too much movement and too much of a mess left behind.

Whatever procedure you choose to use for collecting papers, rehearse the procedure the first time you collect papers.

Your Class Could Learn on Its Own

When students know how the class is run, they will be more willing to do **whatever you want them to do.** You can then have an exciting and challenging classroom with much learning for mastery because procedures and routines manage the classroom.

190

> **The ineffective teacher** begins the first day of school attempting to teach a subject and spends the rest of the year running after the students.
>
> **The effective teacher** spends most of the first week teaching the students how to follow classroom procedures.

✔ Students risk failure because of the lack of STRUCTURE.

✔ Procedures and routines create STRUCTURE.

At-risk students are a topic of concern in the schools. Being at risk has nothing to do with a student's intelligence, gender, skin color, socioeconomic background, or administrative support. The reason students—and teachers—are at risk is that they lack STRUCTURE in their lives. Procedures give both students and teachers structure. Many students come from dysfunctional (unstructured) homes. The effective teacher provides structure so that students have something familiar and secure that they can rely on.

Having special rituals is reassuring to a student—it gives the student something familiar to fall back on. Rituals don't have to be elaborate, but they need to have a certain regularity. They can be as simple as knowing where to line up for an elementary student and knowing where to go quickly in the face of danger for a secondary student. It's ironic that teachers have a lounge that they can retreat to, but students do not have a safe haven that they can retreat to.

Once you have procedures in place, you can have responsible students. **The only way to have responsible students is to have procedures and routines for which the students can feel responsible.**

And once you establish structure and responsibility, you can have the most exciting classroom in school, doing all the challenging and fascinating things students love to do, and you will be able to leave school knowing that if you were not in class tomorrow, the class could responsibly run itself.

If You Were Not in Your Classroom, Could Your Class Run Itself?

Elementary Teacher

I am a single parent and it is sometimes difficult to leave for work on schedule, but I was on time. Alas, my good fortune was not to continue because traffic came to a halt on the freeway due to an accident. As I sat in my car waiting to resume my commute, I tried to imagine the scene in my classroom. I could not call to let anyone know I would be late. What would 25 unsupervised fifth graders do? What would I find upon my arrival? Would the gym teacher be annoyed because we were all going to be late for gym?

What I found in my classroom was a beautiful reward for 20 years of loving students and striving to making them responsible and self-sufficient. To my amazement, I found an empty classroom and the following note left on my desk.

> *Dear Ms. Gould,*
>
> *We took the attendance, did the lunch count, completed our morning math warm-ups, and went to gym.*
>
> *Love,*
> *Your Class*

I cannot agree with you more on the importance of clearly defined procedures and routines. My students are proof of this.

—Sue Gould Flynn
Williamsville,
New York

High School Teacher

I arranged for a substitute teacher and left lesson plans in my grade book (world history and P.E.). Unfortunately, the substitute teacher went to the wrong room and arrived with 10 minutes remaining in first period. He found the students on task, working on their assignment. They had opened the classroom through another classroom, recognized the lack of a teacher, taken the roll book from my desk, taken the roll, found the lesson plan in the book, and proceeded with the lesson for the day.

There's more! On the day that I was absent we were on an assembly schedule. The substitute teacher did not know of the schedule change. During my prep period, he left the campus to run an errand, planning to return by regular fifth period.

Unfortunately, while he was gone fifth period happened. As I arrived the next day, this is what I was told. "When you didn't arrive, Mr. Wall, we took the roll for you. When you still weren't here, we did our calisthenics. Then we went outside to do our activities. When it started to rain, we came back in and played our game in the gym."

It wasn't planned, but my daily procedures had taken hold of my classes and the students never missed a beat. Procedures and routines work!

—Bob Wall
Susanville, California

College Professor

My students range in age from twenty to late fifties, studying to be teachers or school administrators. My classes are "working" classes, highly structured for production and learning. All grading is performance-based. Schedules are set; the classes run themselves. Students know what is expected, and they know how to accomplish the tasks. They work on the team concept. There is no stress, and the results have been overwhelming. I walk into class and everyone is working; many continue working after class is over. Everyone is on time, and no one wastes time.

I can leave my classes "in charge of themselves." By providing structure, I am able to leave . . . to deliver papers. Where are my students? In class, accomplishing their goals! Once, I returned and found the following note.

> *Dear Dr. Walko,*
>
> *Everything went very well. You would have been proud of us. In my group all were present and participated in the activity. I'll give you an update next week.*
>
> *Myra Brown (and all signatures)*

There are waiting lists for many of my courses. Why? Because you are expected to work!

—Ann Walko
Kean College of New Jersey

Procedures to Rehearse with Students

Entering the classroom	Passing in papers
Getting to work immediately	Exchanging papers
When you are tardy	Returning student work
End-of-period class dismissal	Getting materials without disturbing others
Listening to and responding to questions	Handing out playground materials
Participating in class discussions	Moving about the room
When you need pencil or paper	Going to the library or career center
Keeping your desk orderly	Headings on papers
Checking out classroom materials	When you finish early
Indicating whether you understand	Returning to a task after an interruption
Coming to attention	Asking a question
When you are absent	When a schoolwide announcement is made
Working cooperatively	Walking in the hall during class time
Changing groups	Responding to a fire drill
Keeping your notebook	Responding to an earthquake
Going to the office	Responding to a severe weather alert
When you need help or conferencing	When visitors are in the classroom
Knowing the schedule for the day or class	If the teacher is out of the classroom
Keeping a progress report	If you are suddenly ill
Finding directions for each assignment	Saying "thank you"

You seemingly waste a little time at the beginning to gain time at the end.

—Lim Chye Tin

Procedures and routines established early in the school year free up the rest of the year to be devoted to teaching and learning in the content areas.

Remember, it is the procedures that set the class up for success to take place.

The Effective Teacher

1. Has well-thought-out and structured procedures for every activity.

2. Teaches the procedures for each activity early in the year.

3. Rehearses the class so that procedures become class routines.

4. Reteaches a procedure when necessary and praises to reinforce when appropriate.

UNIT D

Third Characteristic — Lesson Mastery

The effective teacher knows how to design lessons to help students reach mastery.

Third Characteristic — Lesson Mastery

The effective teacher knows how to design lessons to help students reach mastery.

Unit D is correlated with **Part 5: Cooperative Learning and Culture** and **Part 6: Lesson Mastery** in the video series *The Effective Teacher*.

KEY IDEA

To increase student learning and achievement, increase the amount of time the student is working.

The Students Must Learn

> If the student cannot demonstrate learning or achievement, the student has not failed—WE have failed the student.

The student must learn or comprehend. The student must master the subject or skill. The student must show achievement. **If the student cannot demonstrate learning or achievement, the student has not failed—WE have failed the student.**

Schools exist and teachers are hired for one reason only: to help students achieve. Teaching is the noblest of professions. We are charged with getting the students to comprehend and achieve. There is no one right way to do this. There are however, some fundamentals and understandings that we as teachers need to know.

The highest stake of all is our ability to help children realize their full potential.

—Samuel J. Meisels

The Three Major Characteristics of Effective Teachers

1. They have high expectations that all of their students will succeed (Unit B).

2. They are extremely good classroom managers (Unit C).

→ 3. They know how to design lessons to help students reach mastery (Unit D).

They Suddenly Make Our Schools and Teachers Look Good

In 1985 a teacher, Edward Janko, wrote, "The evidence shows that a large number of youngsters have never seriously tried the educational system. The success of recent Asian immigrants in our schools reveals **the astonishing truth that highly motivated students who attend school regularly and work conscientiously suddenly make our school and teachers look good. We perpetually rediscover the wheel.**"[1]

Ten years later in a three-year study[2] of 20,000 California and Wisconsin high school students, Laurence Steinberg reported:

- Over one-third of the students said that they get through the day in school primarily by "goofing off with their friends."

- The average American high school student spends about four hours <u>per week</u> on homework outside of school. In other industrialized countries, the average is about four hours <u>per day</u>.

- Fewer than one in five students say their friends think it is important to get good grades in school.

- An extremely large proportion of students—somewhere around 40 percent—are just going through the motions.

- More than one-third of the students showed signs of being emotionally disengaged from school, as indexed by measures of mind-wandering, lack of interest, or inattentiveness.

- Asians average twice the study time of other students. And they pay attention in class. Asian students perform better in school because they work harder, try harder, and are more invested in achievement.

- What Americans have become is not less intelligent, but less interested in being educated.

Archie E. Lapointe of the Educational Testing Service writes, "To be a successful student in Korea does not come only from mothers but from everywhere—**from the nation as a collective entity**—a larger cultural commitment to achieve in school. There is a clear association between success in school and occupational success."[3]

Hard Work Achieves Success

Adam Robinson, co-founder of *The Princeton Review* says, "The universal response to school success in Asian countries was 'hard work'—so they work hard. By contrast, American students replied 'intelligence.' In other words, if you are intelligent, you shouldn't have to work too hard. If you are not, there's no point in trying.

"Let your children know that their success and satisfaction in any field or endeavor is achieved only by diligence and hard work. Teach your children the value of hard work in school."[4]

---

[1] Janko, Edward. (April 22, 1987). "Commentary." *Education Week*, p. 32.

[2] Steinberg, Laurence. (1996). *Beyond the Classroom.* New York: Simon & Schuster.

[3] Lapointe, Archie E. (December 1, 1993). "To Learn or Not to Learn: Opportunity vs. Desire." *Education Week*, p. 28.

[4] Robinson, Adam. (October 15, 1994). "How to Help Your Child Get a World-Class Education." *Bottom Line Personal*, p. 10.

The Learner Must Work at Learning

There is only one way for a student to learn anything. **The student must put in effort; the student must work to learn.** Learning does not come from the teacher's work, such as lecturing, leading a discussion, or showing a video. An effective teacher knows how to manage the time allocated to maximize student time and effort.

Allocated Time: Allocated time is the amount of time given to a student for learning. First, there is the time a school board adopts as the school calendar. The time may be negotiated with the teachers' organization and other interested parties, but once the time is adopted, it becomes the allocated time. Typically, this is about 180 days, some 6 to 7 hours each day.

THE FOUR KINDS OF TIME AT SCHOOL

Allocated Time — 100%
Instructional Time - 90%
Engaged Time — 75%
Academic
Learning Time — 35%

Another kind of allocated time is the time given to an activity. Usually, this is determined by board policy, the administration, or a curriculum committee. So many hours a day or a week may be mandated for spelling, language arts, physical education, math, and science.

Thus allocated time is the total time within which teacher instruction and student learning can take place. It is 100 percent of the available time.

Instructional Time: Instructional time is the time you can observe a teacher instructing. Instructional time is easy to ascertain because the teacher is the focus in the room. All eyes are on the teacher because the teacher is talking, orchestrating, WORKING.

Research has shown that the typical teacher consumes 90 percent of the allocated time. Yes, the teacher is at center stage almost every minute of the school year.

Engaged Time: Engaged time is the time you can observe a student involved or engaged in a task.   The students are now the focus in the room, and the teacher is walking around helping those who are in need. It is easy to identify engaged time. This is the time the students are on task, WORKING.

Research has shown that engaged time is about 75 percent of the allocated time. If this appears to be in conflict with the 90 percent devoted to instructional time (90 and 75 percent exceed 100 percent), it is because the teacher and the students may be working at the same time.

Academic Learning Time: Academic learning time is the amount of time that the teacher can prove or demonstrate that the student comprehended or learned the content or mastered the skill.   According to the research, this provable or demonstrable time is only 35 percent of the allocated time.

Academic learning time has nothing to do with worksheets, boardwork, lecturing, videos, or discussions. The ineffective teacher spends time covering materials.

Conversely, the effective teacher has the students spend time working and earning their own achievement and success.   Academic learning time has to do with answering two questions:

1. Did the student learn what you wanted the student to learn?

2. Can you show that the student learned what you wanted the student to learn?

Academic Learning Time (35 percent)
The time students spend demonstrating comprehension of a skill or content.

Allocated, instructional, and engaged time are all factors in a classroom, but none answers the question "Has the student learned anything?" More days or hours do not guarantee more learning. Just because a teacher is teaching and a student is engaged does not guarantee learning either.

The bottom line in education is ultimately student learning or student achievement.   Achievement is the result of academic learning time.

Why Some Students Are at the Head of the Class

Harold Stevenson, University of Michigan psychology professor, studied 240 students in kindergarten, first grade, and fifth grade in cities in the United States (Minneapolis), Taiwan (Taipei), and Japan (Sendai).

In his six-year study, using carefully devised standardized tests, he concluded, "We didn't find any difference in IQ levels, but we found significant differences in performance." Asian students are no smarter than American students, so why are Asian students so successful in school? He found:

- An American first grader spends an average of 14 minutes a night on homework and hates it.

- A Japanese first grader (in Japan) spends an average of 37 minutes a night on homework and likes it.

- A Chinese first grader (in China) spends an average of 77 minutes a night on homework and likes it.

- Japanese and Chinese students also go to school on Saturday mornings, have fewer holidays, and attend school 240 days a year, in contrast to American elementary school children, who generally go only 178 days a year.

In a survey of 7,836 San Francisco-area high school students, Sanford M. Dornbusch, professor of sociology and education at Stanford University, found that Asian-American boys spend an average of 11.7 hours a week doing homework, compared to 8 hours for whites and 6.3 hours for blacks.

Among girls, the figures were 12.3 hours a week for Asian-Americans, 8.6 for whites, and 9.2 for blacks.

Research has shown that Asian students spend more time on task than non-Asian students.

Asian-Americans also registered the best figures on other measures of work: attendance, cutting classes, paying attention to the teacher, and daydreaming.

Professor Dornbusch said that these numbers, taken together, represent what he termed a "powerhouse statistic in EFFORT." A nationwide study by the U.S. Department of Education, "School Experiences and Performance of Asian-Pacific American High School Students," found:

- Nearly half of Asian-American sophomores spend five or more hours per week on homework, compared to less than a third of whites and a quarter of blacks.

- Half of the Asian-American high school students were never absent from school, compared with only a quarter for whites.

—Fox Butterfield
"Why Asians Are Going to the Head of the Class."
(August 3, 1986). *New York Times.*

The Teacher's Function Is Not to Get Students to Settle Down

"I can't get them to settle down and get to work," so many teachers complain. It is not the function of the teacher to get the students to settle down every morning. Can you imagine what kind of a world we would have if every morning no one would start to work until

- The principal came to every class and told the teachers to settle down and start teaching?

- The boss came to every desk to tell all the office assistants to settle down and start word processing?

- The supervisor asked every worker to settle down and start working?

- The coach hollered at every ballplayer to settle down and start practicing?

The next time you go to a baseball game early, notice the pregame practice sessions. The manager is probably nowhere in sight, yet everyone is practicing or warming up. There is a pregame procedure, and everyone takes part in the procedure without anyone telling him or her what to do.

Effective teachers have opening-of-class procedures. The students know the procedure (Chapter 20) and go about their job without anyone telling them what to do.

In stark contrast, the next page shows the actual scenario of an ineffective teacher.

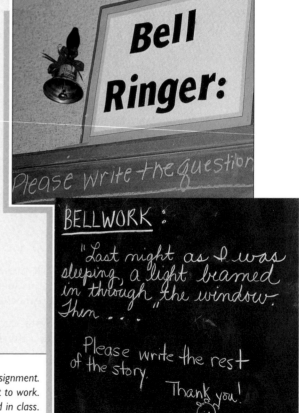

The effective teacher has a posted assignment.
When the students enter class, they go right to work.
It is a routine that has been learned in class.

I Left Them at Home

8:00	Students enter classroom, walk around, and talk.
8:12	One side of front panel on ventilator unit falls to floor (student has been sitting on it, banging it with heels).
8:14	Student continues to "beat it."
8:14.10	Student makes eye contact with principal, who is seated on other side of room.
8:14.11	Student stops "beating it."
8:22	Teacher asks students to be seated and be quiet.
8:24	Students find desks (two in closet area, three in front of room with backs to the board, one in the back corner between wall and filing cabinet).
8:25	Students are told schedule for day.
8:29	Students share news (rock group tour, fight last night, etc.).
8:35	Students are instructed to get books out for silent reading.
8:37	Five students hang on bookshelf trying to find books.
8:40	Two students are still discussing a fan magazine.
8:47	One student returns from very long visit to rest room.
8:48	Two students return carrying 5-inch jar of a mysterious substance.
8:49	Two students hang on bookshelves; principal notices good muscle coordination.
8:50	Teacher asks students to put away reading books; 70 percent are able to do so.
8:51	Teacher starts discussion of worksheet.
9:00	Teacher breaks students into groups for another subject.
9:01	As students group, principal asks teacher for lesson plans or objectives.
9:02	Teacher tells principal, "They are at home."

This is an actual observation of a sixth-grade teacher's class. In addition to wasted academic learning time, the teacher is modeling that young people do not have to be ready to get to work when they come to work.

Successful people prepare themselves daily for their work. That is why they are successful.

You Can Increase Student Learning

llocated time, instructional time, engaged time, and academic learning time all have one variable—**TIME**.

> ### Increase the amount of time the student is working, and you increase learning.

Why do parents berate their children to practice on the piano? Because every parent knows that the more the student WORKS on a piece of music, the better the student will be able to perform it.

What is the one thing all coaches of teams want out of the school schedule, if they can wrangle it from the allocated time? It is practice time, because every coach knows that the more a team practices and WORKS, the better it will be at the game.

What is the one thing all teachers who are directing the annual production want from the school schedule? It is rehearsal time, because every teacher knows that the more time the cast rehearses and WORKS, the better it will be on the night of the performance.

It's common sense—the person who does the work is the one who learns. Yet look into several rooms, especially in a secondary school, and guess who you find invariably working? Yes, the teacher. And what does the research say about learning?

> ### The person who does the work is the ONLY one who learns.

$369,636 Spent to Find Out Who Does Better in School

We taxpayers recently spent $369,636 for a study by a fine organization, the National Endowment for the Humanities. The study, titled "American Memory," found that **students who do more homework, attend school regularly, and read more tend to do better in school.**

It took $369,636 to discover that? Any teacher could have told the government that for a 25-cent telephone call. Who knows what it will cost the government to discover that **students who appear in class with paper, pencil, and textbooks will be able to do the assignments?**

The fact that the teacher does most of the work at school explains why there is so little learning in school. According to the research, only 35 percent of the allocated time is devoted to learning. Any business that operated at 35 percent efficiency would be bankrupt shortly.

I was successful with my students because when they walked into my room, my assignment was posted. They immediately got to work because that was the routine they had learned.

For learning to take place, it is the student, not the teacher, who must be working.

Fifty minutes later, when the period was over, I said, "Have a nice day. See you tomorrow," and they went staggering out of the class huffing and puffing, moaning, "Boy, the guy works us hard, and on top of that, look at all the homework he's given us."

As for me, I leave the school full of energy. Why? Because I haven't done a thing at school other than walk around the room helping students, giving individual attention, and pixieishly snarling, "Stay on task!" or "Stay focused!"

At 4 o'clock I go play racquetball, drink margaritas, and teach my Italian bride how to cook Chinese food. Life and love begin for me at 4 o'clock. You don't see me dragging out at the end of the school day groaning, "I can't take this any longer. I'm going to take early retirement at the end of this school year—and I'm only 29 years old—to sell aluminum siding!"

The reason teachers are so tired at the end of the school day is that they have been working. If I worked as hard as many teachers do, I'd be as tired, too.

But have you ever noticed what happens at 3 o'clock when the students leave? "Yea, yea, yea!" Why are they so full of energy? Because they have been sitting in school all day doing nothing while the teacher is doing all the work.

The person who does the work is the only one doing any learning!

—Harry K. Wong

The next time you go into a restaurant, notice who is doing all the work. It is the cooks, buspeople, and waitpersons, not the owner. The owner is sitting behind a cash register counting money.

The next time you walk past a construction job, notice who is doing all the work. It's the workers, the construction crew, not the foreman. He's standing around with the blueprints in one hand and gesturing orders with the other.

The next time you walk into an office, notice who is doing all the work—the workers again, office assistants, clerks, and bookkeepers, not the bosses. They are all sitting around with phones to their ears.

But walk into a school and notice who is working. Not the students. No, it's the teachers who are beating their buns off. **The research says that the person who does the work is the only one doing the learning.**

To increase the amount of time the student works to learn:

1. Have an assignment posted daily to be done upon entering the classroom.

2. Teach procedures and routines to minimize interruptions and maximize uninterrupted learning time.

3. Constantly monitor students so as to keep them on task.

> People who work and put in effort always achieve more than those who do not.

The only limitations are those you place on yourself and those you allow other people to place on you.

— Jean Driscoll

Four World Records

Jean Driscoll, seven-time wheelchair winner of the Boston marathon, two-time Olympic silver medalist, and holder of four world records in the marathon, excelled because of her famed work ethic. Driscoll takes care of herself, training hard year-around and maintaining such incredible self-discipline that she is world class in her sport. She is living proof that hard work, effort, and a focused work ethic pay off in achievement.

Jean Driscoll, Olympian and world-record holder.

> **The student should be the worker.**
> **Make the student work!**

The truism of work and effort applies not only to students but to teachers and administrators as well. The work ethic is best modeled by teachers who put great effort and work into being effective teachers.

No Substitute for Effort and Hard Work

There is nothing revolutionary or new about how to become an effective teacher. There are only two requirements:

1. You must have an undying belief that every student can and has the ability to learn.

2. You must persevere.

No one ever said teaching was easy. There is no magical instructional method. You need to work and put in effort at developing effective teaching strategies until success is achieved.

Direct Instruction

> When teachers explain exactly what students
> are expected to learn and
> demonstrate the steps needed
> to accomplish a particular academic task,
> **students learn more**.

The procedure stated in the box is called *direct instruction*. Direct instruction takes a person through learning steps systematically, helping the learner see both the purpose and the result of each step.

Direct instruction has been particularly effective in teaching basic skills to young and at-risk students, as well as in helping older and higher-ability students master more complex materials and develop independent study skills. When someone teaches you how to use a word processor or make a cheesecake, what you are getting is structured, direct instruction. Chapters 22 and 23 will show you how direct instruction is done.

—U.S. Department of Education
What Works: Research About Teaching and Learning. (1986).
Washington, D.C.: U.S. Government Printing Office, p. 35.

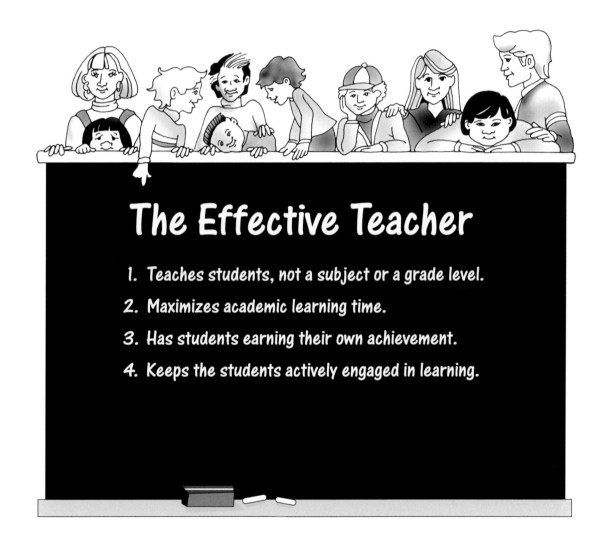

The Effective Teacher

1. Teaches students, not a subject or a grade level.

2. Maximizes academic learning time.

3. Has students earning their own achievement.

4. Keeps the students actively engaged in learning.

KEY IDEA

The greater the structure of a lesson and the more precise the directions on what is to be accomplished, the higher the achievement rate.

A Teacher's Task: To Uncover

The Correct Question to Ask

Stop asking, "What am I going to cover tomorrow?"

Start asking, "What are my students to learn, achieve, and accomplish tomorrow?"

Stop asking, "What video am I going to show? What worksheet am I going to give out? What activity am I going to do?" Danger lurks in the word *I*. That *I*—the teacher—is doing all the work. The students just show up, wondering what the teacher will do next. They have no idea what they are to learn. The teacher "covers" the day's materials.

Start asking, "What are my students to learn, achieve, and accomplish?" You cannot assess or evaluate anything the students have done until both parties know what the students are responsible for performing or learning.

Therefore, you must tell the students at the beginning of every assignment what they are responsible for learning, for achievement, or for being able to perform. **The role of a teacher is not to cover. The role of a teacher is to UNCOVER.**

Ineffective and Effective Assignments

Learning has nothing to do with
what the teacher **COVERS**.

Learning has to do with
what the student **ACCOMPLISHES**.

An **ineffective assignment** results when the teacher tells the class what will be covered—for example, "We will cover Chapter 7 this week, and there will be a test on Friday covering everything in Chapter 7." "Chapter 7," "pages 404 to 414," "Moby Dick," "long division," and "the Renaissance period" are bad assignments. No one—not the students, not their parents who want to help, and, worst of all, not even the teacher—has any idea of what is to be learned.

An effective assignment results when the teacher tells the students, up front, what the students are to have accomplished or mastered at the end of the lesson. In other words, **you teach with the end in mind.**

Steps to Creating an Effective Assignment

1. Think what you want the students to accomplish.
2. Write each step as a single sentence.
3. Write in simple language.
4. Duplicate the list of steps and give it to the students.

Education is not a process of putting the learner under control, but putting the student in control of his or her learning.

—Alison Preece
University of Victoria
British Columbia, Canada

Now that the students have a copy of the assignment, they are responsible for accomplishing each step in it. They are now able to take control of their own learning. The parents also know what the assignment is. Effective teachers send assignments home with a weekly newsletter.

What Teaching Strategy Fosters Student Accomplishment?

> **If students know what they are to learn, you increase the chances that they WILL learn.**

Focusing on goals or objectives makes the most difference in student achievement. The research of Kevin Wise and James Okey showed that "the effective classroom appears to be the one in which the students are kept aware of instructional objectives and receive feedback on their progress toward these objectives."[1] In simple terms, the use of objectives increases the chances that the students will learn.

Only One Out of Twelve

Researchers Kevin Wise and James Okey wanted to know what teaching strategies were most important in helping students achieve. They looked at these 12 possible factors:

1. Audiovisual
2. Grading
3. Inquiry/discovery
4. Focusing on objectives
5. Hands-on manipulation
6. Modifying the textbooks and instructional materials
7. Presentation mode of teacher
8. Questioning strategies
9. Testing
10. Teacher direction
11. Wait time
12. Miscellaneous

They found that **focusing on objectives** made the most difference on student achievement.

The Bottom Line Is Student Achievement

The bottom line in the real world is achievement. The world rewards people who are successful.

- ✔ In baseball, achievement is measured by the batting average.

- ✔ In making cars, achievement is measured by number of defects.

- ✔ In knitting, achievement is measured by dropped stitches.

- ✔ In typing, achievement is measured by errors per page.

- ✔ In selling, achievement is measured in sales.

[1]Wise, Kevin and James Okey. (1983). "A Meta-Analysis of the Effects of Various Science Teaching Strategies on Achievement." *Journal of Research in Science Teaching,* pp. 419–435.

If you make no sales, you are not a salesperson. If your batting average is low, you are traded or released. If the cars have too many defects, the customers buy another brand. The same standards apply in education: **The bottom line in education is student achievement.**

> **If the students do not do their assignments and do not show achievement, no learning has occurred.**

The ineffective teacher is concerned with "covering" history, science, math, art, or language arts. Such teachers spend most of the class time on the textbook and having students fill out worksheets in a mind-numbing environment. They do not teach to objectives, nor do they know how to teach for learning, comprehension, or mastery.

Effective teachers can define three key concepts:

1. **Learning.** The student shows that information or a skill has been acquired. Learning has taken place when you see a student perform a skill or grasp (define, identify, recall) information.

2. **Comprehension.** The student shows understanding of what has been learned. Comprehension has taken place when you see a student interpret, translate, explain, or summarize the information learned.

3. **Mastery.** The student shows the ability to use what has been comprehended. Mastery has taken place when you see a student use or apply what he or she understands. The student can also break down, reorganize, and evaluate what is known and understood.

This chapter shows how to write assignments in which students demonstrate that learning, comprehension, or mastery has taken place.

Are You Teaching for Accomplishment or Just Telling the Students What to Do?

Ineffective teachers do not teach for learning; they tell the students what to do. Often the work that is assigned is used to kill time. Unfortunately, there are teachers who thumb through the teacher's manual, saying to themselves:

What am I to do?	What can I use to keep them quiet?
What can I find to keep them busy?	What can I do to kill the period?

What activity relates to the unit?

As a result, an ineffective assignment tells students what to do; for example:

Read Chapter 24.	Complete this worksheet.
Do the problems on page 34.	Sit quietly and read pages 23 to 30.
Write a paper on Brazil.	Do this activity.

Answer the questions at the end of the chapter.

These are not accomplishments. They are jobs. They tell the student what to do. They do not tell the student what is to be comprehended, learned, or achieved. When the student is told what to do, no sense of accomplishment or responsibility is associated with what the student is to achieve. Assignments like those in the example cause students to say:

What are we doing today?	What's our assignment?
Are you going to show us a video today?	What are you going to do today?
Are we doing anything important today?	What's our assignment for tomorrow?

I'm finished; what do I do now?

The student may be finished, but did the student learn anything? In an ineffective classroom, the students just sit around waiting for the teacher to tell them what to do.

Effective teachers teach for student accomplishment and responsibility. When an assignment tells a student what is to be accomplished, you are also teaching responsibility. Students who are responsible and are working for accomplishment or achievement will ask questions like these:

How am I doing?	Am I first string?
Will I be first chair?	Is this good enough for an A?

Questions like these tell you that the student is constantly and responsibly working to improve.

> **Teach for accomplishment, using structured assignments with objectives,
> and not only will the students demonstrate competence,
> but you will be regarded as a competent teacher also.**

"Your Assignment Is Chapter 24"

Why didn't someone tell me how to give an assignment? I thought giving an assignment was telling the students what chapters to read.

"Students, your assignment for this week is Chapter 24. And the test this Friday will cover everything in Chapter 24."

When I gave them the test a week later, I was horrified at all the poor test scores. And I started to blame the students for their poor achievement.

- *They were not studying "hard enough."*
- *They were not spending "enough time" on their homework.*
- *They were not reading "carefully."*
- *They were not "focusing."*

I had assigned, lectured on, led discussion on, and given them study time on the chapter. I even had a worksheet of questions for homework. It had to be the students' fault.

Little did I know that when the students went home to do their homework, the parents would ask, "What's your assignment?"

The students would respond, "Chapter 24."

Both the parents and the students were at a loss as to what the assignment was. What does "Chapter 24" mean? What is the student supposed to do? How is the parent to help?

It never occurred to me that the problem was me. I did not know how to give an assignment.

I now know how to give assignments that help students achieve. It was not until years later that I learned this:

—A high school teacher

> **The greater the structure of a lesson and the more precise the directions on what is to be accomplished, the higher the achievement.**

Assignments Must Be Clear and Precise

An effective assignment must **HAVE STRUCTURE and BE PRECISE.** Do this and you will have more of your students complete their assignments.

Structure

✔ The assignment must have a consistent and familiar format that the students can recognize as their assignment.

✔ The assignment must be posted daily and in a consistent location before the students enter the room. (See Chapter 15.)

Preciseness

✔ The assignment must state clearly and simply what the students are to accomplish.

✔ The key word is *accomplish.*

The Difference Between a Procedure and an Assignment

Procedures tell what to do.
Assignments tell what to *accomplish*.

A poor assignment tells the student what to do at the BEGINNING of the assignment.

A good assignment states what a student is to have accomplished or achieved when the assignment is FINISHED.

You tell students what you want accomplished. Then you give procedures to help them do so.

The Same Textbook, Yet Only One Class Succeeded

Two teachers taught the same course, used the same textbook, covered the same materials, showed the same videos, did the same activities, and had the same kinds of students. One teacher was a success and the other a failure—in the eyes of the students, the parents, and the administration. Why?

The **ineffective teacher** used units that were two to three weeks long. When asked why, she would say that since there were six to nine weeks in the grading period, she divided her units accordingly into two- to three-week units. And since deficiency notices had to be sent four weeks into the grading period, she structured her units to end at that time; that also suited two- to three-week units.

Her curriculum consisted of following the textbook with 12 to 15 units of two to four weeks each for the year. And her assignments consisted of telling the students that they were responsible for whatever was in the chapter.

Her first test was given on the second or third Friday and taken home to grade. Her students did not know the result of their accomplishment until the third or fourth week of school. By that time it was far too late to help those who needed help. But then, the teacher wasn't interested in helping anyway.

She had covered the material, and it was up to the students to pass the tests.

The **effective teacher** taught single concepts or skills, and her lessons were one to three days long. She knew that it was the students' learning style,[*] not the grading period, that governed the length of the assignments.

Her curriculum consisted of 70 lessons, each teaching a single concept or skill culled from the textbook, activities, media, and current issues. The students completed two assignments a week and took two tests a week. (See Chapter 23.) They experienced four successes a week, and the teacher knew within the first week what had to be done to review, adjust, and correct to help her students succeed.

She had a curriculum that uncovered the material and gave assignments that helped her students succeed.

A teacher's job is to uncover, not cover, the subject matter. **One excellent way to do this is to have short lessons with structured assignments that state precisely what the student is to accomplish.**

[*]For more information on learning style contact Dr. Rita Dunn, St. John's University, School of Education, Jamaica, NY 11439.

The Optimum Length of an Assignment

The shorter the assignment, the MORE likely the student will complete it. The longer the assignment, the LESS likely the student will complete it. Except for term papers and other special projects:

✔ No high school assignment should exceed five days.

✔ No junior or middle school assignment should exceed four days.

✔ No intermediate school assignment should exceed three days.

✔ No primary school assignment should exceed a day or, occasionally, two.

✔ No special education assignment should exceed 15 minutes.

The Most Important Words to Use in an Assignment

The terms objectives, criteria, learning criteria, and specifications are being used to mean the same thing. The outcome for all of these terms is student achievement and performance.

To teach for accomplishment, you must have a series of sentences that clearly and precisely state what is to be accomplished. **These sentences are called objectives or learning criteria.**

Each sentence must begin with a verb that states the action to be taken to show accomplishment. The most important word to use in an assignment is a verb, because verbs show if accomplishment has taken place or not.

> **To teach for learning, use words, especially verbs, that show that learning has taken place.**

Verbs are "action words" or "thinking words." The chart on the next page lists some verbs that can be used. The verbs have been organized into levels like floors in a building. The chart is based on the work of Dr. Benjamin Bloom, of the University of Chicago, and is known as Bloom's taxonomy.[1] His taxonomy arranges the verbs into six related groups:

1. Knowledge

2. Comprehension

3. Application

4. Analysis

5. Synthesis

6. Evaluation

---

[1]Bloom, Benjamin (ed.). (1956). *Taxonomy of Educational Objectives: Cognitive Domain.* New York: David McKay Co.

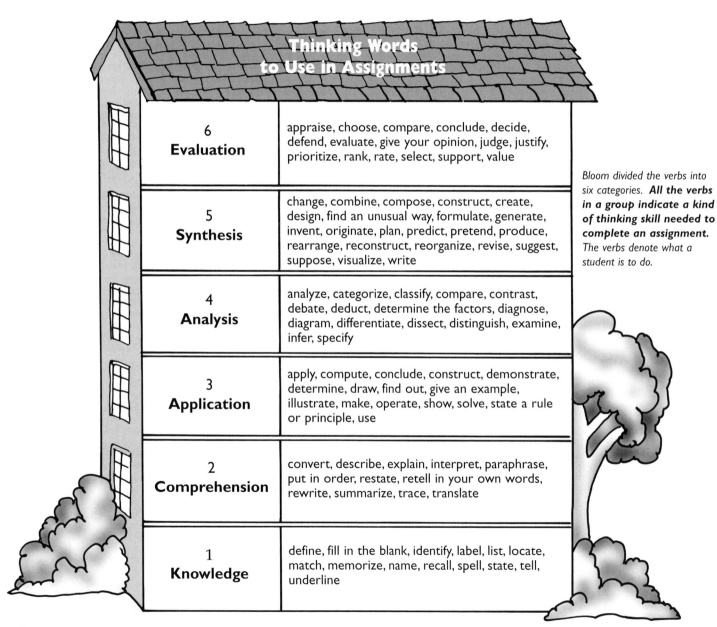

Thinking Words to Use in Assignments

6 **Evaluation**	appraise, choose, compare, conclude, decide, defend, evaluate, give your opinion, judge, justify, prioritize, rank, rate, select, support, value
5 **Synthesis**	change, combine, compose, construct, create, design, find an unusual way, formulate, generate, invent, originate, plan, predict, pretend, produce, rearrange, reconstruct, reorganize, revise, suggest, suppose, visualize, write
4 **Analysis**	analyze, categorize, classify, compare, contrast, debate, deduct, determine the factors, diagnose, diagram, differentiate, dissect, distinguish, examine, infer, specify
3 **Application**	apply, compute, conclude, construct, demonstrate, determine, draw, find out, give an example, illustrate, make, operate, show, solve, state a rule or principle, use
2 **Comprehension**	convert, describe, explain, interpret, paraphrase, put in order, restate, retell in your own words, rewrite, summarize, trace, translate
1 **Knowledge**	define, fill in the blank, identify, label, list, locate, match, memorize, name, recall, spell, state, tell, underline

Bloom divided the verbs into six categories. **All the verbs in a group indicate a kind of thinking skill needed to complete an assignment.** *The verbs denote what a student is to do.*

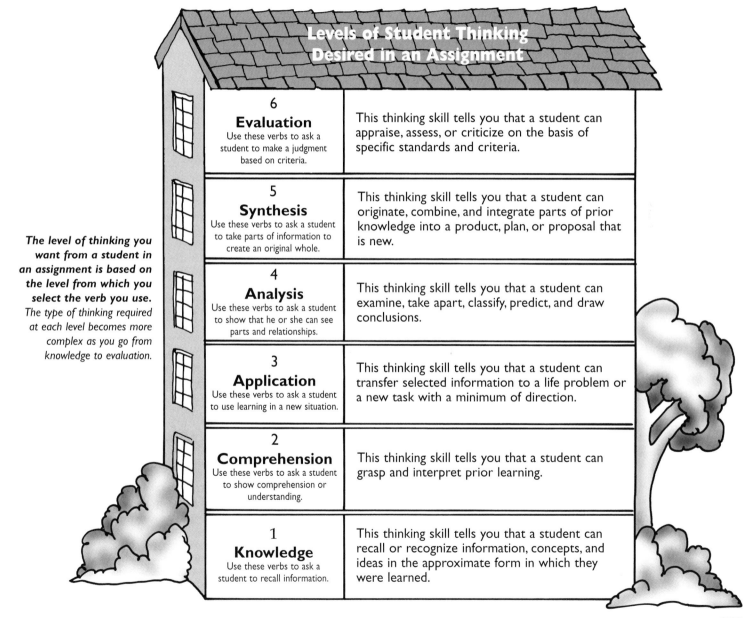

Levels of Student Thinking Desired in an Assignment

The level of thinking you want from a student in an assignment is based on the level from which you select the verb you use.
The type of thinking required at each level becomes more complex as you go from knowledge to evaluation.

6
Evaluation
Use these verbs to ask a student to make a judgment based on criteria.

This thinking skill tells you that a student can appraise, assess, or criticize on the basis of specific standards and criteria.

5
Synthesis
Use these verbs to ask a student to take parts of information to create an original whole.

This thinking skill tells you that a student can originate, combine, and integrate parts of prior knowledge into a product, plan, or proposal that is new.

4
Analysis
Use these verbs to ask a student to show that he or she can see parts and relationships.

This thinking skill tells you that a student can examine, take apart, classify, predict, and draw conclusions.

3
Application
Use these verbs to ask a student to use learning in a new situation.

This thinking skill tells you that a student can transfer selected information to a life problem or a new task with a minimum of direction.

2
Comprehension
Use these verbs to ask a student to show comprehension or understanding.

This thinking skill tells you that a student can grasp and interpret prior learning.

1
Knowledge
Use these verbs to ask a student to recall information.

This thinking skill tells you that a student can recall or recognize information, concepts, and ideas in the approximate form in which they were learned.

What Are Objectives?

> **OBJECTIVES** are what a student must achieve to accomplish what the teacher states is to be learned, comprehended, or mastered.

Objectives or criteria do two things: assign and assess. They should also be written as a single sentence.

> **Just as Tires Need to Be Aligned**
>
> *When goals and objectives are aligned, teachers are able to teach more directly from their objectives.*
>
> —Robert L. Morrison
> Opelousas, Louisiana

1. **Assign.** Objectives give direction or tell a student what is to be comprehended or mastered in an assignment.

2. **Assess.** Objectives tell the teacher if additional study is needed to master an objective. (See Chapter 23.)

Here are examples of typical objectives:

- ✔ Name, in order, the parts of the digestive system.
- ✔ Summarize the class discussion on important study skills.
- ✔ Plan a pizza party.
- ✔ Categorize the contents of the box.
- ✔ Create a new ending for the story.
- ✔ Judge the use of chemical warfare.

*A blueprint gives a contractor directions for building a structure and **the means to align and assess** its construction. Likewise, objectives tell the students what is to be accomplished.*

When and How to Write Objectives

Objectives state what you want the students to accomplish. The students must know before the lesson, assignment, or activity begins what they are responsible for learning.

✔ Objectives must be written before the lesson begins because objectives tell a teacher what is to be taught.

✔ Objectives are to be given to the students when the lesson begins so that the students know what they are responsible for.

It is easy to write objectives. There are only two things to do.

Step 1. Pick a verb. Refer to the list on page 218, and use the verb you select as the first word in a sentence.

Only you know which verb to pick because you know what you want or need to teach, the readiness and level of competence of your students, and what you want to prepare your students to do next.

Refrain from choosing verbs all from one category, as this would challenge your students at only one level of thinking.

Step 2. Complete the sentence. The verb tells the student what action is to be taken, and the rest of the sentence tells the student what is to be performed or mastered.

Make sure that the sentence is precise and easily understood by you, the students, and their parents.

Objectives Begin with Verbs

Verbs are action words that do two things:

1. Verbs tell a student what is to be accomplished.

2. Verbs tell a teacher what to look for to see if the student has accomplished what the teacher specified.

Words like the following are not good action verbs because it is difficult, if not impossible, to determine from them what the student is to do. They are also not on Bloom's list. **Do not use these verbs when you write objectives.**

appreciate	enjoy
be happy	like
beautify	love
celebrate	understand

It is important that a layperson can easily read and understand an objective. **The more understandable the sentence, the greater the chance that the student will do what is intended.**

Do not write complex objectives like the following, taken from a published elementary science program:

Given two different molds growing on the same plate, the student will describe the inhibiting reaction at the interface of the molds.

Write precise objectives that state what you want the student to accomplish. The same objective above could have been written in simple English:

Describe what happens when two molds grow together.

Writing an Objective or Criteria

Step 1. Pick a verb (from the chart on page 218).

Step 2. Complete the sentence.

Examples:

List four collective nouns.

Create a different system to catalog CDs in a library.

Can you explain why saying, "Chapter 5" is not a good assignment?

Can you explain why saying, "List four collective nouns" is a good assignment?

Applying Bloom's Taxonomy to the Studies of Antarctica

Knowledge: Who was the first person to reach the South Pole?

Comprehension: Describe the difference between the Arctic and Antarctic regions.

Application: Give an example of one piece of modern technology that, had it been available to the explorers, would have made a difference in the trip.

Analysis: Compare the weather at the South Pole on December 1 and June 1 in any given year.

Synthesis: Pretend that you made the journey. Write an entry in your diary describing your emotions on the day you reached the South Pole.

Evaluation: Should Antarctica remain a continent free of development and left with its natural habitat? Justify your position.

Objectives do not have to be written; they can be stated verbally, a useful approach in the primary grades and certain special education situations. You need not present all the objectives at one time, either. For elementary students, it may be more appropriate to state the objectives one or two at a time.

Most important, you must look at the objectives continually to make sure the class is aligned and is on course.

Jan Tynan holds a list of verbs during class discussion to keep track of the verbs that have been used.

For instance, if you are driving, you refer repeatedly to your map. If you are building a house, the contractor, inspector, and you refer frequently to the blueprints. And if you are at a conference, you refer now and again to the program to determine the topic of the next session and where it will be held.

Schools typically have an open house about a month after school begins. Since the parents are going to ask you, "How do I tell what my child's assignment is?" tell the parents how you give assignments.

When you show the objectives to the parents, use the analogy of a map, blueprint, shopping list, or agenda. This will help them understand what you are doing. The better they understand what you are doing, the better they can help their children do what they need to do.

How to Write an Assignment for Learning

The assignment on the next page, used with great success for years, is presented as an example only. Ignore the subject and focus on how the objectives for the assignment are written. Then apply the example to your own subject matter.

How to Use the Study Guidelines to Help Students Achieve

Step 1. The first time you give the students the assignment, explain to them why they are called "study guidelines." They are guides that you have prepared to help them complete the assignment. You want to be their guide and help them.

Step 2. Use the analogy of a map, program, agenda, or shopping list to explain the use of study guidelines. Explain to the students, just as a map is used to guide you to a destination, use these sentences to guide you in your study of this unit. The study guidelines are to be presented as "user-friendly," not intimidating.

Step 3. Tell the students that the best way to use the study guidelines is to place them next to whatever source they are studying, such as their textbook, worksheets, or notes. They are to use the study guidelines as their parents would use a map as a guide next to them on the car seat.

Step 4. Tell them that the central concept for the lesson is between the two horizontal lines at the top. They are to focus on this as the key idea for the assignment (as opposed to meaningless assignments like "Chapter 24," "decimals," or "World War II").

The Digestive System

The digestive system breaks down food into usable forms for the cells.

Just as a map is used to guide you to a destination, use these sentences to guide you in your study of this unit.

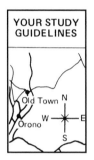

YOUR STUDY GUIDELINES

1. Define all the vocabulary words.

2. State the function of the digestive system.

3. Give examples of the different types of nutrients.

4. Differentiate and give examples of nutritious and nonnutritious foods.

5. Compare mechanical and chemical digestion.

6. Draw the digestive system and state the function of each part.

7. Explain how nutrients get into the blood.

8. Devise a healthy diet for a weeklong trek into the mountains.

9. Assess the effectiveness of different weightloss programs.

Study guidelines tell the student up front what they need to know for achievement.

Step 5. Point out the sentences on the study guidelines. There is no need to use the term *objectives* unless you choose to do so. Tell the students that these sentences are what they are responsible for. They must master these to understand the key idea.

Step 6. Tell the students that each sentence will be the subject of a series of questions on the exam. The students will be tested for their comprehension and mastery of each sentence or objective. (See Chapter 23.)

What About Students Who Need Additional Directions?

Objectives are fine for average to above-average students, people who, when entrusted with a responsibility, will "take the ball and run with it." These students will grow up to be teachers, salespeople, or executives and will be able to translate a plan or a project into concrete results. **They are people who know how to solve problems and achieve on their own. They do not have to be told what to do!**

There are many students (and adults), however, who want to be told what to do. These students are not necessarily below-average students. They may be students who have no background in your subject or face a linguistic or cultural barrier. For these students, write specific questions or procedures for each objective.

Example

Refer to objective 3 from The Digestive System study guidelines on page 224.

Objective

Give examples of the different types of nutrients.

Accompanying Questions

1. Name the different kinds of nutrients.

2. Define and give examples of a protein.

3. Define and give examples of a carbohydrate.

4. Define and give examples of a fat.

5. Explain why proteins are important for your body.

6. Explain why carbohydrates are important for your body.

7. Explain why fats are important for your body.

Accompanying Task

For students who really need lots of direction, next to each question, give the page number or location where the answer may be found.

Rather than giving the page number, have the students write the page number in the left margin after they complete the task or question. This way a student can quickly go back to the source of the answer for review.

YOUR STUDY GUIDE FOR: <u>MAGNETISM</u>
"Nature of a Magnet"

Your textbook has these four objectives at the beginning of the chapter.

1. *Explain how magnets are similar to objects with electric charges.*

2. *Use examples of the action of magnets to explain what magnetic poles are.*

3. *Explain how you can locate a magnetic field.*

4. *Use two magnets to demonstrate the effect of magnetic poles on each other.*

I have prepared this Study Guide to help you learn these objectives. The following break the objectives into smaller questions or tasks. As you do the following, please:

■ Put the page number where you found the answer in the left margin. This will help you when you go back to study.

■ Note the number in the bracket. This tells you which objective it is matched to.

PAGE   Thank you.

(2) What is a magnetic pole?

(1) Three ways magnetic force and electrical forces are alike.

(4) Combinations for attracting and repelling.

     N with N_____

     S with N_____

     S with S_____

(2) What is a temporary magnet?

(2) What is a permanent magnet?

(2) Why does rubbing one end of a steel needle with a magnet magnetize it?

(3) What is a magnetic field?

(2) List five items that are attracted by a magnet.

(2) List five items that have no effect on a magnet.

(4) How can you show that a magnet has two poles?

I hope this lesson does not repel you too much!

The Key to Having Students Do Their Assignments

The Three Major Factors When Writing an Objective

1. STRUCTURE: Use a consistent format.

2. PRECISENESS: Use succinct, clear sentences.

3. ACCOMPLISHMENT: Tell what is to be achieved.

To maximize the frequency with which your students will do their assignments and to maximize your effectiveness as a teacher:

1. Write assignments for accomplishment based on objectives, not coverage.

2. Write the objectives so succinctly and clearly that even outsiders such as parents can understand the assignment.

3. Give the students the objectives so that they know what they are responsible for accomplishing.

The Need for Objectives

1. Setting clear goals for students and making sure they understand those goals is the first component of direct instruction.

These goals or objectives are the groundwork for teacher instruction and student evaluation and achievement.

Chapter 23 will explain and give examples for the remaining four components of direct instruction:

2. Presenting a sequence of well-organized assignments

3. Giving students clear, concise explanations and illustrations of the subject matter

4. Asking frequent questions to see if students understand the work

5. Giving students frequent opportunities to practice what they have learned

The bottom line is—giving them the main objectives of the chapter really helps. Most students look forward to the next "opportunity to make a great grade."

—Sam Morris
Indianapolis, Indiana

The Effective Teacher

1. Writes objectives that tell the student what is to be accomplished.

2. Knows how to write objectives at all levels of Bloom's taxonomy.

3. Writes assignments that will increase the rate of student success.

The purpose of a test is to determine if a student has mastered the objectives.

The Purpose of a Test

> **The major reason for giving a test is to find out if the students have accomplished the objectives of the assignment.**

Telling the students to read a chapter, story, or book involves no accomplishment. Nor does telling the students to read pages 222 to 235, complete a worksheet, or do a report on weather. (Refer to Chapter 22 for the difference between teaching for accomplishment and just telling students what to do.)

> **The students must have been given a list of criteria or objectives at the beginning of their assignment telling them what they are responsible for accomplishing.**

This chapter discusses the tests that are given at the end of an assignment to test for accomplishment of the objectives.

When You Assess, You Help

The purpose of a test is to assess a student's performance against learning criteria,
NOT to provide the teacher with the basis for a grade.

Schools must change from a testing culture to an assessment culture.

When you test for grading purposes, you are labeling a student. When you assess for accomplishment, you are helping the student achieve success.

When you have measurements, you have performance.

When you have no measurements, you have excuses.

—Peter Drucker

When to Write a Test

> **Both the assignment and the test are to be written concomitantly at the beginning of the assignment.**

The reason the assignment and the test must be written at the same time is that they are related and must correlate with each other. Tests are to be used to monitor and assess learning. Tests are not to be used for teacher coverage of materials. **Tests are to be used to determine if the student has accomplished the stated objectives or learning criteria.**

> **These are not valid reasons for writing tests:**
>
> ✔ Passage of time
> ✔ Material covered
> ✔ Need for points on a curve
> ✔ Period to kill

Passage of Time. Learning has nothing to do with a time interval, such as the length of a grading period, the due date for deficiency notices, or the fact that two weeks have passed, "so it's time for a test." If grades are needed for report cards, structure the assignments, not the test, to fall within the grading period.

Material Covered. Tests should not be written simply because "enough material has been covered." Your criteria, not volume of material, should determine when to test.

Stop Covering and Start Accomplishing

One of the most misused and useless phrases in education is "I have so much to cover. How am I going to finish it by the end of the year?" Notice that the word I is used twice and the word student is never used.

> **Tests are given for the students' sake, not the teacher's sake.**

Getting the student to learn is the priority of the teacher. Teaching is not "coverage" because coverage has nothing to do with learning. Why? Because the students do not know what the teacher wants. Worse yet, the teacher probably does not know what he or she wants the students to know.

Learning has nothing to do with what the teacher covers. **Learning has to do with what the student is able to accomplish. Learning occurs only when the students demonstrate accomplishment.**

Need for Points on a Curve. It is a mistake to state arbitrarily, "I want each test to be worth 50 points so that I will have a sufficient point spread to grade the class on a curve." The purpose of a test is not to compare one student to another. Tests are used to help the teacher determine what an individual student needs to learn, not to see who is smarter or dumber than someone else.

Period to Kill. The number of questions on a test is not to be determined by the length of the class period. The length of a test is determined by the number and complexity of the objectives you are testing.

Caution!

Regardless of the method used, grading and reporting remain inherently subjective. Teachers' perceptions of students' behavior can significantly influence their judgments of scholastic performance.

What We Know About Grades

Here are some things research has revealed about grades:

- *Grading and reporting aren't essential to instruction.* Grades are not related to teaching or learning well. Checking with regular and specific feedback on learning progress is essential.

- *Grades have some value as rewards but no value as punishments.* Teachers should never use grades as a weapon as this has no educational value and, in the long run, adversely affects student-teacher relationships.

- *Grading and reporting should always be done in reference to learning criteria, never on the curve.* Grading on the curve pits students against one another and converts learning into a game of winners and losers—with most students falling into the latter category.

—Thomas R. Guskey (ed.)
Communicating Student Learning:
1996 Yearbook of the Association for
Supervision and Curriculum Development.
Alexandria, Va.: Association for Supervision and Curriculum Development.

Show Examples of Your First Assignment and Test

One of the most frightening times for students is when the first assignment is due or when the first test is to be taken. This is because the ineffective teacher never posts examples of what an ideal assignment or a typical test looks like. Students are lost because there are no models or examples. They find out what should have been done or what should have been studied after the fact, and many students are so disillusioned after an initial failure that they do not try again.

The following are ineffective instructions for assignments:

> *Complete the worksheet.*
> *Answer all the questions at the end of the chapter.*
> *Write a report on Amelia Earhart.*
> *Do all the problems on page 57.*
> *Write a summary of the chapter.*

The following are ineffective instructions for tests:

> *The test will cover everything since the last test.*
> *The test will cover everything we've covered this week.*
> *There will be some multiple-choice questions, some true-false,*
> *   and maybe some fill-ins.*
> *The test will be worth about 50 points.*

The effective teacher practices these techniques for assignments and tests:

- **POSTS** many good examples of past assignments and tests so that the students can see what they are to do and what the tests look like.

- **EXPLAINS** how a finished assignment should appear and how the test questions are correlated to the criteria on the assignment.

Not only do the students see excellent models, but by your encouragement, they recognize positive expectations on your part that everyone can achieve perfection.

Comments, Good or Bad, Don't Make the Grade

Grades are only as good as the assessment system from which they are drawn. Grades are clear if clear standards and criteria are used. Narrative comments don't change this fact.

— Grant Wiggins
"Toward Better Report Cards."
(October 1994).
Educational Leadership, p. 29.

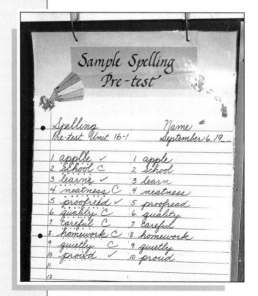

The effective teacher posts examples of tests and explains how they are constructed. This way the students know how to study and what to expect.

Reminder: *The terms objectives, criteria, learning criteria, and specifications are being used to mean the same thing.*

When to Give a Test

Call your assignments whatever you want to: lessons, chapters, units, or topics. To determine achievement for each assignment, you must administer a test.

✔ Each assignment must have a set of criteria or objectives that state the specifics of student achievement to be demonstrated.

✔ Each assignment must have a set of questions written for each criterion or objective.

✔ The test must be written at the beginning of the assignment when the objectives were written.

✔ The test must be given when the students finish the assignment.

How to Write a Test

Every question must correspond to an objective or learning criterion. That makes it very easy to write a test: All you do is write a set of questions for each of the objectives or learning criteria.

> **The objectives govern what questions and how many questions are to be written for a test.**

Step 1. **The basis of every test is the objectives for each assignment.** Have these available as you write the test.

Step 2. Look at the first objective. Write a set of questions for the objective. Avoid writing only one question, because if the student guesses at the answer, you will not know if the student has mastered the objective.

Learning Must Be Crystal Clear

To maximize learning and minimize disruptions, students must understand clearly what is expected of them. They need to know four things:

1. What they are to learn

2. How they are to learn it

3. How they are to demonstrate what they have learned

4. How the quality of their learning will be evaluated

—Lorin Anderson
Timepiece: Extending and Enhancing Learning Time.
(1993). Reston, Va.: National Association of Secondary School Principals.

Two Examples

Objective:

List the steps of the
scientific method.

Test Question:

Which of the following are steps of the
scientific method?

   A. observe, experiment, hypothesize
   B. experiment, study, conclude
   C. hypothesize, think, observe
   D. collect data, state principles,
       draw conclusions

Objective:

Change words ending
in *y* to plural form.

Test:

   pony
   battery
   key
   party
   decoy
   sky
   enemy
   play

**Objectives, Criteria,
Specifications Govern**

1. What students turn in
   for homework

2. How the teacher writes
   the test

Step 3. Use any type of question. The questions do not even have to be on a
written test. The questions can be of the oral or physical type whereby
the teacher asks the student to perform a skill or produce a finished
product.

Step 4. Repeat Steps 1 to 3 for each of the remaining objectives. When you
have written a set of questions for each objective, you have finished
writing the test.

On the next page is an example of a test that might have been written for a chapter
or lesson on OBSERVATION. It has four key parts:

1. Concept
2. Objectives
3. Questions
4. Remediation

This is an example only. Ignore the subject and focus on how the objectives and test questions correlate. Apply the example to your own subject matter.

1. **Concept.** This is the key idea or major point of the lesson.

2. **Objectives.** These are the tasks the student is responsible for accomplishing.

3. **Questions.** Each question corresponds to one of the objectives. Note the parentheses to the left of each question. The first number shows which objective the question corresponds to.

4. **Remediation.** Look at the parentheses again. The second number indicates the part of the textbook in which the answer to the question may be found. (The next section, "The Test as a Corrective Tool," explains how to use this information to help the student study for mastery of the objective.)

Assignment: **Observation**

Lesson Concept:

Observing, or paying attention, is an important step in the scientific method.

Lesson Objectives:

1. Define all the vocabulary words.

2. Explain the importance in your life of studying biology.

3. List the steps of the scientific method.

4. State when and in what order the steps of the scientific method are applied.

5. Explain why the scientific method is useful in daily life.

6. Give reasons why paying attention is important in life.

Lesson Test:

1. Biology is the study of
   (1-1A)
   A. animals
   B. plants
   C. living things
   D. humans

2. Science is
   (1-1B)
   A. the study of biology.
   B. a method of thinking.
   C. paying attention.
   D. making observations.

3. Studying biology may be important to you because
   (2-1B)
   A. you may become a doctor.
   B. you will learn about plants.
   C. you will find out what your body and your environment are trying to tell you.
   D. you will find out about animals.

4. Biology is important to you because
   (2-1A)
   A. you can learn about chemistry.
   B. you can explain birth defects.
   C. plants and animals are important to study.
   D. life is the most precious resource on earth.

5. The first step in the scientific method is to
   (3-1B)
   A. state the problem.
   B. collect data.
   C. conduct the experiment.
   D. make observations.

6. The following are some steps of the scientific method:
   (3-1B)
   A. observe, experiment, hypothesize
   B. experiment, conclude, study
   C. hypothesize, think, observe
   D. collect data, state principles, draw conclusions.

7. The steps of the scientific method can be
   (4-1A)
   A. used only with a scientific problem.
   B. used at any time and in any order.
   C. used only in the proper order.
   D. used after much data has been recorded.

---

8. The scientific method can be used
   (4-1B)
   A. when you make observations.
   B. when you experiment and collect data.
   C. when you state a conclusion.
   D. to accomplish all of the above.

9. The scientific method is used in daily life to
   (5-1B)
   A. solve problems.
   B. make observations.
   C. make discoveries about the world.
   D. do all of the above.

10. Observations can be used in daily life to
    (5-IC)
    A. help you stay alive.
    B. define science.
    C. explain the word biology.
    D. list the rules of the scientific method.

11. In the business world, your boss will want you to
    (6-IC)
    A. conduct experiments.
    B. talk about science.
    C. pay attention.
    D. write about science.

12. When you don't feel well, your body is telling you
    (6-IC)
    A. to go to the hospital.
    B. to work harder.
    C. to pay attention.
    D. to be careful.

13. Paying attention is a valuable life skill. It can help you to
    (1-Key Idea)
    A. memorize the scientific method.
    B. appreciate life.
    C. find a job.
    D. solve problems and make decisions.

14. Paying attention is an important step in
    (1-Key Idea)
    A. the scientific method.
    B. the study of biology.
    C. the study of science.
    D. causing problems.

The test you have just constructed in Step 4 is a **criterion-referenced test**. The kind of test most teachers unknowingly write are **norm-referenced tests**. There is a major difference in the two types of tests:

✔ **A criterion-referenced test** is a test in which each question is written to a prestated criterion. Since the students know what criteria they are responsible for, a percentage grade system should be used. The only person a student competes against in a criterion-referenced test is the student himself or herself. The student knows, for instance, that you have set your standard for an A at 93 percent.

✔ **A norm-referenced test** is a test used to determine placement on a normal distribution curve. Students are "graded on the curve" after a norm-referenced test. Norm-referenced tests are used to determine competitive ranking, such as for position on a team, entrance into a school, or placement on an organizational chart.

> **To teach for accomplishment, you use objectives and a criterion-referenced test.**

Norm-referenced tests have their place, as when you are trying to determine class rank or who will be on the first team. **When you are teaching a lesson, however, you are not teaching for rank. You are teaching for accomplishment, and you want everyone to succeed.**

It's Simple to Record Your Grades

1. Using an alphabetical listing of students, assign each student a number, beginning with 1, in your grade book.

2. When new students join the class, add their names to the bottom of your roll, and assign them the next available number.

3. On all tests, papers, projects, and reports turned in during the school year, students must write their unique number.

4. For consistency, choose one place on papers where this number must be written as a class procedure and routine.

5. For multiple-choice, true-false, and fill-in answers, give your students an answer form so that all answers are in the same place.

6. After the papers are collected, ask a student to arrange the papers in numerical order.

7. Do not grade tests one at a time, while watching television and snacking. Spread the forms on a large table, perhaps 10 across, and correct the answers three to five questions at a time as you move across the forms.

8. Put the papers back in order ready to be recorded in your grade book. Then ask an aide or your spouse to record the grades for you.

You Already Know Before the Test Where Most of the Students Will Fall on a Curve

Benjamin Bloom noted the test scores of thousands of third graders and then followed them for several years. What Bloom found was that the scores of students in the third grade could be used to predict their scores in the eleventh grade with 80 percent accuracy or better. Achievement rank order is highly consistent.

When a teacher says, "I need points so that I can grade the class on a curve," this is not a valid reason for giving a test. According to Bloom, you already know where most of the students will fall on a curve.

When students come into a class, most students already know who will be in the fast or the slow reading group, who will do well and who will do poorly, and who the teacher will treat as a winner and who will be treated as a loser. This is not what education is for, to peg people in holes at an early age and remind them with a succession of bell-shaped curves that they are smart, average, or dumb.

A test should be used to do two things:

1. The TEACHER should use the results of each test item to remediate and correct for student mastery.

2. The STUDENTS should be graded on a percentage system. This way they are competing only against themselves to reach a level of achievement or success.

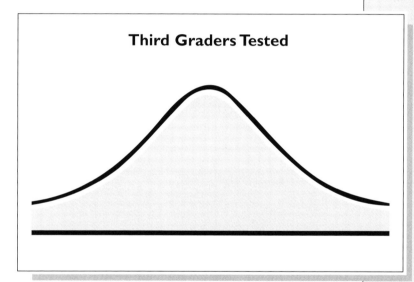

Third Graders Tested

The achievement rank order in the shaded area in the third grade is highly consistent with the achievement rank order in the seventh and eleventh grades.

A teacher does not grade on the curve. A student earns a grade based on percentage mastery of the criteria.

The role of a teacher is not to grade a student. The main role of the teacher is to help every student reach the highest possible level of achievement.

The Test as a Corrective Tool

Assume that you have returned from a visit to the doctor. Your friend or spouse asks you, "What happened at the doctor's today?"

You say, "The doctor is running a test on me."

This does not mean that the doctor is going to grade you on the curve. It means that the doctor is awaiting the results of the medical tests. When the results are studied, the doctor then determines what needs to be done to correct your illness.

A criterion-referenced test is to be used in the same way, as a diagnostic instrument. **A test tells you if the student needs corrective help.**

If you do not correct and remediate, learning gets worse and worse as the year progresses. It's no different from everything else in life. If you do not correct an illness or a bad habit, such as a cold, chain smoking, or drug abuse, your body or your life just gets worse and worse.

After some 10 chapters or units of study, many students have retained only 10 to 20 percent of what has been covered. The poor performance occurs because the ineffective teacher rolls through the school year, covering the chapters and giving tests because the teacher wants points to grade the class on a curve. After the test, the teacher blithely moves on to the next chapter without concern for students who do not comprehend the chapter.

If the student **MASTERS** an objective, do not assign more work. Give the student enrichment materials or ask the student to help another student. Enrichment work could include puzzles, games, software, or leisure reading.

If the student **DOES NOT MASTER** an objective, give the student remediation or corrective help.

Students who are lost or left behind have little chance of getting back on track.

If the Student Misses a Question

If a student should miss a question, give corrective action.** Assume that the student answered question 6 incorrectly on the test shown on page 235.

6. The following are some steps of the scientific method:

                A. observe, experiment, hypothesize
(3-lB)   B. experiment, conclude, study
                C. hypothesize, think, observe
                D. collect data, state principles, draw conclusions

Note the information in the parentheses. This gives you and the student information for remediation or correction.

3 - 1B

OBJECTIVE	REMEDIATION
Objective correlation: The first number tells you which objective the question correlates with. This tells you that the student has not learned or mastered objective 3.	**Answer source:** The second number, 1B, tells you that the correct answer may be found in Chapter 1, Section B of the textbook. Tell the student to review this section, or give the student another form of the same information because learning may be more effective in a different style.

Tests are to be given for the students' sake, not the teacher's sake. The purpose of a test is not to accumulate points to grade the students on a curve. **The purpose of a test is to help the teacher assess what the student has or has not learned.**

A Symbol of Failure

Most studies suggest that student performance does not improve when instructors grade more stringently and, conversely, that making it relatively easy to get a good grade does not lead students to do inferior work.

It is not a symbol of rigor to have grades fall into a "normal" distribution; rather, it is a symbol of failure—failure to teach well, to test well, and to have any influence at all on the intellectual lives of students.

—Alfie Kohn
    "Grading: The Issue Is
    Not How but Why."
    (October 1994).
    Educational Leadership,
    p. 41.

Do You Grade All Tests?

There are two kinds of criterion-referenced and norm-referenced tests, FORMATIVE TESTS and SUMMATIVE TESTS.

✔ **Formative tests** are like drills and practice tests. They are given during the formative, developmental, or teachable period when the student is in the process of mastering an objective. You may not want to grade these tests. These simply let you and the students know how well you are doing at teaching and they at learning the objective.

✔ **Summative tests** are given at the end of a unit when you want to sum up what the student has learned to determine a grade.

Formative and Summative Tests in Our Daily Lives	
Formative Tests	**Summative Tests**
Spring training	Opening day of the season
Dress rehearsal	Opening night
Training wheels on bike	Riding alone on two wheels
The bunny hill	The giant slalom
Driver's ed	Getting driver's license
Student teaching	The first day of school

Formative tests are used to determine what remediation is needed for a student to master the content, skill, or objective.

If it is determined that a student did not master a certain objective, a corrective activity must be given. A corrective activity is one that is given to the student in another form or with a different explanation so that the student can learn the objective through a different approach.

After the corrective activity is given, another formative test or a summative test should be given to determine mastery. **The test should be the same kind of test as first given, but the questions are asked in a different way.**

Some authorities, including Bloom, believe that you should test and retest until mastery is attained. Others believe that testing twice is sufficient because much of the content covered in class is spiral and the student will come around to the content again later on in the school year.[1]

---

[1] Guskey, Thomas R. (1996). *Implementing Mastery Learning* (2nd ed.). Belmont, Calif.: Wadsworth.

The Ineffective Teacher	The Effective Teacher
Covers chapters	Has students learn toward the criteria
Finds busywork for the students	Teaches to the criteria

In the classroom of an effective teacher, the students are focusing on the same criteria toward which the teacher is teaching. The preparation and presentation of all lesson materials, reading assignments, worksheets, multimedia, lectures, and activities must be done for one reason only—to teach to the criteria.

They Beg Me to Test Them

I decide exactly what it is I want my students to know or be able to do. And then I show them how to do it. We practice together. They practice on their own. And then I test them the same way we practice. As we begin each new unit, the first thing I do is tell my students what they will be learning and how they will show me that they have learned it—in other words, how they will be tested. This way we all know exactly what we are learning and how we will know when and if we have learned it. There are no secrets as to what is expected of them. When I do this, they all succeed.

In my class, test is not a bad word. It is something my students look forward to. It is their chance to show me what they have learned. They can't wait for their turn to be tested because after all the instruction and practice, the test is the easiest part—at least that's what my students tell me. They beg me to test them. They even stand in line waiting for their turn to show me what they have learned.

Julie Johnson

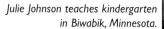

Julie Johnson teaches kindergarten in Biwabik, Minnesota.

The No-Mystery Approach

I know exactly what Julie Johnson is doing. I teach and assess for mastery in my high school class. When I begin a new unit or a topic, I project an outline of my unit on a screen, and it stays up there during the teaching of the unit. On the outline are the lesson criteria. My students see what lesson criteria they are responsible for learning.

I teach to the outline. The students are learning to the criteria, and I am teaching to the performance of the criteria, on the outline. When I finish the outline, I write the test. And every single question that I write on the test is written to the criteria on the outline.

You see, if you don't know what you want your students to learn, how can you write a test or assess to see if they've learned it? My student achievement results are awesome, but then why not? Both teacher and students know what is to be learned. All questions or skills are correlated with the known criteria. That's why my students call it the "no-mystery approach."

—A high school teacher

241

The purpose of formative testing followed by corrective activities is not unique to education:

✔ A doctor does a laboratory test, prescribes medicine, and then repeats this procedure until the patient is cured.

✔ A baseball player watches a video of his or her swing, makes corrections at bat, and repeats this procedure until the batting average improves.

✔ A chef tinkers with a recipe, making changes until a perfect sauce results.

The effective teacher tests and corrects, tests and corrects, because the teacher wants all the students to achieve.

The ineffective teacher delights in giving out only a few A's. Teachers do not give grades; students earn grades. Also, the ineffective teacher is satisfied with grading people on a curve and labeling half the class as "below average" or "failures."

The purpose of teaching is to help all people succeed, not to brand people as failures.

The purpose of teaching is to help all students succeed.

Through testing and correcting, the effective teacher is seeking 80 to 90 percent mastery for each assignment. If each assignment reaches 80 to 90 percent mastery, after some 10 chapters or units of studies, most students will have attained 80 to 90 percent mastery.

The students are successful and happy, and the teacher spends much of the time encouraging the students to do even better.

Your Students Can Outperform 98 Percent of the Regular Students

There are three basic methods of instruction.

1. **Conventional Instruction.** This is the ubiquitous textbook, lecture, worksheet, and test method. The chapters in the textbook constitute the assignment, and the tests are written to determine students' marks only.

2. **Mastery Learning.** The instruction is the same as in the conventional instruction method except the assignments are based on objectives the students are responsible for accomplishing and the tests are criterion-referenced tests. Many of the tests are formative tests used to determine what kind of corrective help the student needs before the summative test is given.

3. **Tutoring.** This is one-to-one instruction, frequently of the conventional form but preferably of the mastery learning form.

We all know that one-to-one tutoring is the most effective form of instruction, but this would be too costly, so Benjamin Bloom set out to find a comparable form of instruction that could be used in standard classroom group instruction. He found it! Here's what he discovered:

The average **TUTORED student outperformed 98 percent** of the students taught under a conventional form (within 2 standard deviations, if you are statistically inclined).

The average student taught under **MASTERY LEARNING outperformed 84 percent** of the students taught under a conventional form (1 standard deviation).

Based on what has been described about assignments (Chapter 22) and tests (Chapter 23), Steps 1 to 4 describe how a teacher could teach very effectively.

Step 1. Base each assignment on a set of objectives.

Step 2. Base each test on the objectives; that is, write criterion-referenced tests.

Step 3. Make the first test a formative test. You are teaching under a mastery learning format when you use Steps 1 to 3. You are now 84 percent more effective than the conventional teacher.

Step 4. After the tests are graded, you note, for instance, that the student has missed question 6.

Look at the information in the parentheses to the left of question 6. (See page 239 for an example.) With this information, determine what corrective activity you need to give to the student who has not mastered the objective. Help the student with the corrective activity, if necessary.

You have just changed from group instruction to individualized tutoring. You are now 98 percent more effective than the conventional teacher.

—Benjamin S. Bloom
"The Search for Methods of Group Instruction as Effective as One-to-One Tutoring." (May 1984). *Educational Leadership*, pp. 4–6.

Mastery Learning + Individual Tutoring = High Student Achievement

---

The Effective Teacher

1. Writes criterion-referenced tests.

2. Gives both formative and summative tests.

3. Uses formative tests to determine the appropriate corrective help.

4. Grades and encourages for percentage mastery, not on a curve.

The greater the time students work together and the greater the responsibilities students take for their work, the greater the learning.

COOPERATIVE LEARNING
is not so much learning to cooperate as it is cooperating to learn.

What Is Cooperative Learning?

Cooperative learning is a win-win situation.

Everyone wins: students, teachers, administrators, community, and humankind.

The students now know how to accomplish their assignments (Chapter 22), and they know how they will be tested (Chapter 23). What occurs between the assignment and the test is what teaching is all about. Effective teachers spend their educational career learning better techniques that will help students succeed in school and in life. This chapter will discuss one of those techniques: **COOPERATIVE LEARNING**.

Cooperative learning refers to a set of instructional techniques whereby students work in small, mixed-ability learning groups. The students in each group are responsible not only for the material being taught in class but also for helping their groupmates learn. In its simplest form, it looks like this:

✔ The teacher presents a lesson to the students.

✔ The student groups are given activities to master the objectives.

✔ The teacher teaches group and study strategies.

✔ The students work together to help one another master the objectives.

In cooperative groups, students help one another complete an activity the teacher has assigned. It is a structured situation. During the activity, the students clarify opinions, compare impressions, share solutions, and develop skills for leadership and teamwork. Cooperative learning is a win-win situation. Everyone wins: students, teachers, administrators, community, and humankind.

The reason cooperative learning is so successful is that the context of a work group is more important than the content of the group. If you have a group of people who care for and are committed to one another, they are going to achieve the goal of the activity much more quickly than if each were to attempt the task alone.

The parents ... see cooperative learning as a bonus because their children are getting the training in leadership, group decision making, and conflict management they'll need to be successful in later life.[1]

—Roger Johnson

Compete Only Against Yourself

If you must hang but two signs in your classroom, let the one shown to the right be one of them.

The message to your students is this:

- There is only one person in the world you need to compete against, and that is yourself.

- Strive each day to be the best person possible.

- Your mission in life is not to get ahead of other people; your mission is to get ahead of yourself.

- But while you are competing against yourself, you are expected to work with everyone else in this classroom cooperatively and respectfully.

- You are responsible not only for your own learning but for the learning of your groupmates as well.

---

[1]Johnson, Roger. (November 1987). "On Cooperation in Schools." *Educational Leadership,* p. 16.

How to Divide Your Class into Groups

The question is not how to divide the class but rather how quickly and effectively the class will divide itself when the students are asked to do so.

Some teachers have no problems dividing their students into groups. When told to do so, the students do it quickly and quietly. Other teachers have problems getting their students to divide into groups. When told to do so, the students whine, complain, and even refuse to work with other people. Why?

Effective grouping is dependent on two major factors:

1. The class climate

2. The explanation

The Class Climate

Quite simply, if the students dislike the class or the teacher or are not successful, grouping will be difficult. **It is important that all the determinants of successful student cooperation be in place before the class is divided into groups.**

The box to the left lists determining factors that may affect student cooperation. The number before the item indicates the chapter in this book where more information can be found.

When students do not cooperate, the ineffective teacher helplessly wonders, "What am I supposed to do?" and looks for a quick fix to resolve the crisis. There are no quick fixes in education. Implicit in the "Factors of Success" list on the previous page is the fact that **it is the teacher who is responsible for the success of the classroom.** The effective teacher knows this.

Telling the students to break up into groups is easy if the students are successful in class. It is the responsibility of the teacher to facilitate this success. In a successful classroom, the students respect the teacher's ability to move them quickly into groups for work.

✔ The teacher's job is to orchestrate all the classroom factors so that they function in harmony.

✔ The teacher is like the conductor of an orchestra, the captain of a ship, or the coach of a team.

✔ The teacher is a problem solver and a maker of decisions responsible for student success.

> **The effective teacher has knowledge and control of ALL THE FACTORS related to the effective classroom that influence student success.**

The brain does not need to be motivated any more than the heart needs to be motivated to pump blood.

—Leslie Hart

Motivation

Humans are born learners. Yet most classrooms demotivate students to learn.

The primary reason for demotivation is THREAT. Everybody BLOSSOMS and learns in a nonthreatening, cooperative, and invitational environment. (See Chapters 9 and 24.)
Is your classroom one of threats or blossoms?

THREATS: Teacher places the students in a helpless position with meaningless assignments.

BLOSSOMS: Students have the power to complete their assignments. (See Chapter 22.)

THREATS: Teacher has the power to give grades.

BLOSSOMS: Students have the power to earn grades based on prior knowledge of lesson criteria. (See Chapter 23.)

THREATS: Teacher can inflict punishment.

BLOSSOMS: Students can be taught how to be responsible. (See Chapter 20.)

THREATS: Teacher threatens students with a disorganized environment that the students cannot trust.

BLOSSOMS: Students feel secure in an organized environment that they can trust. (See Chapters 20 and 24.)

The Explanation

How quickly students move into groups depends on how explicitly the teacher explains how and why groups will be formed. "OK, divide into groups of four" is not how groups are set up. Vague directions like this are sure to provoke comments like these:

> *Can I work with Andrew?*
> *Do I have to work with Charlotte?*
> *How long do I have to stay in this group?*

There is no need to solicit class input on grouping because there will be no permanent groups in the class. Simply tell your students the following:

✔ **Number of People in a Group:** *The class will be divided into groups many times. Each time there is a need for a group, the size of the group will depend on the nature of the activity. Some activities may take two people; others may take four, eight, or whatever. Whatever is the number needed, that will be the number of people in the group. Therefore, there is no need to ask if you can work with any particular person because the groups are not fixed.*

✔ **Length of Time in a Group:** *Each time the class is divided into groups, the length of the group activity will depend on the nature of the activity. Some activities may take two minutes; others may take two days or two weeks.*

When the activity is finished, the group will be disbanded. Therefore, there is no need to ask how long you must be in a group. You will be in a group until the activity is finished.

Prepare yourself for the career world, where you will be working with many different combinations of people on committees, in groups, and on project teams for different lengths of time.

Cooperative learning is not something that will happen overnight. It occurs incrementally and requires time, patience, and constant reinforcement.

In the early grades, teachers should begin by teaching procedures and routines whereby the students move into groups quickly and quietly, speak softly, share the things they use, do their job, and take turns.

Younger children will ask the teacher when activity directions are not understood. Older students will often not ask because they do not like to admit that they do not know. Or if they do ask each other, they will frequently get a put-down response like, "What do you mean you don't understand? You stupid or what?" So rather than admit "stupidity," they withdraw and do not participate, misbehave to distract from their not understanding, or ask to work with someone who will not attack their dignity.

Older students inherently like to work together, so the problem is not student participation or interaction. It is poor teacher instructions. **When the directions, whether verbal or written, do not state what is to be done and what is to be accomplished, the students will start to act up.** The teacher must structure and write the activity for maximum understanding.

> **How quickly students move into groups depends on how explicitly the teacher explains the mechanics and responsibilities of the group assignment.**

They Knew the Names of Only Six Students

Here is part of a letter we received after presenting a workshop to a group of student teachers at a local college.

One of the student teachers tried something in her class to test out one of your ideas. She handed out a blank seating chart to her ninth-grade class and asked all the students to write in the seating chart, giving first and last names. Only about 80 percent of the kids seemed to have more than two-thirds of the names correct. Many of them only knew first names, and there were even a few students who could name only 6 or 8 students sitting right around them out of a class of 35.

The letter was dated May 20, so these student teachers were in a classroom that had been together for nine months. In addition, there were two teachers in the room, a cooperating teacher and a student teacher. Yet at the end of the year, few of the students really knew one another.

When you have a situation like this one, students are sure to misbehave, refuse to work cooperatively, and be reluctant to participate in group activities.

When students refuse to work together, the teacher may be to blame.

Who Is Placed in a Group?

Dividing the class into groups has nothing to do with the number in a group. The number of people in a group depends on the nature of the activity. What is important is who is placed in a group and why you want the grouping done accordingly.

> **Cooperative groups should be heterogeneous in terms of ability, sex, ethnicity, and other personal characteristics.**

Studies show that students are more positive about one another when they learn to work cooperatively, regardless of ability, ethnic background, or handicap.

Cooperative learning teaches the social skills necessary for success in a global economy.

✔ Students who have cooperative skills are more able to appreciate the viewpoint of others.

✔ They are more positive about taking part in controversy.

✔ They have better social skills.

✔ They have more positive expectations about working with others than students from competitive settings.

What you want for every student, especially for those with a lot of ability, is a cheering section helping and urging other students to work to maximum capacity. And you have the high, medium, and low kids in the same group, with the low kid cheering the high one on to boost the group score so that all can get a better grade. **The cooperative system encourages everyone, regardless of ability, background, or handicap, to work at top capacity.**

As students become more skilled in working together, they can practice more sophisticated skills, such as these:

✔ Asking for and giving help
✔ Showing that they are interested in what others are saying
✔ Talking about several solutions before choosing one
✔ Criticizing ideas, not people
✔ Looking for evidence before changing their mind
✔ Asking questions to try to understand another point of view

Over the years in school, learning experiences become richer and richer, and the students build a large repertoire of social skills that are essential in the global economy. The global economy is an economy of diversity. **It is only from working with a diversity of people that students will learn the skills needed in a world of diversity. These skills are learned when students are grouped heterogeneously.** There is nothing simple in such a process, but the results are worth the effort.

What About the Student Who Does Not Work?

> **The number of people in a group must equal the number of jobs in the group.**

Groups are to be divided by the number of jobs, not by the number of people. People do not go through life always working, say, in groups of four. The task always specifies the optimum number of people needed.

The reason some students do nothing or copy from other students is that they do not have specific tasks or jobs. Determine the number of students you need to accomplish an activity, divide the class accordingly, and then spell out the assignments.

For instance, in a group of four

Student 1 is responsible for getting the materials and returning them to the appropriate place when the day or period is over.

Student 2 is responsible for seeing that the steps of the activity are followed.

Student 3 is responsible for making observations, recording data, and taking minutes as the activity progresses.

Student 4 is responsible for overseeing the writing of the group report.

Being responsible does do not mean that the student does all the work. Rather it means that the student is in charge of getting others to help in the task. For instance, it may take several people to get all the materials, everyone to help clean up, several to make observations, and certainly everyone to contribute to the group report.

✔ The teacher may not want to assign who does what job. If no assignments are made, the students are to choose who does which job.

✔ If the students may choose who does which job, you may want to specify that they are not to do the same type of job as they did in the last activity.

✔ Have group procedures, responsibilities, and evaluation. (See the sample activity on page 262.)

What Are the Benefits and Results of Cooperative Learning?

Most of the research indicates that cooperative learning leads to higher achievement for all students.

The research on cooperative learning has the longest history in American social psychology. First done in 1897, a century of research has included hundreds of studies.

There is probably more evidence validating the use of cooperative learning than there is for any other aspect of education—more than for class size, lecturing, age grouping, reading readiness, departmentalizing, or the 50-minute period. And the research applies as much for teachers as it does for students.

These are some examples of the findings from research on cooperative learning:

✔ Many studies have shown positive effects for both high- and low-ability students, dispelling the myth that high achieving students will not progress if they interact with students of lesser ability.

✔ On retention tests, cooperative learners score at least as well as high achievers from competitive learning situations.

✔ Cooperative learners use higher-quality reasoning strategies, higher-level processing, and deeper thinking than isolated students.

The idea that people working together toward a common goal can accomplish more than people working by themselves is a well-established principle of social psychology.[2]

—Robert Slavin

What Determines an Individual's Success?

My daughter recently graduated from Michigan Technological College and was hired by IBM as a computer scientist in the company's "think tank" in Owego, New York.

She was immediately placed into a group and the group was assigned projects. The success of each individual (higher pay, promotions, etc.) was dependent on the success of the GROUP to a significant extent!

—Dick Kyro
Oak Park, Michigan

Self-Directed Work Teams

The effective teacher prepares students for the world. Ineffective teachers discipline their students, controlling their every action. Effective teachers teach their students how to be responsible to appropriate procedures—how to succeed in self-directed work teams.

---

[2]Slavin, Robert. (November 1987). "Cooperative Learning and the Cooperative School." *Educational Leadership*, p. 7.

✔ Cooperative learners develop the skills of leadership, communication, decision making, and conflict management they need for future success in school and in a career.

The NUMMI Story

When the General Motors plant in Fremont, California, closed down in 1982, it had the highest absenteeism and lowest productivity levels of any General Motors manufacturing facility.

It reopened in 1984 as the New United Motors Manufacturing, Inc. (NUMMI), a partnership between General Motors and Toyota. It is a United Auto Workers plant with 4,600 employees producing Geo Prizms, Toyota Corolla sedans, and Toyota Tacoma pickup trucks.

Its business style is vastly different from that of other factories:

- It is based on the team concept, emphasizing participation, sharing of ideas, and problem solving together.

- Teams of four to eight, under a team leader, are responsible for all the jobs in a given area on the production line.

- All team members learn all the jobs in a given team and rotate among them.

Today the NUMMI factory is among the most productive in North America and has placed among the top three plants for quality in 1994, 1995, and 1996 according to J. D. Power and Associates.

✔ Cooperative learners develop a sense of interdependence. Students learn to care about and become committed to others' success as well as their own. In a competitive classroom that lacks cooperative groups, students really have a stake in one another's failure. That includes making sure that the worse other students do, the better it is for them to get a higher grade. In an individualistic classroom, students have no stake in other students whatsoever. Each student works independently on his or her own agenda. What happens to others is irrelevant.

In cooperative groups, students have a vested interest in making sure that other people do well. Anything they can do to help their group or groupmates learn the material better, retain it longer, get a better grade on the test, or learn new skills benefits them all. They celebrate when other people learn.

✔ Cooperative learning produces committed relationships in which students really care about one another and provide assistance and help when needed. It promotes more positive peer relationships, better social skills, more social support, and, partly for that reason, higher self-esteem. Students like the class better, they're more interested in the subject and each other, and they're more self-disciplined.

✔ In cooperative learning, students take more responsibility for helping one another with assignments and problems. That alleviates some of the stress on the teacher to maintain order and to keep the students on task.

✔ Cooperative learning improves self-confidence for many students. Because the groupmates become responsible for one another's learning and have a vested interest in the others' success, all students tend to be more successful. Success builds self-confidence. By working together, the students find out that their ideas can be useful to others, and they become more self-confident.

How to Make Cooperative Learning Work

The Four Basic Elements Needed to Make Cooperative Learning Work

1. Positive interdependence
2. Social skills
3. Individual accountability
4. Group evaluation

1. **Positive Interdependence.** Interdependence refers to the relationships that individuals have to others' success in a group. **For cooperative learning to be successful, the students really have to believe that they are in it together and to care for one another's learning.**

In cooperative groups, each student has a responsibility to the team. Goals or tasks are structured so that the students concern themselves with the performance of all members of the group, not just their own performance. When students understand that they are part of an interdependent group, they usually find ways to work together for the benefit of all.

The Monsanto Story

Alvin K. Allison is a worker at the Monsanto Chemical Company in Greenwood, South Carolina. He leads a team of mechanics who divide the work and make key decisions themselves. There is no foreman peering over a worker's shoulder. The mechanics are involved in decision making and quality control.

"I knew 20 years ago that I could direct my own job," says Allison.

The result of cooperative work? Quality improvement and productivity is 47 percent higher than four years earlier.

—"Monsanto Is Teaching Old Workers New Tricks," (August 21, 1989). *Business Week*, p. 67.

2. **Social Skills.** The basis of cooperative learning is social skills that help students share leadership, communicate effectively, build trust, and manage conflict. Generally, the students do not come to the classroom with those skills; the skills must be defined clearly and taught in much the same way that academic subjects are taught.

   Lots of verbal face-to-face interaction, explaining, arguing, resolving of conflicts, elaborating, consensus forming, and summarizing will occur and should be encouraged.

3. **Individual Accountability.** Each member of the cooperative group is held accountable for the performance of all. It must be clear that every member of the group has to learn, that there's no free ride. No one can sit on the sidelines and let others do the work; everyone has to be in there, pulling equal weight.

   The teacher can stress accountability by calling on one groupmate at random to give the group's report at the end of a task. If the student can report the group's conclusions, procedures, or solutions, the group has been successful. If the student called on cannot report the group's results, the group, not the individual, suffers. Therefore, it becomes the group's responsibility, not the teacher's, to ensure everyone's participation.

4. **Group Evaluation.** Periodically, the groups must assess how well they are working together and how they could do better.

How to Structure a Cooperative Learning Activity

Structure your lessons for cooperative learning. Industry spends millions of dollars to find and train people to work cooperatively. The effective teacher takes time to teach and train students to work cooperatively.

How to Structure Lessons for Cooperative Learning

1. Specify the group **NAME**.
2. Specify the **SIZE** of the group.
3. State the **PURPOSE, MATERIALS,** and **STEPS** of the activity.
4. Teach the **PROCEDURES**.
5. Specify and teach the **COOPERATIVE SKILLS** needed.
6. Hold the individuals **ACCOUNTABLE** for the work of the group.
7. Teach ways for the students to **EVALUATE** how successfully they have worked together.

---

1. **Specify the Group Name.** Want something better than calling your groups teams, squads, or groups?

    Learning together is epitomized by the concept of a support group. There are support groups for people trying to lose weight, stop addictions, overcome fears, and learn parenting skills. There are support groups for single parents, senior citizens, abused children, battered wives, and war veterans. Power groups, or business support groups, exist to help such people as businesswomen to achieve leadership roles and secretaries to become executives.

    Consider calling the groups **support groups** and each member of the support group a **support buddy**.

    A support group is formed by people, with like needs and goals, who join together to care for and help one another solve problems and achieve success. Support groups in the classroom are formed for the same reason.

2. **Specify the Size of the Group.** The size of the group is a factor of how many jobs are needed to complete the activity. (See "What About the Student Who Does Not Work?" on page 252.)

3. **State the Purpose, Materials, and Steps of the Activity.** The students must be given an activity that is structured enough so that the students know what is to be done and how. (See the sample activity on page 262.)

4. **Teach the Procedures.** Here are four procedures for you to consider with your students. They should be posted, taught, modeled, rehearsed, and monitored. (See Chapter 20.)

   ✔ **You are responsible for your own job and the results of the group.** (In the working world, you are responsible for your own job and the results of the people you work with.)

   ✔ **If you have a question, ask your support buddies. Do not ask your teacher.** (In the working world, you do not raise your hand for help. You seek, ask, and research because you are expected to act on your own initiative.)

   ✔ **You must be willing to help if a support buddy asks you for help.** (In the working world, you are expected to apply teamwork skills.)

   ✔ **If no one can answer a question, agree on a consensus question and appoint one person to raise a hand for help from the teacher.** (In the working world, negotiating and reaching agreements are the keys to success.)

5. **Specify and Teach the Cooperative Skills Needed.** Teach, model, and monitor the group procedures for the sample activity on page 262.

6. **Hold the Individuals Accountable for the Work of the Team.**
The teacher acts as consultant to the group after setting the objectives, assignments, and procedures. Problems are turned back to the group for resolution. That aspect of cooperative learning is often difficult at first, but it is crucial to the success of cooperative learning in the classroom.

The support groups are to write reports cooperatively and give team presentations. The students are accountable for the quality of their group work and the results of their work.

The support group will get a group grade, and that grade will be each individual's grade, so it is important that each member of the group support the others' achievement efforts.

7. **Teach Ways for the Students to Evaluate How Successfully They Have Worked Together.** Tell your students to write down the group procedures. (See page 263.) After each procedure, state whether the support group followed the procedure most of the time, sometimes, or not at all.

For each procedure, have the support groups discuss how they can improve their cooperative skills. The procedures that truly need to be discussed are those that received a rating of "most of the time." By being aware of why they followed the procedures most of the time, they can review and apply the success of how they worked together to improving the procedures rated lower.

The Honda Story

Honda has a factory in Marysville, Ohio. The company employs more than 10,000 "associates" (not workers).

The associates work in groups. The procedure is for each group to submit complaints and suggestions to management at the end of each shift. In the United States, management generally does not want to hear about problems, and workers do not want to get involved with problems.

The Honda procedure requires answers to three questions:

1. What was the problem?
2. What did you do about the problem?
3. What is your suggestion for long-term solution of the problem?

Honda works on quality through empowering workers, within groups, to solve problems, to search for ways of improvement so that the group can achieve excellence.

Overall, the average Japanese employee submits 24 suggestions a year, compared with 0.14 per U.S. worker (that's the same as $24 vs. 14 cents, no comparison in a competitive environment).

—Thomas Peters
San Antonio Light,
February 7, 1989.

The Benefits of a Structured Cooperative Activity

✔ Peer pressure severely limits achievement in many schools. Students who do not do well scorn those who do well, and these students join together, socially, to limit each other's success. In cooperative classrooms, by contrast, **students encourage their teammates to do well because they all benefit.**

✔ **All members of the group share leadership responsibilities.** Each member has a job to do, and the group has no formal leader.

✔ In their groups, **the students focus on both the academic assignments and the skills they need to work together.** They review the success of their assignment and their cooperation, and they try to improve both.

✔ The teacher benefits from cooperative learning because **the students take more responsibility for classroom management.** Hands-on participation requires that the students interact with the materials, and cooperative learning is structured so that the students, not the teacher, manage the materials.

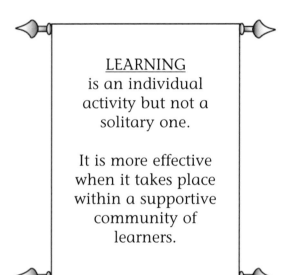

LEARNING
is an individual
activity but not a
solitary one.

It is more effective
when it takes place
within a supportive
community of
learners.

**The greater the time students work together
and the greater the responsibilities
students take for their work,
the greater the learning.**

Sample Activity

In this activity you will be working in support groups of four. Your teacher will choose the members of the **support group**. The reason you work in support groups is because when you discuss new ideas with your classmates, you understand the ideas better.

Sometimes you will work with your friends, and sometimes not. No matter who your support buddies are, your responsibility is to help one another understand and complete the activity. This is why you are called **support buddies**.

Your teacher will explain what jobs need to be done. Either the teacher will choose or you will be asked to choose who does which job.

You need to work together and talk about your assignment so that each member of the support group understands what your group has done and why. When it is time for your support group to report to the class, your teacher will call on only one member of your group. That member will explain the support group's results, so make sure that you all know what is happening before you get called on. When your support group looks good, you look good!

How Do Propellers Work?

Background

Some airplanes and helicopters fly because of propellers. As the shape and pitch (angle) of the blade change, different results are obtained.

Problem

How many different ways can you design a propeller blade?

How does each design perform?

What is your evaluation of each design?

Support Group Jobs

Equipment Manager: Your job is to obtain the materials needed for the activity and to make sure that they are returned to the appropriate place at the end of the designated time.

Facilitator: Your job is to make sure that the group is following each step of the activity carefully and correctly.

Recorder: Your job is to observe, take minutes, and record data. You need to see that the support group has the proper forms to record the results of the activity as they occur.

Reporter: Your job is to coordinate the writing of the group report.

Materials

Binder paper, scissors, and a paper clip

This is an example of a cooperative learning activity. Substitute your own activity. Begin by rewriting sections: background, problem, materials, and activity steps. Apply the example to your own subject matter.

Activity Steps

1. Cut a piece of binder paper across its width into 2-inch strips.

2. Cut and fold the paper as shown. (Fig. 1)

3. Hold and release the paper as shown. (Fig. 2)

4. Try different versions of the helicopter.

5. Observe and record each result.

Support Group Procedures

Move into your groups quickly and quietly.

Stay with your group in your area.

Do your job.

Help each other.

Follow the Activity Steps listed above.

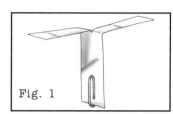

Fig. 1

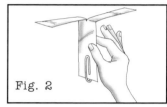

Fig. 2

Support Group Responsibilities

1. The **facilitator** needs to make sure that everyone has read and discussed the activity before beginning to work. Do not start until everyone knows the purpose of the activity, what needs to be done (Activity Steps), and what everyone needs to do (Support Group Procedures and Responsibilities).

2. The **equipment manager** needs to see that the materials are collected.

3. The **recorder** needs to see that a record page is set up on which to record what is to be observed. This can be a form for taking minutes, a table for recording numbers, or a chart for writing observations. Do not start until the record page has been set up.

4. The **facilitator** takes the group through the activity steps, as a moderator would take a meeting through its agenda.

5. At all times the members of the **support group** must cooperatively and respectfully help each other by following the Activity Steps and the Support Group Procedures.

6. The **support group** must help the recorder record the results of the activity.

7. The **reporter** coordinates the writing of the group. Make sure that everyone in the support group can explain the activity: its purpose, steps, and results.

When everyone can explain the purpose and results of the activity, all the members of the group should sign their name to the group report.

Thank You

Applying Cooperative Learning to Teachers and Administrators

Cooperation is especially important for teachers because much of what they learn is procedural. This is similar to learning how to play bridge or how to perform surgery. Procedural learning differs from the simple learning of facts and acquiring knowledge. It relies heavily on receiving feedback about performance and modifying one's implementation until errors are eliminated.

Cooperation must start at the classroom level because that determines the organizational climate in the school. There are teachers who spend five to seven hours a day advocating a competitive, individualistic approach, telling students:

"Do your own work."   "Don't care about each other."
"Don't talk to your neighbors."   "Just try to better yourself."
"Don't share; don't help."   "Think for yourself."

These are the same values these teachers will exhibit in their relationships with students, administrators, and colleagues.

Conversely, there are teachers who spend five to seven hours a day saying:

"Help each other."   "Put your minds together.
"Share."   "Discuss the material in groups."
"Work together."   "You're responsible not only for your
"Explain things to each other."   own learning but for the learning of
"Figure it out together."   your support buddies as well."

Based on these values, these teachers will look to their colleagues as potential cooperators. What you want are teachers supporting one another so that if a teacher has a particular strength or plans a new unit or comes in with new materials, the other teachers will provide support and encouragement.

Staff-Development Support Groups

Form staff-development support groups to help you implement success. Collegial support groups offer a formal structure for learning from colleagues. This is called **collegial learning**. Consisting of small groups of teachers and perhaps administrators, the goal of the support group is to improve one another's professional competence and ensure the professional growth of all.

Tangible and Measurable Results

Three characteristics exemplify continuous school improvement and serve as the foundations for school results:

1. Working as a productive team

2. Setting clear and measurable goals

3. Regularly collecting and analyzing performance data

—Mike Schmoker
Results: The Key to Continuous School Improvement. (1996). Alexandria, Va.: Association for Supervision and Curriculum Development.

The Cooperative School

Whatever happens in the classroom with students will hold true at the building level with teachers. **The most effective schools are those where there is a cooperative staff that pulls together.**

School A—for Apathetic
- Teachers do not discuss their practice of teaching with one another, nor do they help one another improve their skills.
- Teachers are quick to point out areas for improvement to their students but pay no attention to evaluations that point out areas for their own improvement.
- When new programs or ideas are suggested, teachers respond with apathy and indifference.
- The faculty seldom unites around any effort to improve the school.

School C—for Cooperative
- Teachers are working toward a common goal of school improvement.
- Teachers observe one another's teaching and strive to help one another improve.
- Experienced teachers regularly share with new colleagues the practices that have worked effectively for them.
- The principal provides the support that teachers need to work together, and the teachers look to one another as resources for solving problems.
- The teachers are proud to take part in decision making.

—Inspired by Stuart C. Smith
"The Collaborative School."
(November 1987). *Educational Leadership,* p. 4.

Members of collegial support groups serve many functions:

✔ They discuss new teaching practices and problems connected with their implementation.

✔ Together they plan, design, prepare, and evaluate curriculum materials.

✔ They observe one another's teaching and offer helpful feedback.

The support groups consist of dedicated, caring, and knowledgeable colleagues willing to share techniques for beginning the first days of school and continued teaching in the most effective ways.

The quality of education is largely determined by what happens at the school site. Cooperation is needed at the professional level from everyone at the school site.

> **Education is a helping profession. There are professionals out there willing to help. Help each other, and we all profit.**

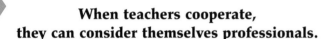

> **When teachers cooperate, they can consider themselves professionals.**

Doctors are professionals because they invite their colleagues to evaluate their techniques. When they develop a new surgical technique, for example, colleagues are invited to watch and provide suggestions for improvement.

✔ If support groups of teachers and administrators at schools can operate in this way, then, and only then, can teachers be called professionals.

✔ For educators to be professionals, we must learn and grow together and ON OUR OWN without constant prodding from the administration or the public. When that happens, collegial learning is taking place.

A support group for collegial learning.

266

Why Some Schools Succeed

The Rand Corporation conducted a study in 1990 comparing three high schools in the same urban area. All of the students were the same, at-risk, low-income, minority students, so the students were not the variable. The variable was the high school the students attended. (The Ford Foundation paid the tuition for some of the students to attend the Catholic high school used in the study.) Here are the results:

Traditional high school: 55 percent graduated
Magnet high school: 66 percent graduated
Catholic high school: 82 percent graduated

Traditional high school: 33 percent took the SAT
Magnet high school: 48 percent took the SAT
Catholic high school: 85 percent took the SAT (these students scored the highest on the SAT)

The factors that caused the magnet high school and Catholic high school to succeed: The school formed a kind of unified family that had a shared vision and focused on meeting that vision and fulfilling its mission.

The factor that caused the traditional high school to fail: It housed a bunch of loose cannons. Administrators, counselors, librarians, and teachers were all in their own rooms doing their own thing. They had no sense of family, no vision, no impetus to improve, and no purpose other than to put in time and to do a job.

When Teachers Work Together, Students Benefit

A 1992 study at Stanford University based on 16 schools in seven districts in California and Michigan found that the most effective teachers had hooked up with a network of like-minded colleagues who addressed problems and found solutions together.

As an example, the study cites the case of two high schools in the same California district. Both served roughly the same student population, and both lived under the same rules and regulations. One of the schools, however, had high student failure and dropout rates, while the other had among the highest test scores in the state and sent 80 percent of its students to college.

The difference was reflected in the professional characteristics of the schools. In the school with high failure rates, teachers complained frequently, came to work late, left early, and held meetings in front of the school mailboxes, if at all.

By contrast, the successful school held frequent schoolwide meetings to solve problems together and, as a result, developed unusual solutions.

—Milbrey McLaughlin and Joan Talbert
Contexts that Matter for Teaching and Learning.
(March 1993). Stanford, Calif.: Stanford University.

Successful schools are distinguished from unsuccessful schools by the frequency and extent to which teachers learn **together,** plan **together,** test ideas **together,** discuss projects **together,** reflect **together,** work things out **together**—all solely in the interest of developing students to their fullest potential.

The Effective Teacher

1. Applies all the factors discussed in Chapters 1 to 23 to set a cooperative class climate.

2. Writes structured cooperative activities.

3. Works cooperatively and shares with colleagues.

4. Helps establish and enhance the school culture.

UNIT E

Future Understandings —
The Professional

The teacher who constantly
learns and grows
becomes a professional educator.

Future Understandings — The Professional

*The teacher who constantly learns and grows
becomes a professional educator.*

Unit E is correlated with **Part 7: The Professional Educator**
in the video series *The Effective Teacher*.

KEY IDEA

How a person chooses to behave will greatly determine the quality of that person's life.

I CAN HAVE IT ALL!

- CAREER
- HAPPINESS
☆ SUCCESS
- ACHIEVEMENT
- POPULARITY
- MONEY
- GOOD HEALTH
- A JOB
- FREEDOM FROM STRESS
☆ REPUTATION AS A PROFESSIONAL

You can have anything you want from life.

What Do You Want from Life?

> **You can have anything you want from life.**

The first 24 chapters contain information to help you begin school successfully. Turn back to these pages frequently to help you during your daily work. This chapter and the next are written to help you with the rest of your life. **Chapters 25 and 26 are designed to help you prepare for your career as a professional educator.** You have choices:

✔ You can be a worker or a leader.

✔ You can have a job or a career.

✔ You can become a teacher or an educator.

Depending on your choices, you can have anything you want from life. What do you want?

Are You a Worker or a Leader?

There are two kinds of people: **WORKERS** and **LEADERS**. They each have their distinctive characteristics, and these characteristics will give a person certain results in life. **You can predict your life as a teacher 10, 20, even 30 years from now on the basis of these characteristics.**

Worker

> ### The two things that matter the most to a worker are time and money.

Workers are preoccupied with time for breaks, holidays, overtime, and work hours. They will do everything to negotiate for longer breaks and shorter work hours. There are teachers and teacher organizations who will negotiate away in-service meetings, negotiate the number of minutes allotted to in-service, or negotiate to have in-service on a Friday before a three-day weekend. Time and money, not learning or growing, are the primary concerns of a worker.

A worker will agree to put in more hours or agree to in-servicing if there is additional pay or some form of perk.

Money and other tangible rewards are understood by workers.

Workers have jobs and can earn more money by putting in more time, as teachers who moonlight do, or they can increase their skills to be placed in a higher job category.

> ### Workers Have No Future

Workers who do not increase their skills run the risk of being the first to be laid off or fired because they have failed to stay abreast of changing job skills in a technological society. Workers have no future. Similarly, there is no future for a teacher who knows how to teach but one subject, one way; and that one way may be suspect.

Workers are concerned about time and money.

You Are Paid for Your Skills

In today's global economy, you are paid well for your skills, not because you have a college degree. For an office worker position listed in the classified ads, the applicant was asked to provide evidence of the following skills:

Strong analytical and organizational skills

Scheduling and staffing skills

Word processing and spreadsheet skills

Creating effective presentation materials

Phone skills

Skill in working on own

→ *Skill in a professional, team-oriented environment*

Outstanding verbal, interpersonal, writing, and organizational skills

Charm, a sense of humor, excellent judgment, and grace under pressure

Ability to react quickly with sound judgment

→ *Initiative, mature judgment, discretion, independence, focused skills*

The more skills you possess, the greater your pay will be and the better your future. Not only do effective teachers have the skills listed here, but they also acquire additional skills. (A chart of effective teacher skills appears on page 297.)

Teaching is used by many teachers as a way to earn money to pay the bills and support the family. Their commitment to teaching stops at the dismissal bell, with no time and little desire to partake of growth and learning opportunities.

In reality, the worker-teacher has already been fired from within the system. These are the teachers who retired in their own classrooms and have fired themselves from life. These are the teachers to whom early retirement is offered or who are transferred from school to school or job to job so that they will do the least amount of damage or at least spread the damage evenly and as thinly as possible throughout the district. These are the teachers the parents have fired because they complain long and hard to have their children placed with another teacher elsewhere.

The worker profile is not unique to teachers in education. There are many worker-administrators. It is unfortunately too common to see worker-administrators sitting out in the hall or in the back row while the teachers are attending in-service, too many administrators whose attitude is "I'll sit by the door so that I can leave after the meeting gets started."

Leader

The two major concerns of a leader are enhancement and cooperation.

Like workers, leaders have a job and put in time to earn money. But leaders are willing to put in additional time to improve themselves, the people they work with, and the environment in which they work. As a result, leaders also make more money. They make more money not because they put in more time on the job but because they put in more time to improve their skills and enhance their life. **Life rewards the competent, not the clock watchers.**

Leaders also have the ability to work with other people and can lead or get other people to work cooperatively and productively. **Anyone who can work cooperatively and productively is always rewarded to a greater extent.**

Leaders have careers. People who are constantly enhancing their work lives have careers rather than jobs.

> **Whereas a job is something a person does specifically, a career is what a person pursues as a lifetime.**

A person who has a career can do a variety of jobs because through constant learning and growing, a person acquires many talents and skills.

Anyone who has talents and skills is valuable as a thinker, a problem solver, and a decision maker. These people, of course, are more valuable to a community, school, or organization and are rewarded for their contributions.

Leaders are professionals. A person who has a career, who has many talents and skills, who is a thinker, a problem solver, and a decision maker is a professional. **The professional teacher recognizes that the classroom is a complex environment; the most successful teacher is the one who is capable of making decisions and solving problems in that environment.**

People with careers can do many jobs and, should they lose a job, can move to another job because they are qualified to do several things. Therefore, leaders are not concerned with time and money; they have their mind set on growing and working cooperatively with others.

Educational leaders have a variety of careers from which to choose.

A WORKER is concerned with **time** and **money**.
A LEADER is concerned with **enhancement** and **cooperation**.

A WORKER has a **job**.
A LEADER has a **career**.

A WORKER is hired to **do a job**.
A LEADER is hired to **think, make decisions**, and **solve problems**.

A WORKER is an hourly **laborer** with a skill.
A LEADER is a **professional** with talent.

A WORKER **can** be fired from a job.
A LEADER **cannot** be fired from a career.

A WORKER **cannot** find another job because of training in only one job.
A LEADER **can** always find another job because he or she possesses versatile skills.

A WORKER has **no future** in having a job.
A LEADER has **a great future** because he or she is oriented toward a career.

Job Titles Do Not Reflect Worker or Leader Status

A teacher wrote:

New teachers are not the only beneficiaries of induction programs. The involvement of the education association with the administration has a positive impact on students, colleagues, and administrators. We model teamwork as a way of achieving mutually desired goals.

— Mary Ecker, Executive Board
Port Huron Education Association,
Michigan

An executive said:

The in-service went five minutes over. You owe me five minutes.

— President
Local education association,
New Jersey

More Characteristics of Workers and Leaders

You Can Recognize Workers

You see them in the morning. They're tired.

They manage by crisis.

They are full of excuses.

They dress like laborers.

You see them at lunch. They're tired.

They sit at the back of meetings.

They complain about why they have to be in-serviced.

They complain about other people, places, and things.

You see them after school. They're tired.

They blame other people, places, and things.

They are frequently late.

They chitchat.

You see them at a meeting. They're tired.

They are always asking, "What am I supposed to do?"

They do not subscribe to or read journals.

They do not belong to professional organizations.

They seldom, if ever, go to conferences and even complain about district in-service meetings.

They speak negatively of their obligations, as in "Do I have to do this?" and "I'm only doing this because I've got to."

They talk about not getting respect.

They decide to do what others do.

They worry about their jobs and their job conditions.

They are victims.

They are unwilling to learn or turn elsewhere for help.

You see them while shopping. They're tired.

Their outlook on life is "Another day, another dollar."

You Can Recognize Leaders

You see them in the morning. They're helping someone.

They manage by leadership.

They have plans, goals, and vision.

They dress for success.

You see them at lunch. They're on their way to a meeting.

They sit where they can learn.

They enjoy being part of a meeting.

They compliment people, places, and things.

You see them after school. They're waiting for a parent.

They work cooperatively with people, places, and things.

They are prompt and have their materials ready.

They pay attention.

You see them at a meeting. They have a report ready.

They are able to make decisions and help solve problems.

They subscribe to and read the professional literature.

They belong to professional organizations.

They attend and may even contribute academically at conferences.

They speak enthusiastically about their options, as in "I want to go to the conference" and "It is my choice to do a workshop and share with others at a meeting."

Their success earns them respect.

They choose to do what they have determined is best.

They have a career and have options to choose from.

They have power and are in control.

They are knowledgeable and can turn elsewhere for help.

You see them while shopping. They're smiling!

Their outlook on life is "You strive to be a peak performer and pursue life, love, and happiness."

Will You Decide or Will You Choose?

> **What counts is not the number of hours you put in but how much you put into those hours.**

Now that you just read and know the difference between a worker and a leader, which will you be?

Will you DECIDE to be a WORKER?

or

Will you CHOOSE to be a LEADER?

If I Didn't Read This, I'd Go Broke

Al Sisson ran the corner service station and was my mechanic for over 20 years. He was outspoken and often brusque but unafraid to do what he believed was right. He was both admired and disliked for these very attributes. He was good at fixing cars and honest to boot.

I got some insight into why he was so good when I was in his waiting room one day. There was a melange of automotive magazines, mostly filled with ads from automotive parts houses, strewn on a table.

I said to Al, "You read this stuff?"

He said, in his brusque voice, "I wish they would stop sending me that garbage." But then he looked at me over his glasses and said authoritatively, like a mentor who knew what was right, "You bet I read it. If I didn't, I'd go broke!"

Al Sisson was a professional. He enhanced his own life without anyone telling him what he had to do.

When you walk into teachers' homes, look at the end tables or the coffee table. More often than not, not a single education magazine or journal will be in sight. Ask them to produce one from their home office, and they cannot. Ask them the last time they read *Educational Leadership*, *Teacher*, or some similar journal, and you get a look that seems to say, "What are they? I've never heard of them."

In many a teacher's lounge you will find duplicating machines, vending machines, a bulletin board of notices, and teacher mailboxes but not a single professional journal.

This is why lots of teachers are already bankrupt and the Al Sissons are not. Knowledge is power.

Decide

Look at the two parts of the word *decide.* The prefix, *de-*, means "off" or "away," as in *defeat, destroy, denigrate,* and *deemphasize.* It is a negative prefix. The stem, *cide,* means "cut" or "kill," as in *suicide, pesticide, insecticide,* and *herbicide.* To *decide* is thus to "cut away" or "kill off"—not a very happy activity.

Many people make decisions by deciding. Have you ever dined with someone at a restaurant who cannot select what to order from a menu? While everyone at the table waits for this person to place an order, someone impatiently barks out, "How long does it take you to decide? When will you decide? Can't you decide?"

And does the person order? No. Instead the person asks the others at the table what they plan to order and will then decide to do the same.

Oh, you're going to have a turkey sandwich? I'll have the same. No mayonnaise? Oh, OK, make mine the same way. I'll have the same thing.

Monkey see, monkey do, just as kids and adults tease.

And what happens to people who decide in this way? **Deciders become victims because they allow other people to make decisions for them.**

When you study a menu, do you choose or do you decide?
Workers let other people make their decisions.

VICTIMS are people who are suffering because they have no control over their own lives.

Many teachers are victims:

✔ You don't stand at the door to greet the students? I don't have to either.

✔ You take roll at the beginning of the day or period? I'll do it that way, too.

✔ You write tests that equal 50 points, three times a grading period? If everyone else is doing it that way, so will I.

✔ I see that almost everyone is coming to school dressed in a sweatshirt and jeans. I'll decide to come to school looking like that, too.

✔ Look at all the people who sit at the back of the in-service meeting. None are taking notes; many are reading magazines, knitting, or grading papers; and several are talking and reading the morning paper. Since most of the teachers are sitting in the back doing these things, I'll decide to do the same.

It's Our Choice to Make

The world owes no one a living.

You owe the world the opportunity to make a living.

If you listen to enough people bemoan the fact that they are tired and underpaid and get no respect, you will believe that you, too, are tired and underpaid and have no respect.

If you listen to enough people who vilify administrators, parents, and students, you will believe that administrators, parents, and students are the cause of your being a victim.

 When you see in a given situation what everyone else sees, you become so much a part of that situation that you become a victim of that situation.

Choose

Leaders CHOOSE! Leaders do not decide.

Leaders have control over their own lives. They know that life comes from what they earn for themselves. They generate their own happiness, and much of that comes from serving and sharing with others. Leaders enjoy problems, obstacles, and challenges.

Leaders are achievement-oriented. They have visions that help them see beyond their task or job. They know what the word *choose* means and how to use it.

> ✔ *Choose* means that I am responsible for my choice.

> ✔ *Choose* means that I am accountable for my choice.

> ✔ *Choose* means that I have control over what I do.

> ✔ *Choose* means that I accept the consequences that accompany my choice. If it fails, blame me. But if it succeeds, reward me.

A Leader

Leaders control their own lives and are achievement-oriented.

Leaders seek their own means to reach a goal.

Worker-decider teachers do not strive for success, happiness, money, or respect. This is why they never receive anything in life.

Leader-professional educators are rewarded with whatever they are striving for—be it happiness, success, money, achievement, popularity, or respect as a professional. **Leaders are people who strive, reach for excellence, and seek achievement.**

People who are rewarded know the difference between deciding and choosing.

Some people go through life adding years to their life. Others go through life adding life to their years.

Workers Decide	Leaders Choose
Life comes from what others get for me.	Life comes from what I earn for myself.
I expect others to bring me happiness.	I will generate my own happiness.
Life comes from some other source.	Life comes from within me.
Life will be better when I get a new x or more y.	Life is better when I share or serve others.
Life will be better if I didn't have to do all these things.	Life is fine because I want to or choose to do these things.
All I want is some peace and quiet.	I enjoy challenges; they are the elixirs of life.
I can't do this. You know I have to go home and cook.	I can't wait to go home and have a candlelight dinner with my family.
I can't wait for the weekend.	I can't wait for the reading conference.

Now that you know the difference between deciding and choosing, what will you decide or choose to do?

Because of our district's new teacher induction program, I was able to CHOOSE to be an effective or ineffective teacher.

—Michele Boyd
Ashland, Wisconsin

Life Begins When You Make a Choice

Laura was a worker-teacher. She was typical of the countless number of sweet, kind, average people who teach. Laura was a maintainer, a survivor. She did her work: taught class, gave assignments, wrote tests, showed movies, passed out worksheets, supervised lunch, attended faculty meetings, and baked cookies for the textbook selection committee she was on for the year. She had a family and sang in the church choir.

She took early retirement at 53, having "put in" 30 years. During that time she never read a journal, joined a professional organization, or attended a conference.

During her 30 years, Laura never caused any problems, did not abuse her sick leave, and seldom said a word at faculty meetings. She always sat at the back of meetings and knitted. She didn't really harm any children, but then she never really lit fires under any of them either. She did her job and felt, as workers are prone to tell you angrily, "I did my job, didn't I? What more do you want me to do? I wish they would end this meeting. I have to go home and take care of the kids."

One day several years after Laura's retirement, I ran into her at a shopping mall. It was a nice reunion. After all, she was sweet and kind and generally well liked by the staff. I certainly liked her. I asked her what she had been doing and she said, "Well, I go to see my grandchildren, watch television a lot, and walk the malls. Walking is good for me, and the malls are safe. That's about all. I've been taking it easy."

Then she asked, "And what are you doing?"

I said, "I'm teaching part-time with students but seemingly full-time with preservice and in-service teachers. In addition I have a book coming out later this year, did a workshop at the regional International Reading Association conference, and for my fifty-fifth birthday, my family surprised me with a raft trip down the Colorado River."

We sat down on a nearby bench, amid passing shoppers, and she looked into my eyes, with her eyes glistening, and said to me, **"When does life begin?"**

I could not bring myself to say it, but I wanted to say, **"Laura, life begins when you start making choices."**

The Choices We Make Determine the Quality of Our Lives

> **What a person *chooses* to do will greatly determine the quality of that person's life.**

A **person's behavior will determine what choices that person will make**. The normal distribution curve, the bell-shape curve, will be used to explain this concept. The normal distribution curve describes, graphically, how events or things occur. **The tall part of the curve in the middle says that more things or events are average in occurrence.**

For instance, if the heights or shoe sizes of people are measured and plotted on a graph, the results state that most people have average heights or shoe sizes. Fewer people have small or large shoe sizes or are short or tall; their results are shown at the two ends of the curve. This is how people are normally distributed on a graph when it comes to comparing shoe size or heights.

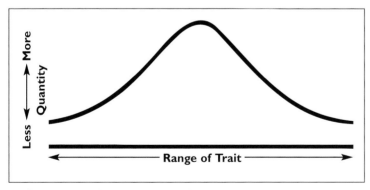

Traits in nature do not occur in equal proportions. The shape of a bell more accurately describes how traits are normally distributed.

The phenomenon of a normal distribution curve holds true for countless other examples in life:

✔ Speed of cars on the highway—some go fast, some go slow, most travel at the speed limit.

✔ Length of recitals—some are too long, some are too short, most are of tolerable length.

✔ Week in which the snow first falls—sometimes early, sometimes late, mostly predictable.

✔ Grades students receive in class—some A's, some F's, mostly C's.

✔ Work fulfillment—you can have a job or a career.

✔ Life fulfillment—you can become a teacher or an educator.

283

The normal distribution curve can be used to describe the behavior of people. People normally fall into one of three categories, according to the behaviors they exhibit:

1. **Protective behaviors**

2. **Maintenance behaviors**

3. **Enhancement behaviors**

Protective Behaviors

Protective people spend most of their time complaining or rationalizing to protect themselves.

People who use protective behaviors are full of excuses and are prone to complain about people, places, and things. They are good at explaining, rationalizing, or even lying to justify their position. When they talk about others, they never dignify people or groups with their appropriate names. It's typically, "these people" or "those administrators." **By complaining, rationalizing, or putting others down, they avoid doing what is expected of them, and they divert your thoughts from the task at hand.**

Protective people are easy to spot. They frequent the teachers' lounge more than others and can be heard complaining and moaning about everything on the school grounds. And if anyone tries to do something positive, they are convinced that the only reason is to make them look bad or create more work for everyone.

> **The surest path to decline is to blame others for your problems.**

Maintenance Behaviors

Maintenance people spend most of their time coping and hoping that life and work will improve.

People who use maintenance behaviors are the great survivors of life. They even tell you, "I'm a survivor." They don't complain, rationalize, lie, or put people down (well, most of the time). Instead, they hope, cope, and survive. They hope that the lottery will pay off or that they will receive an inheritance from a heretofore unknown relative. They are primarily concerned with themselves and their own survival, safety, health, and welfare.

Maintenance people are the hardworking backbone of society. They work to pay the bills, feed the mouths, and clothe the children. They wonder where the college tuition will come from, and if only, if only someone would knock on their door with the $10 million sweepstakes award, their worries would be over.

Maintenance people do a lot of wishing. They wish for a new car, a new husband, four fewer kids in class, and the day to go by faster. They like to fantasize, so their day is preoccupied with watching the soaps, reading the tabloids, playing the lotteries, and consulting their horoscope.

Because they are maintainers and survivors, they do nothing to rock the boat. They are pleasant and unassuming people who get along fine with others. Some of their favorite phrases are "Go with the flow," "*Que será será*," and "Whatever you guys want to do will be fine with me."

The surest path to stagnation is to do nothing or just get by.

You must become an advocate of what you believe, otherwise you will become a victim of what others want you to believe.

— *Jesse Jackson*

Distributed Prior to an In-Service Meeting
(Shown exactly as it was printed)

According to our Collective Bargaining Agreement, article 7 section 7.2 states that the school workday for teachers shall consist of not more than 7 hours. Therefore your workday ends at 2:45 P.M. FOLLOW YOUR CONTRACT, ENJOY THE WORKSHOP AND HAVE A GREAT WEEKEND!!!!!!!!!!!!!!!!!!!!!!!!

Enhancement Behaviors

Enhancement people spend most of their time participating, learning, and growing.

People who use enhancement behaviors are "we" people. They enjoy participating, so they go to conferences, conventions, and meetings. They go to meetings because they know that they can learn by interacting with, sharing with, and listening to other people.

These are the people the protectors and the maintainers wish would just sit down, rest, and smell the roses, right? Every time you look up, there they are on some committee, going to some conference, getting some award, or having their picture taken.

It's easy to identify the people with enhancement behaviors. You keep hearing them use the word *we*, as in "We need to find a solution to reduce the dropout rate," "Do we have some people who would like to volunteer to answer the phones at the educational television station pledge night campaign?" or "We can do it—I know that we can do it—so let's all go out and give it the best try we have ever given."

People who use enhancement behaviors are leaders and professionals. Enhancement people are easy to spot. They are the active people at school and in the community. They get the work done, and they make contributions to society. They are achievement-oriented and have vision. They are called enhancement people because they enhance the lives of all the people around them.

> **The surest path to success is with an attitude of enhancement and cooperation.**

The Most Vulnerable Teachers

The most vulnerable people on the staff are the maintenance people, the middle 60 percent of the curve. They know that they should be enhancing lives, first their own and then those of the people they teach. They know that they should work cooperatively with the enhancement people of the staff.

But at the faculty meetings, the protective people stand up and start to shout about the pay, the conditions, the parents, the publishers, and the crummy administrators (remember, protective people need to blame others to protect themselves). The needs of the people with a maintenance behavior to survive are so great that they decide to follow the protectors.

Because maintainers do not choose, they go through life vacillating, one day deciding to follow the enhancers and the next day deciding to follow the protectors. Which group should they follow?

If only they would make a choice!

How to Succeed with a Minimum of Effort

> **Teachers**
> **Eighty percent are affiliation-oriented.**
> **Twenty percent are achievement-oriented.**

Research has shown us that 80 percent of teachers are affiliation-oriented. They join organizations, specifically the teachers' organization or union, and expect the affiliations to obtain rewards for them. Their happiness, money, fringe benefits, and parties are all gotten for them in exchange for the dues they pay. Their attitude seems to be, "Let others get my rewards for me."

They even expect the teacher organization to write newspaper releases and run television commercials about the good deeds being done by teachers and the schools. "Let others bring me respect."

Twenty percent of the teachers are achievement-oriented. Teachers who are achievement-oriented do more than belong to a teacher's organization. They may attend workshops or conferences or serve on an education committee. Their dues are the opportunities they look for in life. They derive great satisfaction from getting their own rewards in life.

Because the 80 percent of the teachers who are affiliation-oriented so willingly step aside, it is fairly easy for the 20 percent who are achievement-oriented to excel without too much effort.

Teachers who are successful are self-driven people who put in effort and have an achievement-oriented attitude.

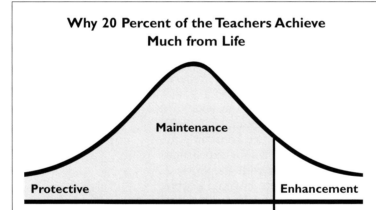

Why 20 Percent of the Teachers Achieve Much from Life

Maintenance

Protective | Enhancement

Eighty percent of people spend most of their lives complaining or just trying to survive. They are affiliation-oriented, expecting others to get them what they want from life.

Twenty percent of people spend most of their lives improving their quality of life. They are achievement-oriented, getting what they want from life.

287

Normal Distribution of Human Behaviors

The Choices We Make Determine the Quality of Our Lives

20 Percent	**60 Percent**	**20 Percent**
⟷	⟷	⟷
PROTECTIVE BEHAVIORS	MAINTENANCE BEHAVIORS	ENHANCEMENT BEHAVIORS
Rationalize and complain	Cope, hope, and survive	Participate and grow
HAVE TO	WISH TO	WANT TO
They	*Me or I*	*We or us*
SELF-DEFEATING	GETTING-ALONG, COPING	SELF-ENHANCING
PEOPLE	PEOPLE	PEOPLE

EXAMPLES OF TYPES OF BEHAVIORS

The kids can't read.	If only I could make it through the week.	May I share this article with you?
The administration is not supportive.	I need a raise, newer materials, less work, more help,...	What can I do to contribute?
The young (old) teachers don't know anything.	I wish I had a new principal, different coworkers,...	I volunteer.
In-services are boring. They are a waste of time.	End this meeting; I have to shop, cook, and go to aerobics class.	Let's work on this project together.
The new program will never work. I tried it years ago.	I wish I had the materials to follow this program properly.	Let's go to the conference together.
Where does it say that in the contract?	I'll just go with the flow and do what the group wants to do.	Tell me about your new idea.
I'll sit on the fringe, in the back, alone, or not come at all. I'll do my own thing.	Where will you sit? I'll sit with you and knit and read to pass the time.	We need constantly to strive for excellence.
I'm taking early retirement.	My problems are unique.	I'll sit with and work with involved people.
People bother me.	People don't understand or appreciate me.	I believe in opportunities.
Do I have to do this?		People are our most precious resource.
		I want to learn.
		I choose to learn.

RESULTS OF THE THREE BEHAVIORS

HAPPY ⟶
SUCCESSFUL ⟶
PRODUCTIVE ⟶
WELL-LIKED ⟶
PROFESSIONAL ⟶
FINANCIALLY SECURE ⟶

Now that you know the difference between people who use protective, maintenance, and enhancement behaviors, which kind of person do you choose to be?

Why It Is Easy to Succeed in Life

Have you determined which kind of behavior you exhibit most of the time? If not, here's another way of telling. People with similar behaviors or values tend to group themselves.

> **Seize the Moment**
>
> Life is a series of opportunities.
> Most opportunities come only once in a lifetime.
> An opportunity is a moving target, and the bigger the target, the faster it moves.
> Opportunities always come in when the doors are left open for them.
>
> Research shows that if you do not use an idea or an opportunity within three days, you will never use it.
> And if you use it within 24 hours, you are more likely to integrate it permanently.

✔ **Protective people** form their own group at school, although they will deny it. They can usually be found sitting in the back row of meetings, in the lounge complaining, or at association meetings filing grievances.

✔ **Maintenance people** form their own cliques also, although they will not recognize it. They are characterized by being tired much of the time. They hope that they can make it through the week, always seeking sympathy.

✔ **Enhancement people** form their own group also. Whereas the protective and maintenance people will not recognize or accept the fact that they are in a group, enhancement people acknowledge this and give their groups names.

They say things like this:

"We have this support group organized to help each other."

"We go out once a month to a power breakfast and share our successes and problems."

"We have this self-help group, and our purpose is to help mentor the beginning teacher."

"We need to work together with the administrators, the classified staff, the community, and the business sector."

"Jan is my support buddy."

Because of their behavior:

✔ **Protective people are self-defeating people.** Because their behavior can spread, they can cause an organization to defeat itself also.

✔ **Maintenance people are coping people.** They do not destroy an organization, like protective people do, but it is necessary to light a bonfire under these people to get them to contribute to and be a part of an organization.

✔ **Enhancement people are self-enhancers.** They are self-motivated, self-disciplined people who contribute to the quality of life, first their own and then that of the organization.

As a result, enhancement people are happier.

✔ They are more productive.

✔ They achieve higher status.

✔ They make more money.

✔ They earn more rewards.

✔ They are more professional.

✔ They get greater respect.

✔ They get whatever else they strive for.

Protective and maintenance people make up 80 percent of the teaching population. Since 80 percent of the teachers are self-defeaters and survivors, they forfeit their happiness and success to others. **The enhancers are successful not because they are such great strivers but to a great extent because 80 percent of their colleagues are not striving, seeking, or growing.**

CHOOSE

- I **choose** to invest in myself so that I may increase my value to others.

- I **choose** to learn and grow as a professional.

- I **choose** to read professionally.

- I **choose** to go to conferences.

- I **choose** to avoid thoughts and people who limit me.

- I **choose** to work cooperatively with colleagues, family, and self-directed workteams.

- I **choose** to stop BLAMING my circumstances and take the initiative to CREATE my circumstances.

- I **choose** to take risks to provide opportunities for growth.

- I **choose** what I want to do with my life and then DO IT.

- I **choose** to **CHOOSE**.

The Pareto Principle

Twenty percent of the people own 80 percent of the wealth.
Eighty percent of the people own 20 percent of the wealth.

— Vilfredo Pareto
Italian economist

Enhancement and the Four Stages of Teaching

Recall from Chapter 1 that teachers may pass through four career stages:

1. **Fantasy**
2. **Survival**
3. **Mastery**
4. **Impact**

Teachers who practice protective and maintenance behaviors remain in the SURVIVAL stage most all of their life.

Teachers who practice enhancement behaviors reach the MASTERY stage quickly and then make an IMPACT not only on the lives of their students, but also on their own lives and the life of the community.

A coach will tell you that a winning team does not necessarily win a game. Most often, a losing team botches itself into defeat from all the mistakes team members make. Look at the statistics for a football game. The team with the greater number of turnovers (errors such as fumbles and intercepted passes) is usually the loser. The team with the greater number of takeovers (fumble recoveries and interceptions) is usually the winner.

Vic Braden, the tennis teacher, tells his class, "Just lob or dink the ball over the net. You don't have to smash, and you don't need top spin. Just lob or dink the ball over the net. Why? Because the average player on the other side of the net will hit the ball back into the net or out of bounds 70 percent of the time. Do not beat yourself when playing tennis. The odds are that your opponent will do that for you."

Such is life with teachers. Eighty percent of the teachers are turning over their lives because of their protective and maintenance behaviors, while 20 percent of the teachers walk away with the opportunities life offers them because of their enhancement behaviors. These teachers just keep lobbing the ball back into play.

Professionals understand this concept of keeping the ball in play. You keep striving, growing, making choices, and staying focused on enhancement opportunities—consistently developing your career as a professional educator as well as enhancing your life. Do this and you will achieve happiness, success, and effectiveness as a teacher.

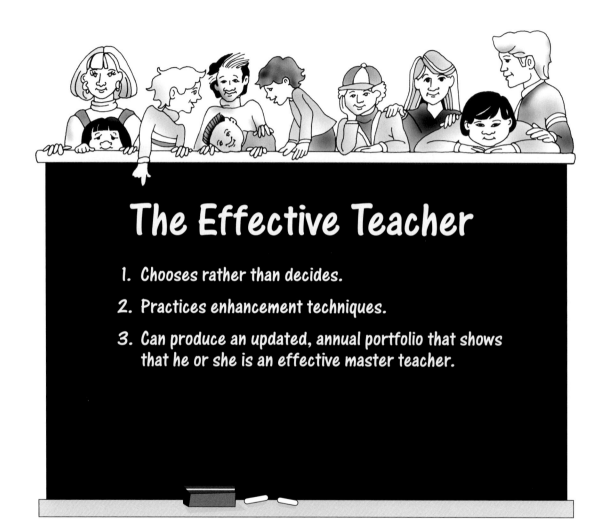

The Effective Teacher

1. Chooses rather than decides.

2. Practices enhancement techniques.

3. Can produce an updated, annual portfolio that shows that he or she is an effective master teacher.

KEY IDEA

The rewards in education and life go to the person who is a professional.

The Rewards Go to the Professional Educator

> **A professional is defined not by the business a person is in but by the way that person does his or her business.**

The Rand Corporation reports that teacher reform still leaves a major question unanswered: "Are teachers full-fledged professionals or merely semiskilled workers who constantly need supervision and regulation?"[1] It can be argued late into the night as to whether teaching is a profession or not. We maintain that it is, but only for teachers who perform as professionals.

As with any group, the competence of the people in the group will range from inept to masterful. There have been good and bad presidents, ballerinas, television evangelists, athletes, auto mechanics, teachers, and administrators.

The debate over whether teaching is a profession will be resolved when all teachers, or at least a significant number of them, are professional in their own lives.

---

[1]Darling-Hammond, Linda, and Barry Barnett. (1988). *The Evolution of Teacher Policy.* Santa Monica, Calif.: Rand Center for the Study of the Teaching Profession.

A professional is someone who, without supervision or regulation:

✔ Is a responsible person

✔ Has a continuing growth plan to achieve competence

✔ Strives continuously to raise the level of each new group of students

All some teachers want is a job. They want a job working 180 days, 8 a.m. to 3 p.m., closed in a room with no worry of a supervisor, reluctant to be in-serviced, and free to belittle people (children, administrators, and parents) to cover their ineffectiveness. Making money to pay bills is the primary concern of such a worker-teacher.

> *The totally inept go in one of two directions. They either leave the profession of teaching or develop a repertoire of defense mechanisms that protect their fragile self-concepts. These teachers become bitter blamers, constant critics, despondent despots, and managers of monotony. Worst of all, they stay in the classroom and believe they are doing a good job.*[2]
>
> —Douglas Brooks

The truth is that some people who teach do not want to be professionals. It takes work and effort to be a professional. It takes time to go to conferences, read the journals, work actively on committees, and give extra help after school to students who need it. But the rewards go to the professionals.

> **The rewards go only to the professionals. They are the happiest, make the most money, get the most respect, and are the most successful.**

Are you a worker or a leader?

---

[2]Brooks, Douglas. (Summer 1986). "The First-Year 'Gap'." *Kappa Delta Pi Record,* p. 99.

The Thin Margin for Success

The margin for success is so thin that getting across it is frighteningly simple.

Take baseball as one example. The difference between being an all-star and an average player in baseball is so slight that it makes baseball seem like a silly game.

Consider the difference between a great year and an awful year.

The season is 26 weeks long. A player gets 500 at-bats between April and September. That's about 20 at-bats per week, or five games per week. The difference between a .300 average and a .250 average is ONE hit per week—ONE more every 20 times you bat.

At the end of the season there will be fewer than 25 players in each league (National and American) batting above .300. From about 400 players playing full-time on all the teams, only 12 percent, 48 out of 400, will be batting .300. If you bat .300 per year, you are in an elite crowd that is able to earn millions of dollars more per year. **And all you have to do is get ONE more hit per week!**

Likewise, for any team, the difference between a miserable season with a 66-96 record and a terrific season with a 92-70 record is ONE more victory per week.

Individual Batting
(Based on 450 plate appearances)
Player/Team

	AB	H	AVG
Gwynn, San D.	592	220	.372
Walker, Col.	568	208	.366
Piazza, L.A.	556	201	.362
Lofton, Atl.	493	164	.333
Joyner, San D.	455	149	.327
Grace, Chi.	555	177	.319
Gallarraga, Col.	600	191	.318
Alfonzo, N.Y.	518	163	.315
Mondesi, L.A.	616	191	.310
Biggio, Hou.	619	191	.309
Blausser, Atl.	519	160	.308
Bichette, Col.	561	173	.308
Castilla, Col.	612	186	.304

13 players batted .300 or above during the 1997 season in the National League.

In the same way, success in life is simple. Try one or two new ideas or techniques each year:

- Go to a conference.
- Move up six rows at an in-service meeting.
- Share an idea with another teacher.
- Welcome students at the classroom door with a smile.

Notice the active verbs of successful people: go, move, share, welcome. It takes just as much effort and you use exactly the same amount of energy to perform these activities:

- Sit in the faculty lounge with the negative people who moan, complain, and belittle.
- Hide from people who may ask you to do something.
- Gaze at your watch wondering when the day will be over.
- Sit in the back rows at a meeting.

Notice the sedentary type verbs of unsuccessful people: sit, hide, gaze. Which verbs best describe your attitude toward life?

The difference between a great year and an awful year is so slim! Life is no different. **All that separates a person from SUCCESS or FAILURE is one word: *ATTITUDE*.**

The Rewards Go to Those Who Continue to Learn

The first days of school may be history for you now, but the school year continues. What does the teacher do after the first days of school?

The worker-teacher will do nothing except read stories, cover the basal text, hand out worksheets, lecture, show movies, and give tests—a pattern to be repeated decade after boring decade.

The professional educator is always learning and growing. The professional educator is constantly on an endless journey of looking for new and better ideas, new information, and improved skills to succeed with students. Here are some specifics to learn.

This Is Teaching: Promoting Student Growth

The professional educator learns how to promote student growth in the following ways:

Seeing that students perform at or above expectations
Solving problems so that students receive the best possible services
Using recent research and technological advancements
Applying higher-order learning skills
Applying information-processing strategies
Applying increasingly complex learning tasks
Using cooperative learning
Using invitational learning
Applying classroom management research

This Is Not Teaching

There is no research to support this model of teaching:

- Read the assigned chapters.

- Answer the questions at the end of the chapter.

- Sit and take lecture notes.

- Watch a video.

- Complete the worksheet.

- Take a test.

This Is Teaching: Making Good Use of Time

The professional educator learns how to make good use of instructional time in the following ways:

Following lesson plans
Focusing student attention
Communicating the purpose of every lesson
Setting high expectations for student achievement
Applying study guidelines
Using guided practice
Using materials, media, and technology appropriately
Planning according to types of students
Planning instructional strategies
Optimizing time on task

Studying and demonstrating the subject being taught
Maintaining a smooth flow and momentum of events
Being aware of class activities
Managing several events simultaneously
Articulating information clearly
Giving effective directions for activities
Providing logically sequenced instruction
Revising and augmenting instruction on the spot
Managing aides, tutors, and parents
Evaluating and improving classroom instruction

These are some general areas in which knowledge brings power.

[1] *Survey, Question, Read, Recite, Review*
[2] *Academic Learning Time (on-task time)*
[3] *Criterion-Referenced testing*
[4] *Teacher Expectation, Student Achievement*

This Is Teaching: Recognizing That Knowledge Is Power

Knowledge is power. Knowledge, like money and status, is a form of power. Power is not force but rather the ability to do things. For instance, the more money a person has, the more a person can do. The more horsepower in a car, the easier it is to climb a hill. The more knowledge a person has, the more the person is able to accomplish. **The ability to achieve and accomplish accrues to those with the knowledge.**

Knowledge gives a person options. A person with no options is helpless in life. You can see this in the ineffective teachers. Because they do not read the literature or attend conferences, their fund of knowledge is minimal. People with a poor knowledge background are not aware of the options they have to solve problems. They repeatedly run into brick walls and then helplessly yell into the world seeking specific answers.

Options give a person the power of choice. Professional educators have no brick walls. Their life is spent adding the fuel of knowledge to a power cycle. As more knowledge is added, more learning takes place, more options are generated, and more power to accomplish is unleashed.

Rewards Go to Those Who . . .

✔ Have the knowledge

✔ Have the power

✔ Have options

✔ Can make choices

✔ Have control

✔ Continue to learn

Knowledge to help you become a more effective teacher is at your fingertips, waiting to be accessed.

Thank You for Expanding My Awareness

Professional persons, leaders, are always alert, searching for opportunities, and looking for ways to move forward in life. They may not agree with everything they hear or see. They even will look for information not in their present realm of influence. However, their attitude is always, "Thank you for expanding my awareness."

The worker-teacher is not interested in any expansion of awareness. Awareness means looking ahead, beyond, and into the future. Beware of worker-teachers who try to prevent you from expanding your awareness. They sit at meetings belittling and ridiculing the proceedings. They are no different from the problem students who belittle the teacher, the subject, and the students who do well.

Worker-teachers expend energy to prevent you from learning. If you expand your realm of awareness, you threaten their existence. They have trapped themselves, like lobsters, in a cage. Their goal each day is to drag others into the cage with them. And if you get caught and try to escape, they will reach up with their claws and pull you back down.

Do not allow people who cannot control their own lives to control your life. Rather, proceed through life expanding your awareness, searching for opportunities, working and sharing with the professionals who are also expanding their awareness.

Professional educators believe that within every great teacher, there is an even better one waiting to come forth.

The Basics for a Beginning Teacher

The most crucial time in a new teacher's life is the first one to three years. During this time, some 40 percent of the new teachers will decide to leave teaching. But regardless of the reasons they give, the fact is that the successful ones don't quit. The professional accepts the responsibility of personal growth and invests time to become an effective and successful teacher.

Fundamental People and Programs You Need to Know:

People

> **Jack Canfield** on self-esteem
> **Barbara Coloroso** on discipline
> **Art Costa** on higher-order thinking skills
> **Rita Dunn** on learning styles
> **Carolyn Evertson** on classroom management
> **Thomas Guskey** on evaluation
> **Madeline Hunter** on effective teaching strategies
> **David and Roger Johnson** on cooperative learning
> **Harry Wong** on classroom management

Audio and Video Programs

> *How You Can Be a Super Successful Teacher*, see page 336
> *I choose to CARE*, see page 337
> *The Effective Teacher*, see page 335

Books and Magazines

> **Fuery, Carol L.** (1986). *Winning Year One.* Sanddollar Publications, P.O. Box 461, Captiva Island, FL 33924
> **Jones, Fredric H.** (1987). *Positive Classroom Discipline/Instruction.* Fredric H. Jones and Associates, Inc., 103 Quarry Lane, Santa Cruz, CA 95060
> **Shalaway, Linda.** (1989). *Learning to Teach.* Scholastic Professional Books P.O. Box 7502, Jefferson City, MO 65102
> **Zike, Dinah.** (1996). *Classroom Organization, K–6.* Dinah-Might Activities, Inc., P.O. Box 39657, San Antonio, TX 78218
> *Educational Leadership,* the journal of the Association for Supervision and Curriculum Development
> **Journal** from your own discipline or area of responsibility

The Rewards Go to Those Who Share

Professionals consult and help one another. Physicians who have difficulty diagnosing an illness routinely consult with other physicians. Lawyers who are stumped by a case get help from colleagues in their firm. Athletes seek advice from coaches. Most teachers, sad to say, seldom seek or get help from anyone. **Though the essence of a teacher's work is helping others learn, teachers are the worst learners when it comes to improving their own performance.**

<u>**Join or Organize a Support Group.**</u> Find the effective and professional teachers. Chapter 25 describes how to recognize these teachers. The effective teachers are well respected in professional circles. In turn, they are regarded with great jealousy by the worker-teachers.

The most effective support group strategy is known as peer coaching. Attend a seminar, or have your district contract with a group to teach coaching techniques. In peer coaching, each person helps others grow. Work and socialize with the professional teachers. You not only will learn much from them, but also will learn a professional ethos that will bring you much respect, too.

Support groups are common outside of school, but they are normally not formalized in schools. You will have to look for pockets of successful teachers. You may find them at your school, at another school, or at conferences. Conferences are the best places to find the superprofessional teachers, the ones who are educational leaders. Make these people your support group. They already have their own support groups, so adding another professional will be easy.

Your support groups are your best source of information and emotional support from which you can learn and gather strength to be an effective teacher.

<u>**Listen to Others.**</u> **Listen to your support group.** These are teachers and administrators with years of experience and are active in professional circles. They are well read, know people, have contacts, can suggest references, and know about future conferences.

To Be a Professional Educator . . .

✔ Join or organize a support group.

✔ Listen to others.

✔ Read the literature.

✔ Observe other effective teachers.

✔ Participate in conferences.

✔ Use the research.

<u>Listen to Tapes and Watch Videos.</u> Buy your own, borrow from your mentor, check out the media center in your district or local educational service center, inquire what the school of education has, and see if your district subscribes to a satellite in-service program. Invest time in teaching yourself.

<u>Read the Literature.</u> Subscribe to at least one professional journal. This is the easiest way to know how, who, and what is happening in education. There is nothing more disconcerting than a teacher who does not know the names, the terms, or the trends in the profession.

It can be downright embarrassing when you mention Madeline Hunter, William Glasser, performance assessment, hemisphericity, or learning styles and get a glazed look. Would you tolerate this lack of knowledge from your doctor, pharmacist, or accountant?

Be knowledgeable. **Knowledge is power, and knowledge gives professionals options on which to base decisions.**

Attending conferences is one of the best ways to grow and learn as a professional.

<u>Participate in Conferences.</u> Go to conventions, conferences, seminars, and workshops. National, state, and local groups have their meetings near you. These conferences typically have speakers, workshops, seminars, exhibits, sample materials, parties (yes, parties), socials, and field trips. You will return to school with bags of free samples, papers other teachers have shared at workshops, and pages of notes on how to be a more effective teacher.

Give a paper or conduct a workshop and share your materials. Don't just attend a conference; be on the program and participate or serve on the convention committee. Become an officer and contribute to the profession. Join the organization and receive its magazine and materials. **Professionals share.**

Use the Research. Learn how to use ERIC, the Educational Research Information Center. ERIC is an electronic library of all educational research and papers in the United States.

The box on this page explains how to access this information. Use the research to increase your teaching effectiveness.

Observe Effective Teachers. **Observe other teachers.** The effective teacher can be the best source of knowledge because you will be able to observe a strategy being implemented in a classroom. Such teachers are easy to spot and have much to share. Ineffective teachers have nothing to share and will be reluctant to have you visit. They will even negotiate to prevent or greatly regulate supervision.

Effective teachers welcome visitors and are not afraid of evaluations. Effective teachers do not regard evaluations as supervision; rather, they regard evaluation sessions as a way of finding out how they can improve.

Effective teachers exist right in your own building or district. Start by observing the effective teachers in your own support group. Consult with your administrators, supervisors, and coordinators. Many were outstanding teachers when they were in the classroom. There is plenty of talent in your own building.

A Wealth of Research at Your Fingertips

Vast amounts of educational information are available on the World Wide Web. Begin with the **AskERIC** home page (http://ericir.syr.edu/) to find everything from ERIC documents to subject area lesson plans. Another source is the **U.S. Department of Education** home page (http://www.ed.gov/) for government documents and reports on education.

Try the **Global SchoolNet Foundation** home page (http://www.gsn.org/), which has links bringing schools together from around the globe. Many other sites can be found on the Internet that provide links to other interesting educational sites.

—Courtesy of Max Frazier
Manhattan, Kansas

Before You Start Your First Day of School

1. **Watch** *The Effective Teacher*, and *I choose to CARE*, and **listen** to *How You Can Be a Super Successful Teacher*. These are the most popular tapes on classroom management and lesson mastery. See pages 335–337 for the source.

2. **Read** "The First Day of School" by Douglas Brooks, "What Helps Students Learn" by Margaret Wang, and "Making the Grade" by Thomas Guskey, all in *Educational Leadership* (May 1985, December 1993, and October 1994, respectively).

3. **Participate** in a workshop or a college class that will stress classroom management skills.

4. **Find** a mentor, support buddy, or support group of experienced professional educators, not a fellow new teacher, who can share with you.

5. **Insist** that your district have an induction or in-service program to help new teachers with classroom management and lesson mastery. You have every right to expect a program to help you succeed.

6. **Believe** in yourself. Regardless of who you are or what you have been, you can be what you want to be!

The Greatest Civil Right Is the Right of Equal Opportunities

Professional educators or teachers in the process of becoming professional educators do not sit in the back at a meeting.

The back of an auditorium is the worst place to sit.

- It is the hottest location.
- It is the most crowded.
- It is the most uncomfortable.
- You can't see or hear well.
- You will be distracted by every movement around you.
- You will be surrounded by all the negative people who do not want to be at the meeting to learn and cooperatively participate.
- The handouts will run out before they reach you.

It is common knowledge that the students with the poorest attitudes and grades, if allowed open seating, will sit at the back of the room. In fact, they will sit at the back corners, nearest the doors. Their body language tells you that they do not want to be in class and are anxious to get out first and fastest.

Being at the back is the same in life as being at the end of the line, the back of the pack, the rear of the group, the last in class, the bottom of the league.

There was a time in history when certain groups of people were forced to sit at the back of the bus, the back of the meeting, and the back of church. Why? Because if you want to discriminate against a group of people, you put them at the back, where you reduce their chances of partaking or achieving.

Thanks to one little lady, Rosa Parks, who refused to sit at the back of a bus in Montgomery, Alabama, all people are now free to sit where they choose to sit.

The worker-teachers who do not want to learn decide to sit in the back with all the other worker-teachers.

The leaders and professional educators choose to sit nearer the front, where they can see, hear, pay attention, not be distracted, and receive handouts. It's also a lot more comfortable because people are not packed in.

TESA (Teacher Expectation, Student Achievement) research has discovered that the best students sit in class in the shape of an inverted T—across the front and down the middle. If you plot this on a graph, you get a bell-shaped curve. The worst students sit at the far corners. Note this of your students; note this of your colleagues.

The next time you go to a conference, a place where professionals go to enhance their lives, notice the teachers who arrive early at workshops, sit up front, and badger workshop leaders for handouts. These are the people you want for role models.

Thanks to Rosa Parks, we now have equal access to all the opportunities that are available in a free society. Professionals understand and make use of this concept.

Rosa Parks

303

The Rewards Go to Those Who Take Risks

There can be no accomplishment **without taking some risk.** The professional educator understands the concept of taking risks. Risk taking is not the same as gambling.

Gamble is a dangerous word. Gamble means that the odds are against you but you are taking a chance that the odds will roll in your favor. Betting on a game, playing the lottery, and smoking cigarettes are examples of gambling. You know that the odds are against you, but you are betting that you will beat the odds.

Risk is a safe word. Before you try something in your class, you do the following:

1. Identify what you need to resolve.

2. Read to see what technique is available.

3. Observe other teachers using the technique.

4. Ask questions about the technique.

5. Discover that many others are using the technique.

6. Determine that the technique is a commonsense approach supported by research.

After careful consideration of these six items, you choose to implement a new technique. You take a risk knowing that the odds are in your favor for success. **Accomplishment and rewards go to those who take risks.**

There is one thing perhaps more dangerous than gambling, and that thing is doing nothing.

> **Nothing will ever be accomplished by sitting around doing nothing, making butt prints in the sands of time.**

One of the hardest things about your life when you're over a half century (old), as I am, is to realize what you should have done 20 years earlier.   I blew it.

— Dustin Hoffman
Newsweek,
December 11, 1989.

Rollie Fingers, a Hall of Fame pitcher who earned millions playing baseball, is broke at age 43. When asked if there was anything he would wish for Christmas, he replied:

Yeah, to be 10 years younger and know what I know now.

— *San Jose Mercury News,*
December 2, 1989.

Your Chances of Success Are One to One

Your odds of winning a state lottery are 14 million to 1.

Your odds of jumping out of an airplane with two parachutes and not having both open are 1.2 million to 1.

Your odds of getting hit by lightning are 600,000 to 1.

Your odds of success in whatever you choose to do are 1 to 1—far better than winning a lottery or getting hit by lightning.

> **Your odds of succeeding are 1 to 1. There is only one person you ever need to compete against, and that is yourself.**

Reward Yourself with a Career Risk Plan

If you put money into an investment or savings plan that has an interest rate of 10 percent, compounded semiannually, you will double your investment every 7.2 years. For instance, if you save $2,000 each year, at the end of seven years you would have not $14,000 but $20,000.

At the end of 14 years, you would have not $28,000 but $56,000.

And at the end of 28 years, you would have not $56,000 but $260,000, over a quarter of a million dollars. Investment people call this a compound growth curve. At the beginning nothing seems to accumulate, but as the years progress, the sums jump forward in leaps and bounds.

The professional educator invests in his or her career. After three years of investing in your own life, you can be 33 percent better than you were when you started. After four years, you can be some 45 percent better than you were when you started.

After three to five years, growing 10 percent each year, you should be in the top 20 percent of the teaching profession. Why? Because 80 percent of your colleagues will have been sitting, doing nothing. Some are even regressing and destroying the organization they are in.

Start a 10%
Risk Plan

Try 2 to 3 new
ideas each year.

In 3 to 5 years,
you can have
anything you
want in
education.

✔ The research shows that 80 percent of the teachers have not been to a conference on their own time and money for an average of 10 years.

✔ Forty percent of the teachers have not been to a conference for an average of 16 years.

✔ Simply put, the great majority of teachers refuse to learn and grow, yet they expect their students to do so.

The rewards in education and in life go to the professionals. The rest get paid a salary for putting in time.

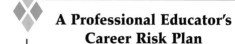

A Professional Educator's Career Risk Plan

Each year try two or three new ideas or techniques.

- ✔ Start with one, perhaps one from this book.
- ✔ A few months later, try another one.
- ✔ A few months later, try another one.
- ✔ Aim for two or three new ideas a year.
- ✔ Continue to learn.

How to Be at the Forefront of Your Profession

I first heard you speak five years ago. I had just transferred from a nice, small Catholic school to a much larger Detroit public elementary school. I also went from teaching 21 fifth graders to running a library and seeing over 500 students a week, including Special Ed. I was overwhelmed, discouraged, and unsure of myself as a teacher.

When I heard you at Seaholm High School in Birmingham that year, I felt recharged, inspired, and understood. I used your classroom management plan and modified it for my situation, and it worked wonderfully. I had my diploma framed and hung it in my library.

But the one message that helped me the most was when you said, "Every year do one thing that is different, above and beyond your job. If you do this, in five years you will be at the forefront of the profession."

I began that year to dress up as a book character from the story "Miss Nelson Is Missing." I posed as Viola Swamp, the meanest, oldest, and ugliest substitute teacher in the world.

A year later, my supervisor started asking me to speak at reading conferences and in-services in Detroit. Two years later, I was speaking around the state. Last year I spoke in Texas, Indiana, Alabama, and Washington, D.C. I was asked back a second time to Houston to be the keynote speaker at the Greater Houston Reading Council. This summer I will be speaking in Georgia, Arkansas, and again in Alabama.

Because I dared to be different, I am at the forefront of my profession. But far more important, I am happy with myself. I love teaching. I know I am a great teacher. I know I can inspire other educators to be innovative, loving, humorous, and proud of themselves.

Sincerely,
Mary Kay Stark

Mary Kay Stark is a media specialist at Walled Lake Central High School in Michigan.

The Rewards Go to Those Who Implement a Risk Plan

You can have anything you want in education in three to
five years:

- ✔ The school of your choice

- ✔ The district of your choice

- ✔ The job of your choice

- ✔ A salary greatly improved from what it is now

- ✔ Happiness, success, and respect

> **The Biggest Secret for Professional
> Growth in Education**
>
> If you invest 10 percent into your life
> each year, you will go zooming by most
> of your colleagues and be an
> accomplished professional educator in
> three to five years.

You can have it all in three to five years—and with no special effort! This is how
and why.

The scope of this book has been restricted to a small but very significant part of a
teacher's life, the first days of school. The book does not pretend to be a
comprehensive textbook, nor should it be used to evaluate a teacher. There is still
much for a professional educator to learn.

Since there is no scope or sequence to the content and the information does not
represent a model, there is really no beginning or ending to this book. Plunge in
wherever you may need help, just as you would use a cookbook or a repair manual.
As for an ending, the professional educator never stops learning.

> *A woodsman who has been lost in the forest for several weeks has been rescued. Tired
> and hungry, he is taken to a restaurant featuring an eat-all-you-want buffet.*

> *Staring at his first sight of food in weeks, a rescuer asks, "You seem puzzled. Do you not
> know what to do?"*

> *The woodsman replies, "Oh, I know what to do. I just don't know where to begin."*

The professional educator says, "What do I need to know in order to do what I need to do?"

The Three AREs

Teachers ARE important.
Teachers ARE influential.
Teachers ARE able to
make a difference.

—Helen Morsink

Begin by asking yourself what you need to do. Are you having problems with discipline, classroom management, roll taking, seating assignments, homework, collecting papers, assignments, tests, something else? Until you know what you need to do, you will never do anything.

After identifying what needs to be done, turn to the appropriate chapter and begin.

Just begin! Begin anywhere, but take a risk and begin.

Which one of you will be the next great teacher? If not you, someone else will.

The rewards go to those who implement a risk plan.

- ✔ The rewards go to the professional educators.

- ✔ The rewards go to those who continue to learn.

- ✔ The rewards go to those who share.

- ✔ The rewards go to those who take risks.

- ✔ The rewards go to those who implement a career risk plan.

Professional educators continue to learn and share.

Risk

To laugh is to risk appearing the fool.
To weep is to risk appearing sentimental.
To reach out for another is to risk involvement.
To expose your feelings is to risk exposing your true self.
To place your ideas, your dreams, before a crowd is to risk their loss.
To love is to risk not being loved in return.
To live is to risk dying.
To hope is to risk despair.
To try is to risk failure.

But risks must be taken, because the greatest hazard in life is to risk nothing.
Persons who risk nothing do nothing, have nothing, and are nothing.
They may avoid suffering and sorrow, but they cannot learn, feel, change, grow, love, or live.
Chained by their attitudes, they are slaves, for they have forfeited their freedom.

Only a person who risks is free.

The Effective Teacher

1. Implements a career risk plan.

2. Can document annual professional growth.

3. Is able to explain why he or she is a professional educator.

If you touch a rock, you touch the past.
If you touch a flower, you touch the present.
If you touch a child, you touch the future.

Although we have taught in American schools, our many speeches and workshops have taken us to schools worldwide in Canada, Asia, Europe, South America, and Africa. The ideas and techniques used in this book may have come primarily from American schools, but our message is applicable to the children of the world.

We ask our friends in neighboring Canada and abroad to take a serious look at the crisis in America, a nation that went in a few short years from being the world's leading creditor nation to the world's leading debtor nation, a nation of scientific and technological giants but ethical and moral midgets. If you suspect that the same crisis is looming on the horizon for your country, this closing epilogue applies to you also.

Our Children Are an Endangered Species

✔ Each year 700,000 students drop out of school, equivalent to the school population of Minnesota. At this rate, 40 percent of our population into the next century could consist of citizens who dropped out of school.

✔ Each night 100,000 children are homeless, and this does not include children who have run away from home or have been kicked out of the house.

✔ The intact family, of responsible parents who teach values, seldom exists. Only 4 percent of families in America consists of a married couple with two children.

✔ An estimated 25 million Americans are illiterate. The business world knows that the next generation of workers will not be as qualified as this generation.

✔ Children are caught in a maelstrom of cultural and social problems: drugs, permissiveness, poverty, teenage pregnancy, broken homes, and falling academic standards.

We are very pleased and honored that *The First Days of School* has an international audience. Copies can be found in the following countries:

Canada	Philippines
Singapore	Namibia
Israel	Sweden
China	Ecuador
Taiwan	Bermuda
Japan	Saudi Arabia
India	Italy
Korea	Sri Lanka
Netherlands	Germany
Grenada	Mexico
Australia	Colombia
South Africa	Poland
England	Bahamas
Hong Kong	Samoa
Thailand	Belize
Malaysia	Spain
Kenya	

Thank you!

✔ Never before in the history of a country have so many children been raised by strangers. First the parents transfer their responsibility to a caretaker or care center; later they transfer it to the schools. The result is that schools are struggling to deal with the increasing numbers of at-risk youth.

✔ Whereas each generation has had a better life than each past generation, the next generation in America could quite possibly be the first generation to be worse off than the previous generation.

It doesn't make sense. The teachers of today are better than the teachers of yesteryear. So are the administrators, the schools, and the curriculum. Yet the product is worse than ever before. **The reason is societal.**

The schools are being blamed, incorrectly, for the ills of society. Why do certain nations succeed while others fail? It is a complex question with many answers, but there is one common answer—culture. Countries that create wealth (economically, socially, and politically) stress education, freedom to create, delayed gratification, mutual trust, and hard work. Those that don't stay poor, remain in debt, or head toward bankruptcy.

Within the American culture, groups whose culture stresses hard work and learning succeed in disproportionate numbers to those who do not. It isn't a lack of talent but the lack of values and culture that too often results in failure. Culture overcomes discrimination and poverty if it sends the right signals.

We are blaming the schools for faults that lie deeper within our society. In the long run, the habits, values, and behavior of citizens determine national strength. The truth is that culture, not politics, religion, money, or skin color, determines the success of a society.

America did not become strong by eating junk food, watching TV, or by crowing "We're number one." **America became strong with its cultural values: hard work, effort, and integrity.** One of the causes for the current problems with youth is the inability of the culture to pass on its values.

The family is the bulwark of culture. Schools merely help the family pass culture along. But when you no longer have intact households, a family dinnertime, or clear-cut societal values, the next generation will never acquire culture.

Our children—humanity's most precious resource—are an endangered species. They are our most precious resource because they are our future. We need leader-teachers, professional educators who will begin this revitalization of our culture and values.

For many of our students, we play an extraordinarily important role:

✔ We may be the only stable adult in their lives.

✔ We may be the only people able to pass culture on to them.

✔ We may be their only hope, the only ones who dream of a brighter tomorrow for them.

Teachers Create Their Own Culture

By the next decade there will have been an 80 percent turnover of the teachers. We are faced with the opportunity to redefine our culture.

✔ **This is a challenge, a charge, a mission for the veteran teachers to leave a legacy of positive expectations with the new teachers.**

✔ **This is a challenge, a charge, a mission for these new teachers to create a revolutionary change in the cultural attitude of teachers.**

It is not money, class size, or a new textbook that determines the success of a group of teachers or the esteem in which they are held. It is culture. People tend to look at each other's wallets instead of each other's eyes and hearts. You can't buy a look into someone's heart. The best things in life are not things.

**When I Look
at Them . . .**

*When I look at them,
When I smile at them,
When I hold them,
I realize that I have
    the universe in my hands.*

*They are the light of my life.
They are the love of my life.*

They are life.

Teachers play a dramatic role in the life of a child. Are you up to the part?

Money can't buy health, and it can't buy hope. Money can't buy a nice conversation around the family dinner table. Money can't buy freedom, time, peace of mind, equality, justice, love of your children, or an end to loneliness.

Money cannot buy integrity or respect.

> **A principal thanked a teacher for sending her transcript but needed her vita also. Her response was telling and a reflection of the attitude of many teachers.**
>
> **"I don't have a vita," she said. "What would I put on it? I'm just a teacher."**

Just a teacher. Indeed. The lack of integrity or respect we have for ourselves is a reflection of cultural attitudes toward teachers.

Teachers see themselves as "just teachers." The fact is that teachers express the worth of their work humbly, modestly, and apologetically. The learned helplessness of some teachers is pitiful.

The reflection of people toward the work they do is a reflection of their own worth. Teachers need a different set of values from which to construct their self-worth. Teachers need to construct a whole new culture for themselves, not one where the public knows us only as a group of people forever whining about insufficient pay.

We are not against better pay; rather, we are appalled that teachers view themselves as a group of people who are poor and forlorn. Walk out to the parking lot and see if any teachers are driving old wrecks; go to the homeless shelters and see if any teachers are bedded down; go to the rescue mission and see if any teachers are in line for a meal.

The TRUTH About Teachers

- Only 22 percent of the general population has a college degree, but all teachers have one. We are an intelligent group of people.

- The teaching profession is the ONLY profession in which over half of its members have voluntary advanced degrees. As of 1995, some 52 percent of the teachers had degrees beyond a bachelor's degree. Teachers are the intellectual elite of America.

- Every tenured teacher has a teaching credential. Teachers are an intelligent, certified, licensed, and competent group of people.

—U.S. Department Education National Center for Educational Statistics

The truth is far rosier. Yet you would never know it by looking at many teachers. Some come to school dressed like they have just finished cleaning the house or repairing the car. Even more complain about getting an education, such as attending in-services, conferences, and college classes. Then you look around their classrooms and their diplomas and credentials are nowhere to be seen.

When you walk into a doctor's office, you see degrees, certificates, and licenses nicely framed and neatly hung on the wall in columns and rows. The same is true in the offices of accountants, pharmacists, and even mechanics, with their Mr. Goodwrench certificates.

Effective Teachers Display Their Diplomas with Pride

> *How often I have looked at my college degrees sitting in a box in my attic gathering dust. And just to think about the years and time spent in earning them. Thanks to you mine are in the process of getting framed to be displayed with pride like those of people in other professions.*
>
> —Sandra Knecht
> Marion Center, Pennsylvania

Members of every profession display their diplomas, licenses, and certificates—every profession but teaching. The tragedy is that teachers are in the diploma business. On Graduation Day, the student receives a diploma, the only tangible proof of years of schooling. Yet teachers are reluctant to hang up a diploma that says to the world, "Look at me; I am an educated person." Why? Because teacher culture has taught teachers to practice learned helplessness, planned pitifulness.

317

All of our national problems, from international competitiveness to improving our standard of living to the future of our children, ultimately rest on one important word: education.

Through the history of civilization, the concept of education has remained stable. Colors fade, temples crumble, empires fall, but education endures. Societies that succeed respect their teachers, and the teachers respect themselves.

We must begin with ourselves.

Leaders Begin with Themselves

Leaders begin with respect for their own worth. Society needs models of leadership. What better models of leaders are there than the teachers of a community?

> ✔ Teachers can be compared productively with business executives in that teachers, like executives, develop, manage, and evaluate the work and productivity of a relatively large number of individuals on a daily basis.

> ✔ When comparing teachers and doctors, teachers make more complex decisions than doctors do and make them far more frequently.

> ✔ More teachers go into teaching because of the influence of another teacher. This is not true for other professions. Teachers have influence.

> ✔ Teaching is the profession that makes all other professions possible. We are the only profession dedicated to making the world a better place for our future generations. They are our legacy.

> ✔ We are the only profession concerned with all youth and the realization that our children today are our most precious resource, that through them we will realize a better tomorrow.

> ✔ We realize that the degree of civilization of any nation is equivalent to the civilization of its youth.

Goal of Graduation

One of our teachers really zeroed in on your "diploma" comments and has arranged for all her Chapter I students to spend a day at our local university. They will attend classes, eat lunch, visit with one of the university administrators, and then get a "diploma" with the future date of their graduation indicated. In the students' individual goal conference, they will refer to their goal of graduation from college and so on.

—Trish Marcuzzo
Omaha, Nebraska

Our mission is to teach students the important skills, knowledge, and values necessary to be a success in tomorrow's world. What better way to teach these important skills, knowledge, and attitudes than to have ourselves as models?

Our children need models of success. Teachers who are considered successful work at being successful. There is no other way. There is no simple, foolproof, easy way—not even in this book. Every suggestion in this book must be worked at and worked at. Having a well-managed class, a class of academic achievers, a class of students who perform well at the annual musical, a team of students who are perennial league champions, requires constant work.

Commitment, dedication, and hard work make a person a leader. Ability and talent are not enough. Leadership is not created; it is achieved. It is the product of ability and talent combined with relentless practice and tempered by years of training. But even then, leaders give more. They give their heart and soul.

Accomplishment begins with teachers who are leaders. You do not want someone else's accomplishments, and you cannot give your accomplishments to someone else. What you can do is share how you achieved those accomplishments so that others may work toward and have pride in achieving their own successes. And that is why we are teachers.

The effective teacher knows that all children are capable of success.

The best results are the results you earn, acknowledge, look back on, and take pride in. You have to compete only against yourself to achieve the results you want from your life. The very second you commit yourself to work on a goal, you are a success.

Success of any kind requires you to take responsibility. In the final analysis, the one quality that all successful people have is the ability to take on responsibility.

319

Some people can give thousands of reasons why they cannot succeed at something when all they need is one reason why they can succeed. Knowing that any person can succeed is the responsibility and spirit of a leader.

You are a leader, a professional educator. Your challenge is to change the image and culture of the teaching profession. Your challenge is to revitalize and preserve the culture and restore and maintain the values of the nation.

> **With desire and commitment the leader builds a fire inside that causes others to glow brightly. No matter what the odds, the leader knows that any task can be accomplished.**

Never be satisfied with even a good job, because good is not good enough. You need to be brilliant, to excel, to go beyond, to be preeminent.

Going far beyond the call of duty, doing more than what others expect—this is what the children need from our teachers.

Striving, maintaining the highest standards, looking after the smallest details, and going that extra mile—these are the values a nation needs from the leadership of its professional educators.

You can do it.

The ultimate joy, happiness, nourishment, and reward lie within yourself. Get in touch with your own magnificence.

One hundred years from now it will not matter

What kind of car I drove,
What kind of house I lived in,
How much I had in the bank account,
Or what my clothes looked like.

But the world will be a better place because
I was important in the life of a child.

Teaching

The art of teaching is the art of assisting discovery. ♥ You can teach a lesson for a day but if you teach curiosity, you teach for a lifetime. ♥ It's too bad that the people who really know how to run the country are busy teaching school. ♥ When truth stands in your way, you are headed in the wrong direction. ♥ When teaching the love of truth, never lose the truth of love. ♥ Teacher's task: take a lot of live wires and see that they are well-grounded. ♥ The mediocre teacher tells, the good one explains, the superior one shows, the great one inspires. ♥ Nothing improves a child's hearing more than praise. ♥

Calligraphy by M.E. King

About the Authors

Who are Harry and Rosemary Wong?

They are teachers.

◆ CREDITS

PHOTO CREDITS

Reavis Z. Worthum, Communications Department, Garland Independent School District, Garland, Texas, pp. 7, 43, 47, 49, 53, 74, 78, 86, 98, 117, 130, 205, 220, 266, 280, 312, 315, 319, 321
Aaron Rosander, p. 58
Robert Messick, p. 83
A/P World Wide Photos, p. 303

ACKNOWLEDGMENTS

Grateful acknowledgment is made to the following people and institutions for permission to use their pictures, illustrations, or facilities:

Alicia Escobar, p. v
Henry County Schools, p. xiv
Jane H. Smith, p. 10
Roberta Ford, p. 11
Pam Ware, p. 12
Richelle Dodoo, p. 13
Gaston County Schools, p. 16
Marita Lacey, p. 17
Jim Heintz, pp. 17, 110, 176
Elouise Bettis, p. 27
Oklahoma City Public Schools, p. 37
Flowing Wells School District, Tucson, Arizona, pp. 39, 45, 67, 176, 185, 317
Alexia Clamp, p. 46
Crystal Anderson, Mary Anne Wiegard, p. 47
Phil Grant, p. 56
Luisa Velasco, p. 58
Yokota High School, Japan, pp. 72, 202
Eric Abrams, p. 78
Wanda Bradford, p. 82
Laurie Jay, pp. 82, 124
Alice Waters, p. 83
Gloria M. Houston, p. 86
Aaron Rosander, p. 88
Arthur Kavanaugh, p. 89
Yokota East Elementary School, Japan, p. 92
Sherry Sather Braaten, p. 104
Shirley Lanham Elementary School, Japan, p. 106
Debbie Curtis, Leanne Magnotto, pp. 107, 176
Julie Johnson, pp. 107, 241

Sherril Henrie, p. 109
Anita Richardson, p. 113
LaContenta Junior High School, Yucca Valley, California, p. 117
Shirley Bert Lee, p. 125
Colby Charko, Hilton Jay, p. 133
Merle J. Whaley, p. 139
Betty J. Behic, p. 148
Cheryl Rodgers, pp. 163, 176
Linda Banducci, p. 170
Judi Gustafson, p. 172
Susan Fortino, p. 176
Sharon Searle, p. 176
Julie Joubert-Guillory, p. 181
Cindy Wong, p. 186
Sue Gould Flynn, p. 192
Ann Walko, p. 192
Bob Wall, p. 192
Jean Driscoll, p. 206
Janelle M. Tynan, p. 223
Kimberley Wong, p. 225
Ruth Yamatoda, p. 232
Richard Crewse, p. 242
Ken Schaefer, p. 242
Yokota West Elementary School, Japan, p. 251
Dick Kyro, p. 254
Brian Colbert, Elayna Tami Wong, p. 278
Margaret Whaley, p. 301
Mary Kay Stark, p. 307
Beth Dixon, Kim Migliore, Barb Stark, p. 310
Rocio Inclán, p. 319

INDEX

R

Ralston, Cheryl, 56
Rand Corporation, 267, 293
Readiness, 94, 100
Reading, extensive, 31
Records, three basic, 136
Remediation, 239
Reputation, 101
Research process, 27, 28
Research-based practices, 30
Responsibility, 23, 161
Results and responsibilities, 18
Reward, ultimate, 164
Rewards, 151, 163, 164
    go to, 298
    professional, 296
    risk, 304, 308, 310
Rickards, John P., 29
Risk, 304, 310
Risk plan, 10%, 306
Robinson, Adam, 198
Role, understand your, 23
Roll taking, 127
    effective, 130
    three ways, 131
Room, how to enter, 109
Rosander, Aaron, 88
Rosenthal, Robert, 38
Routines, 170
Rule, chose to break, 158
Rules, 141
    for behavior, 146

Rules (cont.)
    classroom, 148
    district and school, 149
    general, 145
    introducing, 147
    number of, 147
    specific, 145
Running grade total, 138
Ryan, Kevin, 5

S

Salary, raise in, 19
Saphier, Jon, v
Schmoker, Mike, 265
School, concept of, 48
Scores, 138
Seating arrangements, 116, 117
Seating assignments, 116, 119
Seating chart, 108, 119
Security, 85
Self-directed work teams, 254
Self-discipline, 161
Seven things students want
    to know, 105
Shalaway, Linda, 299
Simon, Sid, 142
Sission, Al, 277
Skills, compensation for, 273
Slavin, Robert, 254
Smiling, 73
Smith, Jane H., 10
Smith, Vernon, 49

THE FIRST DAYS OF SCHOOL
How to Be an Effective Teacher
by
Harry K. Wong
Rosemary Tripi Wong

The First Days of School

This is the leading book on classroom management and teaching for lesson mastery. Over 1.4 million copies have been sold.

There is overwhelming evidence that the first two to three weeks of school are critical in determining how well students will achieve for the remainder of the year. What the teacher does on the first days of school will determine the teacher's success or failure for the rest of the school year.

- Full color cover
- Two color print
- 352 pages
- 10 x 8 inches
- 123 illustrations
- 131 photographs

✔ If you had to buy only one book in education to help you become a successful teacher, *The First Days of School* is the book you want.

✔ If you are having trouble with your students and you are not getting the results you want, *The First Days of School* is the book you want.

✔ If you are a staff developer or an administrator and you want to help your teachers be the best that they can be, *The First Days of School* is the book you want.

✔ If you are a college professor and you want to help your preservice teachers be the best that they can be, *The First Days of School* is the book you want.

Order direct from Harry K. Wong Publications, Inc. Call for immediate shipment at sale prices. Quantity discounts are available.

Also, "That Noble Title Teacher," the inspiring essay celebrating educators on page iv of *The First Days of School* is available as a large, full color poster. Contact Harry K. Wong Publications, Inc., for pricing and quantity discounts.

Produced by:
Harry K. Wong Publications, Inc.
943 North Shoreline Boulevard
Mountain View, CA 94043
TEL (650) 965-7896
FAX (650) 965-7890

I tried everything and nothing worked. After reading **The First Days of School***, I had the best year I've ever had. Wish I had this book 23 years ago.*

—Carolyn Schramka
Anna, Illinois

The Effective Teacher

- Eight VHS video tapes, over 5 hours
- One book, *The First Days of School*
- One binder
- *Facilitator's Handbook* with complete transcript of videos
- Transparency reproducibles
- Attractive storage case

- Award winning
  1st Place Gold Award,
      US International Film and Video Festival
  Silver Statuette,
      Telly Awards
  Bronze Award,
      Columbus Film & Video Festival

Produced by:
Harry K. Wong Publications, Inc.
943 North Shoreline Boulevard
Mountain View, CA 94043
TEL (650) 965-7896
FAX (650) 965-7890

Using the book and the video, we have completed the most effective, most beneficial, most comprehensive staff development program we have conducted in our system.

—Charles McDonald
Gainesville, Georgia

THE EFFECTIVE TEACHER
with
Harry K. Wong

You will be AWESTRUCK! Even if you have seen Harry Wong speak at various meetings, you haven't seen anything until you see this production. Using broadcast-quality cameras and state-of-the-art editing, an in-service presentation has been created of such a high level of excellence and quality that you will be awestruck by the production.

Best Investment—*The Effective Teacher* will be your best staff development investment. *The Effective Teacher* shows you what effective teachers do to incite student achievement. It showcases the commonsense, research-based, noncontroversial, successful techniques used by effective teachers.

SCOPE AND SEQUENCE OF *The Effective Teacher*

Part 1: **The Effective Teacher -** 32 minutes
✔ How to use research-based practices to be a happy, effective teacher

Part 2: **The First Days of School -** 36 minutes
✔ How to invite students to succeed

Part 3: **Discipline and Procedures -** 36 minutes
✔ How to have a well-managed classroom

Part 4: **Procedures and Routines -** 55 minutes
✔ How to have students follow classroom procedures

Part 5: **Cooperative Learning and Culture -** 47 minutes
✔ How to prepare your students for tomorrow's world

Part 6: **Lesson Mastery -** 33 minutes
✔ How to increase student learning and achievement

Part 7: **The Professional Educator -** 41 minutes
✔ How to become a professional

Part 8: **Positive Expectations -** 20 minutes
✔ How to increase positive student behavior

HOW YOU CAN BE A SUPER SUCCESSFUL TEACHER
with
Harry K. Wong

How You Can Be A Super Successful Teacher is the most widely used set of tapes on classroom management, discipline, and self-esteem. Some 50,000 tapes have been sold, and they continue to inspire and help teachers. No bull, all beef. Little theory, all substance. Harry Wong has been called "Mr. Practicality." Invest in these tapes for your own success.

How to Achieve Maximum Success in the Classroom (tapes 1 and 2)
These tapes present dozens of immediately useful techniques to achieve maximum success with your students. All techniques are proven, tested, and easy to implement. You will learn how to:
- ✔ begin a class with success
- ✔ increase the homework turn-in rate
- ✔ increase students' test scores, reading, and retention rates
- ✔ teach students to teach themselves
- ✔ be a caring and loving teacher

Once and for All You Can Solve Your Discipline Problems (tape 3)
Here is a simple three-part plan to help you greatly reduce your discipline problems, reduce your stress level, and increase the achievement level of your students. You will learn how to:
- ✔ reduce 80 percent of your discipline problems
- ✔ discipline students who break your rules
- ✔ reward students who obey your rules
- ✔ reduce your stress level
- ✔ include other teachers in your discipline plan
- ✔ increase students' academic learning time

You Are a Marvel (tape 4)
Listen to this tape when you need a shot in the arm to remind yourself of your importance, dignity, and respectability as a teacher and a human being. This tape explains how to move from being an ordinary teacher to becoming a super successful teacher. You will learn why:
- ✔ every person is unique
- ✔ people make excuses
- ✔ some people are always happy and fulfilled
- ✔ some people can't decide while others make good choices
- ✔ YOU, as a teacher, are so important!

**How You Can Be A
Super Successful Teacher**

- Four audio tapes, 4 1/2 hours
- Vinyl case
- Lifetime replacement guarantee

Contact Harry K. Wong Publications, Inc., for additional information, current prices, or quantity discounts.

Produced by:
Harry K. Wong Publications, Inc.
943 North Shoreline Boulevard
Mountain View, CA 94043
TEL (650) 965-7896
FAX (650) 965-7890

I recently took over a class that had somewhat poor discipline. This being the first class I could call my own, I have found the information and advice contained in your tapes to be invaluable. In just three days I have managed to gain some semblance of order where before chaos had reigned supreme. Thank you for having produced these tapes.

—Jim Orth
Wendell, Idaho

I *choose to* CARE

- 60 minutes
- 1/2" VHS format
- Studio-quality production
- Unconditionally guaranteed against manufacturing defects

Contact Harry K. Wong Publications, Inc., for additional information, current prices, or quantity discounts.

Produced by:
Harry K. Wong Publications, Inc.
943 North Shoreline Boulevard
Mountain View, CA 94043
TEL (650) 965-7896
FAX (650) 965-7890

Dr. Wong, now I know why you are the most sought-after speaker in the country. I have invited and listened to a number of speakers in the last 12 years, and you rank number one. You are not only a master teacher but an exciting and dynamic speaker.

—Dante Thurairatnam
Bowling Green (Ohio) University

I *choose to* CARE
with
Harry K. Wong

I choose to CARE is a one-hour motivational video tape for your personal and immediate growth. It will excite and renew your professional soul. It offers concrete, practical, and applicable classroom suggestions that you can use every day. In a stirring presentation recorded live before an audience of 3,200 district employees, Harry K. Wong will make you laugh and make you cry. When it's over, you'll be more determined than ever to strive for excellence.

Harry K. Wong brings out the best in educators. His in-service and keynote convention speeches are legendary. He has given thousands of them, all over the United States, Canada, and elsewhere in the world. Half a million people have seen him in action. No one is better than Harry K. Wong as an educational speaker. Many more consider him the most exciting and motivating speaker in education. He is in a class by himself.

What is the difference between *I choose to CARE* and *The Effective Teacher*, listed on page 335? *I choose to CARE* is motivational, with research-based classroom effectiveness material, but is designed for personal use. *The Effective Teacher* is instructional but highly motivational and is designed for pre-service and staff development use. Think of *I choose to CARE* as your personal shot in the arm.

Contents of *I choose to* CARE

A. The Four Beliefs of Effective Teachers
- ✔ The teacher makes a difference.
- ✔ The teacher is competent.
- ✔ The teacher is a good classroom manager.
- ✔ The teacher uses research-based practices.

B. Effective Teachers Use Research-Based Practices to Ensure Student Success
- ✔ Questions for comprehension
- ✔ Maximizes time on task
- ✔ Uses procedures and routines for efficiency
- ✔ Teaches to objectives
- ✔ Teaches responsibility
- ✔ Has a discipline plan

C. Effective Teachers Teach Leadership
- ✔ Leaders make choices.
- ✔ Leaders are risk takers.
- ✔ Leaders have curiosity.
- ✔ Leaders work cooperatively.
- ✔ Leaders have a work ethic.
- ✔ Leaders care.

Please Share with Us

Every 20 years, education cycles itself. There are really no new ideas in education. Newer ideas are refinements of older ideas.

Everything we have shared in *The First Days of School*, we have acquired from years of research, visiting schools and classrooms, and interacting with teachers, administrators, and college professors. Teacher-specific ideas and techniques are given to us and mailed to us after our in-service meetings. We thank these professional educators for their contributions.

Please share with us your ideas, your techniques, your strategies.

Please share with us your:
- ✔ Worksheets
- ✔ Assignments
- ✔ Criterion-referenced tests
- ✔ Study guidelines
- ✔ Discipline plans
- ✔ Procedures and routines
- ✔ Invitational messages
- ✔ School and classroom pictures

We'd like to hear from:
- ✔ Teachers—your personal stories of success
- ✔ Staff developers—your professional development programs
- ✔ Administrators—your beginning teacher induction programs
- ✔ College professors—your preservice class experiences

Send to:
Harry and Rosemary Wong
943 North Shoreline Boulevard
Mountain View, CA 94043

Thank you for sharing and enhancing our profession.

Sharing

If you have a dollar and I have a dollar and we exchange dollars, we still each have a dollar.

But if you have a teaching technique that works and I have a teaching technique that works and we exchange these techniques, you still have your technique, but you have mine also, and I still have my technique, but I have yours also.

We are now both 100 percent better off because we shared.

Between pages 18 and 19 of this book is a certificate that was shared with us. It's our pleasure to share it with you. Best wishes.